ALAN WOODS

BEING NAKED PLAYING DEAD THE ART OF PETER GREENAWAY

Being Naked Playing Dead
the art of peter greenaway

manchester university press

For my Father and in memory of my Mother

COPYRIGHT © ALAN WOODS 1996

PUBLISHED BY:

MANCHESTER UNIVERSITY PRESS, OXFORD ROAD, MANCHESTER M13 9NR, UK

DISTRIBUTED EXCLUSIVELY IN THE USA BY:

ST. MARTIN'S PRESS, INC., 175 FIFTH AVENUE, NEW YORK, NY 10010, USA

BRITISH LIBRARY CATALOGUING-IN-PUBLICATION DATA

A CATALOGUE RECORD FOR THIS BOOK IS AVAILABLE FROM THE BRITISH LIBRARY

LIBRARY OF CONGRESS CATALOGING-IN-PUBLICATION DATA

WOODS, ALAN, 1942-

BEING NAKED-PLAYING DEAD : THE ART OF PETER GREENAWAY / ALAN WOODS

P.   CM.

ISBN: 0 7190 4771 4 HARDBACK - 0 7190 4772 2 PAPERBACK

1. GREENAWAY, PETER - CRITICISM AND INTERPRETATION. 1. TITLE.

N6537. G695W66 1996

709'.2--DC20

96-8350 CIP

FIRST PUBLISHED 1996

00 99 98 97 96   10 9 8 7 6 5 4 3 2 1

PRINTED IN THE UNITED KINGDOM

DESIGNED BY: SUNBATHER (0171 255 3003)

ACKNOWLEDGMENTS

I should like to thank: Paul Melia, both for his help in the formative stages of the project and for reading one of the earlier final versions of the text; Katherine Reeve, Vanessa Graham, Matthew Frost and Rebecca Crum at Manchester University Press; Jane Raistrick, for her copy-editing; William Julien, the designer of this book, for his ability, on this and other projects, to understand what I want either before I know what it is, or when I know what it is but can't explain it; and finally Peter Greenaway and Eliza Poklewski Koziell for their help throughout the writing of this book, most particularly in regard to their work on the interviews which form its final section.

I am also grateful to Peter and Eliza for granting me access to their photographic archives, from which all the illustrations are gathered. The credits for the material reproduced here are: Film stills: BFI Stills, Posters and Designs (*The Draughtsman's Contract, A Zed and Two Noughts, Drowning by Numbers*); Marc Guillaumot (*Prospero's Books, The Baby of Mâcon, Darwin, M is for Man, Music and Mozart, Death in the Seine*); Jacques Prayer (*The Cook, The Thief, His Wife and Her Lover*); Channel 4 (*A TV Dante*); Charles MacDonald (*The Pillow Book*); Peter Greenaway (*The Belly of an Architect*). Exhibitions: Claudio Franzini (*Watching Water*); Graham Matthews (*Some Organising Principles*); Maru Luksch (*100 Objects to Represent the World*); Peter Cox (*The Physical Self*); Peter Greenaway (*The Stairs Geneva*). Opera: Deen Van Meer (*Rosa*).

I have received financial support, both for the production of the book and for travel, from Duncan of Jordanstone School of Fine Art Research. My thanks go also to my friends and colleagues at the University of Dundee, in both the School of Fine Art and the college library.

Contents

A Walk Through G

SOME ORGANISING PRINCIPLES

ring United Sta...
the art of Peter Greee

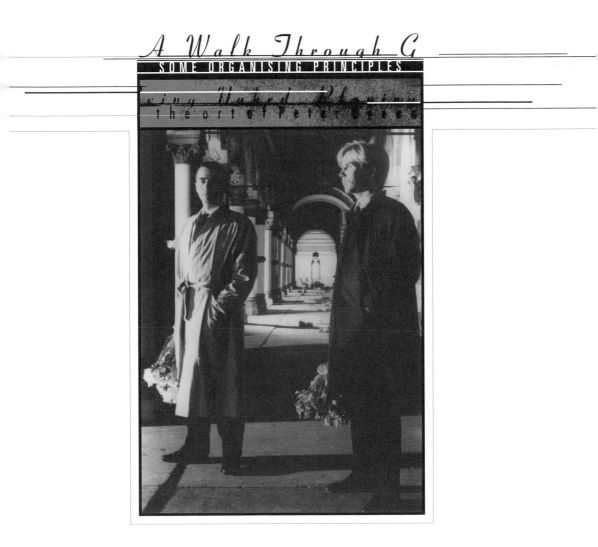

A CINEMA OF IDEAS, NOT PLOTS

Naturalism is based on a lie. Why try to be natural in what is a totally artificial environment? Be artificial, and that becomes natural.

ROBERT WILSON [1]

A specter is haunting the cinema: the specter of narrative. If that apparition is an angel, we must embrace it; and if it is a devil, we must cast it out. But we cannot know what it is until we have met it face to face.

HOLLIS FRAMPTON [2]

I am speaking of what might have been done and what cinema alone can do. I mean those specific and unique things that can be done and created only in the realm of the cinema. The problem of the synthesis of the arts, a synthesis realizable in the cinema, has not yet found its full solution.

SERGEI EISENSTEIN [3]

Reading and considering what film comment seems to want to see ... make[s] me often feel like a hippopotamus in a giraffe race, or when I'm feeling superior, like a giraffe in a hippopotamus race ... it is more interesting for me to talk to a painting historian or an art critic ... because my terms and attitudes are rooted in what [they] know and have studied. My ambition has always been to try and bring that sort of language, those criteria, that vocabulary, those processes into cinema - and not ivory-tower cinema - but mainstream cinema.[4]

Both favourable and unfavourable criticism, at least in English, of the cinema of Peter Greenaway tends to isolate him as a maverick figure: brilliant (or elitist, or too clever by half) but an unclassifiable one-off.

'British film culture' can produce, for example, Stephen Frears's British Film Institute-commissioned personal history of British cinema, *Typically British*, in which Greenaway is represented only by the poster for *The Draughtsman's Contract*.[5]

Greenaway is certainly a distinctive figure, and he takes a certain amount of pleasure in his distinctiveness; he has repeated Sacha Vierny's remark to him, 'Vous n'est pas un réalisateur, vous êtes un "greenaway"'.[6] But his difficulty is overrated.

It is possible that it is because he is in many ways such a typically English *artist* that he can appear to be an impossibly unEnglish film-maker; but it is certain that when his work is considered

Prospero's Books: McCay's Grid
MIXED MEDIA ON PAPER 81 X 112 CM

in the context of the contemporary international art world it cannot plausibly be considered as eccentric. His interest in corporeality, in the body and representations of the body, in sexuality and mortality; his foregrounding of artifice, his detachment, his irony; his comparisons and distinctions between painting and photography; his interest in the relations between images and texts, and in the lives of texts as images; his visualisations and representations of vision and representation; his 'difficult' or extreme subject matter - all these place him in the mainstream of contemporary art practice.

What is most individual about his work in this context is the range of artists by whom he has been influenced or to whom he might usefully be compared - painters such as Kitaj (when he discusses the influence of Kitaj, it is usually at the level of Kitaj's liberating mix of images and ideas, text and paint, sex and politics, but his influence as a draughtsman on Greenaway is also clear), Bacon and Tom Phillips (with whom he worked on *A TV Dante*); photographers and artists using photography such as Joel-Peter Witkin, Andres Serrano, Cindy Sherman and Gilbert and George; land and public artists such as the Boyle family, Richard Long, and Christo and Jeanne Claude; the conceptual and minimalist traditions, which he puts to maximalist use. Some of these links - with Kitaj, in particular - were decisive, others were useful; some are parallels and coincidences; but most are stronger, and more relevant, than any which can be made with contemporary cinema. The parallels between Greenaway's film-making and the art world are maintained throughout his career; as a part of it, he changes with it. And he is, increasingly, a part of it. His paintings and drawings are not merely included within his films - *A Walk Through H*, *Vertical Features Remake*, *The Draughtsman's Contract*, and the animated painting/collages in *Prospero's Books* - but are exhibited and catalogued as independent works within a multi-media oeuvre. His exhibitions, although explicitly extensions of his own film projects and critiques of cinema as a medium, are also clearly relatable either to the vast but transient projects of Christo, spectacles of, for and within cities rather than galleries; or else, where they are gallery-based, equally clearly relatable to the many contemporary projects which frame the gallery as a site for viewing art, or the museum as a site for viewing objects, rather than accepting them as frames within which objects and art objects are unproblematically displayed. Perhaps because contemporary cinema itself, whether European or American, commercial or art-house, has largely lost its excitement (and, with it, its importance to theory), there seems to be no equivalent set of continuing dialogues between Greenaway and contemporary film directors. It is true, of course, that Jarman was also a painter who turned to cinema, who frequently referred to the history of painting, who often avoided traditional narrative, who offered representations of sex and violence which were often controversial, who used artifice, theatricality and, indeed, theatre; both directors filmed *The Tempest*. There does not appear, however, to have been any mutual sympathy between the two; and, while clearly this does not rule out a critical comparison, I am myself so out of sympathy with the bulk of Jarman's work that if I attempted such a comparison it could only read, pointlessly, as a one-sided put-down of Jarman. It may, I suspect, become clearer in time that a more pertinent parallel and dialogue is with the Brothers Quay, who are obliquely present, indeed, in *The Falls* and *A Zed and Two Noughts*. They are comparable in their range of projects, which extends into stage design as well as cinema; in their suspicion of narrative; in their artifice, reference (particularly to European sources) and self-reference (not just to cinema, but to the pre-history of cinema); in the importance of music and dance in their work, and, generally, in their visual style and richness. Their animation *The Cabinet of Jan Svankmajer* (1984) suggests many points of comparison with Greenaway: the interest in maps (repeated in *Street of Crocodiles* (1986)); the metaphorical fusion of books and bodies (mostly the head); the simultaneity of past and present (Svankmajer's atelier, one caption suggests, is 'XVIth and XXth century simultaneously'); and the construction of systems, classifications, exhibition spaces for arcane knowledge. One sequence, 'The Child Receives a Lesson in 1/24th of a Second', an animation about the process of animation which includes, as does Greenaway's *Rosa*, a frame counter, recalls one of Greenaway's favourite remarks: Godard's definition of cinema as truth at twenty-four frames a second. Greenaway is also fond of repeating Eisenstein's suggestion that Disney's animation was the truest cinema, because it was totally self-contained.

Consider Greenaway, therefore, as an artist who makes films as a (central) part of his practice, and one is beginning to put him in the right race. More specifically, although painters by no means dominate the list of contemporary artists to whom he might profitably be compared, Greenaway trained as a painter and paints and draws still, and his deep love for the history of painting - a history beside which he regards the history of cinema as ludicrously brief, although possibly already almost over - structures all of his image-making, including his films. Most significantly - beyond the myriad references and quotations, important as they are - his ambitions for the images he creates for the cinema screen are closer to those of the most ambitious, ideas-driven artworks, from Raphael's *School of Athens* to Duchamp's *Large Glass* to Kitaj's *Specimen Musings of a Democrat*, than they are to conventional (or almost any kind of) cinema. Greenaway makes demands - of the medium as well as of the viewer - which might ultimately be impossible, utopian, but which have opened up a whole new range of possibilities for cinema, a medium which he regards with great excitement, but also with ambivalence. (Cinema as, literally, *film* is of course being transformed, modified, replaced by the new technologies which Greenaway is enthusiastically exploring.)

Greenaway has often compared cinema to opera, and with *Rosa* - published as a book which describes a production of an opera before it was actually realised on stage - he moved into a music theatre clearly indebted to, above all, Philip Glass and Robert Wilson's *Einstein on the Beach*; while *Prospero's Books* and *M is for Man, Music, and Mozart* both involved collaborations with contemporary dancers. His longest collaboration, save for that with Sacha Vierny, was of course with Michael Nyman. Although their proposed opera - of which *Rosa* is a fragment - was never completed, by working with Nyman Greenaway was able to produce *Gesamtkunstwerke* which did not merely translate the ideas of, above all, John Cage into visual systems and sequences and homages, but can properly be regarded alongside, and indeed within, a predominantly American strand of contemporary music, music theatre and even (remembering Philip Glass's involvement with cinema) music cinema.

Cinema was always parasitical upon the other arts: theatre, the novel, and also painting. Cecil B. De Mille was the last of the epic Victorian painters; and there has been a long tradition of cinematic pictorialism, apart from and alongside the biopics of artists (usually Van Gogh), in which cinema (usually absurdly) re-creates from paintings versions of the subjects and motifs which 'inspired' them, and then fakes the originals as works in progress on the easel. Greenaway is not exactly outside these traditions, which can be traced right across Hollywood, heritage movies, the genres of 'art' cinema and the avant-garde, but he is distinctive within it; partly through his familiarity, as a practitioner, with contemporary art, which cinema generally either parodies or ignores, its pictorialism being generally nostalgic, a warding-off of the modern. (Advertising, on the other hand, is currently - as it has often been before, from Lautrec to surrealism - closely linked to the art world, plagiarising not just, lazily, the Pop old masters, Warhol and Lichtenstein (which never works), but also, in recent campaigns, Christo, Damien Hirst (though here the influence cuts both ways), and Greenaway himself. Moreover, when an ad as sophisticated as those in the Guinness series ends with a tableau of a Renoir, the true reference is to the presence of such photographic recreations in contemporary photography. Impressionism in the cinema is potentially interesting - in many ways the Impressionists aspired to the condition of the camera, which, unlike most linear systems of perspective, operates purely through light, is 'just an eye', unable to abstract light into line, vision into the stable geometries of perspective diagrams; and Warhol's film of the Empire State building is an Impressionist film of sorts, comparable to Monet's series of Rouen Cathedral. But, lazily referenced, it is generally the worst kind of sentimental pictorialism.) He is distinctive also through his love and knowledge of Western painting, which has forced a genuine exploration of cinema as a medium linked to painting. Almost all the interests which, I have suggested, place him in the mainstream of current art practice are also central to the traditions, obsessions and anxieties of Western painting. The combinations, familiar in Greenaway, of spiralling, intricate ideas and references, of the importance of text as a skeleton or driving force of image-making, with an intense fixation on the body, its physicalities, embarrassments, pleasures and cruelties, a body displayed within an often self-referential framework and represented without either 'realism' or idealism - all these are conscious echoes of mannerist and Baroque painting in particular. Nor does Greenaway asset-strip art history; he thinks through it, learns from it with an appropriate humility; he seeks, indeed, to join it. The artist most often present in Greenaway's films is Greenaway himself, sometimes ironising, sometimes examining, sometimes collapsing the relations between painting and cinema.

While it is essential to establish Greenaway's reference points outside cinema, it would of course be absurd to consider his work without reference to cinema history. He can be dismissive of much of its canon. Frears wanted to call *Typically British* 'Bollocks to Truffaut', in response to Truffaut's remark that British cinema was a contradiction in terms; Greenaway (re-)wrote that very remark into the dialogue of *The Draughtsman's Contract*, substituting 'painting' for 'cinema', and would clearly have much sympathy with it. He can also be scathing about much European cinema (one wonders whether Truffaut himself interests him much), although he clearly takes it seriously in a way in which he does not take American film. I can think of no other director so apparently uninterested in, impervious to, almost the whole range and history of Hollywood product. When he refers to 'dominant cinema' (a term suggesting, perhaps nostalgically, the possibility of a genuine avant-garde opposed to it), he mostly means, sweepingly, American cinema - from *Kramer vs Kramer* to *Terminator 2*; although at his most extreme he can wonder 'have we seen a film yet?' 'Have there really been films of which it can be said, their content could not be presented in any other way as effectively?'[7]

The only reply to this 'deliberate provocation' is - surely - well, yes, *thousands*. Nor, of course, is Greenaway outside the history - or pre-history, as he suggests and hopes it may one day be seen - of cinema. A handful of European directors - more accurately perhaps, one European director and a handful of European films - have, however, inspired him, and continue to do so. The director is Eisenstein, for his range, his intelligence, his presentation through cinema of a 'world-view', and for his 'genius', the intuitive creativity which Greenaway, temperamentally sympathetic with clever and thoughtful artists and performers, values not least in the actors he uses. *Drowning by Numbers*

includes a homage to Bergman's *The Seventh Seal*, the film which first alerted the young Greenaway to the possibilities of cinema. He has also often referred to his debt to Resnais's *Last Year at Marienbad*, a film of unreliable story telling but no straightforward narrative, of statues in a formal garden, of (literal) theatricality, of deep perspectives, of games-playing, of repetitions, which lies more obviously behind many elements of Greenaway's cinema. (There is also a more direct connection; Sacha Vierny worked on *Last Year at Marienbad*. Vierny also worked with Resnais on *Hiroshima Mon Amour,* in which the lengthy tea room scene makes great use not only of water, but of the reflected light from water which is one of Greenaway's trademarks.) Greenaway has referred less often to individual films by Godard, though he frequently quotes him in interviews; in conversation, he mentioned particularly *Les Carabiniers*[8] and *Les Petits Soldats.* Godard's reformulation of Brechtian devices for the cinema, his investigations of the non-realist possibilities of the soundtrack, his irony and humour, his simultaneous critiques of film and power, so that self-reference, far from being a device of art for art's sake, is, precisely, a means of attacking the complicity between the 'natural' languages and genres of cinema and political power - all these fed into, enabled, Greenaway's work. He is also keen to acknowledge his debt to Hollis Frampton's films, and also to Frampton's writings, collected in *Circles of Confusion*; he first saw his work as in an area between Frampton and Resnais, with Eisenstein and Godard as massive presences around it. Fellini was also important; increasingly, it seems that the films made in the seventies, after the 'classic' films, offer the most telling points of comparison to Greenaway's feature films - *Casanova*, for example, with its shameless theatricality and artifice (black plastic sheeting as water), or Fellini's *Roma*, with its ecclesiastical fashion show.

This mix of contexts, influences and reference points involves, within the excess, the surplus, the over-determinations characteristic of Greenaway's projects, which are invariably far wider than the particular films, texts, artworks or exhibitions which emerge from them, inevitable paradoxes, ironies, overlappings, overreachings, contradictions. Text, for example, is at once resisted, overwhelmed by the visual, and embraced by a cinema and mega-cinema which is hybrid but not illustrative or derivative, which seeks at once to include everything and to be dependent on nothing but itself. But there are common threads discernible in the works which Greenaway admires, which feed into his own. His cinema of ideas, above all, includes the idea of cinema: self-reference, artifice, a rhetoric of representation which uses the realities of the medium to ridicule and denounce all 'realisms' which depend upon a pretence that media can be 'transparent'. These are Greenaway's basic assumptions, held variously in common with modernism - certainly with most of the forms of modernist painting - with mannerism and the Baroque, with the avant-garde cinema, and theory of cinema, current as he began to make films, with the work of Robert Wilson and with (for example) Cindy Sherman. This is inseparable from an art which makes the viewer self-conscious of viewing, and thereby prevents empathy, any emotional identification with character or action - or even pictorial space - which stands in the way of a proper understanding of both art and life. Unless art first holds a mirror up to art, it cannot begin to include nature within its frame.

And it is, precisely, nature which is central to Greenaway's world-view: Darwin's nature, as we shall see. Greenaway uses Darwin as Brecht, Eisenstein, and Godard used Marx, which leads to a comparable critique of genre, of character, of narrative - though art in the service of evolution has fewer problems relating itself to the future than art in the service of revolution. This gives Greenaway a particular take on his universal themes of birth, copulation and death - broadly, the kind of take on tragedy which Felipe Fernández-Armesto applied to history by considering wheat as the dominant life form on earth, a life form which has cunningly exploited man. In practice, this insistence on man as animal, and on animal as bearer of the selfish gene, is balanced by a fascination with religious myths, primarily Greek and Christian - although, as the figures of Greenaway's cinema carry, or pass through, a succession of archetypes, the disruption of character is maintained.

This opposition/doubling of evolutionary theory and creation myths (most persistently the myth of Adam and Eve) is echoed, paralleled, sustained by the ways in which bodies and objects are represented - and, in the exhibitions, displayed. They are simultaneously presented (to use a word poised between representation and display) as palpably, stubbornly physical, and as emblems, ciphers. Objects are themselves, are what is there to be seen; but are also images (including the images, the definitions, we have which order our seeing), and symbols, and props, and clues, and items to be catalogued. They are at once matter and spectacle, idea and thing.

Such opposites are held in suspension by art itself, and above all by irony. It is time, perhaps, to allow Greenaway to introduce his work himself; here is a passage from his introduction to a British Film Institute booklet cataloguing his early films:

I began my film-making when I was an art student studying to be a mural painter, and had ambitions to make every film-image as self-sufficient as a painting. As with painting, so with cinema;[9] I wanted to make films that were not illustrations of already existing text, or vehicles for actors, or slaves to a plot, or an excuse to provide material for any emotional catharsis - mine or anybody else's; cinema is not therapy, both life and cinema deserve better than that. My ambitions were to see if I could make films that acknowledged cinema's artifices and illusions, and demonstrate that - however fascinating - that was what they were - artifices and illusions. I wanted to make a cinema of ideas, not plots, and to try to use the same aesthetics as painting which has always paid great attention to formal devices of structure, composition and framing, and most importantly, insisted on attention to metaphor. Since film is not painting - and not simply because one moves and the other doesn't - I wanted to explore their connections and differences - stretching the formal interests to questions of editing, pacing, studying the formal properties of time intervals, repetitions, variations on a theme, and so on. Which was all rather convenient for I couldn't pay actors or build sets. I had no money. All of those very early films were made for twopence; I was my own cameraman and my own editor. If I could have written the music, I would have done that too. Such ambition and such lack of resources makes for irony or disaster. The irony has become endemic.

My paintings had largely concerned themselves with landscape, I was interested in all forms of natural history, my literary interests were strong on lists, classifying, encyclopedias, and the *nouvelle roman*, and my twentieth-century heroes outside of cinema were John Cage, Duchamp and Borges. Inside cinema they were Hollis Frampton and Alain Resnais and all those film-makers in between whose intelligences were wholly cinematic which, as far as I could see, was no-one. The influence of all this - nature and nurture - can be seen in the early films from *Intervals* to *The Falls*, and indeed can be seen ever since, right up to *Prospero's Books*. However, after *The Falls*, the cultural baggage has proliferated. Conspiracy theory, de-romanticised sex, equal participation of the female, the trauma of death, and an unapologetically Baroque view of the world in all its richness and complexity have now become some of the constant characteristics - but they are there in embryo in *Vertical Features Remake*, in *A Walk Through H*, in *Windows*.

What is also constant - then and now - is the irony - irony as tolerance, as non-dogma, that 'this is only cinema, not life', that there are no longer any certainties - if indeed there ever were

- and surely no single meanings - except to the very simple-minded who endearingly want things kept straightforward and clear-cut. If a numerical, alphabetical or colour-coding system is employed, it is done so deliberately as a device, a construct, to counteract, dilute, augment or complement the all-pervading obsessive cinema interest in plot, in narrative, in the 'I'm now going to tell you a story' school of film-making, which nine times out of ten begins life as literature, an origin with very different concerns, ambitions and characteristics from those of the cinema.[10]

LOSING COUNT

The pretence that numbers are not the humble creation of man, but are the exacting language of the universe and therefore possess the secret of all things, is comforting, terrifying, and mesmeric.
Fear of Drowning [11]

This book first arose out of a passage in Borges, out of the laughter that shattered, as I read the passage, all the familiar landmarks of my thought - our thought, the thought that bears the stamp of our age and our geography - breaking up all the ordered surfaces and all the planes with which we are accustomed to tame the wild profusion of existing things, and continuing long afterwards to disturb and threaten with collapse our age-old distinction between the same and the other. This passage quotes a 'certain Chinese encyclopædia' in which it is written that 'animals are divided into: (a) belonging to the emperor, (b) embalmed, (c) tame, (d) sucking pigs, (e) sirens, (f) fabulous, (g) stray dogs, (h) included in the present classification, (i) frenzied, (j) innumerable, (k) drawn with a very fine camelhair brush, (l) et cetera, (m) having just broken the water pitcher, (n) that from a long way off look like flies'. In the wonderment of this taxonomy, the thing we apprehend in one great leap, the thing that, by means of the fable, is demonstrated as the exotic charm of another system of thought, is the limitation of our own, the stark impossibility of thinking *that*.
MICHEL FOUCAULT [12]

But why should we need to seek clarification, when a plethora of meaning is desirable?
Flying Out of This World [13]

To quote the catalogue introduction [from *100 Objects to Represent the World*]: [14]

> This list of 100 objects seeks to include every aspect of time and scale, masculine and feminine, cat and dog. It acknowledges everything - everything alive and everything dead. It should leave nothing out - every material, every technique, every type of every type, every science, every art and every discipline, every construct, illusion, trick and device we utilise to reflect our vanity and insecurity and our disbelief that we are so cosmically irrelevant. Since every natural and cultural object is such a complex thing, and all are so endlessly inter-

connected, this ambition should not be so difficult to accomplish as you might imagine.

For example, to indicate both the brevity and the irony of this ambition, the fountain-pen inside my pocket is a machine that can represent all machinery; it is made of metal and plastic which could be said to represent the whole metallurgy industry from drawing-pins to battleships, and the whole plastics industry from the intra-uterine device to inflatables. It has a clip for attaching it to my inside jacket pocket and thus acknowledges the clothing industry. It is designed to write, thus representing all literature, belles lettres and journalism. It has the name Parker inscribed on its lid, revealing the presence of words, designer-significance, advertising, identity.
The Stairs Geneva [15]

New art forms - which indeed, at first, are not quite *forms* - are in advance, often well in advance, of critical language. This was true of Renaissance painting, and is true of the plethora of art practices within the twentieth century which were provoked by dissatisfaction with traditional media or inspired by the ever-accelerating possibilities of new media - performance, happenings, installations, video, and cinema itself. Greenaway is at present increasingly interested in CD-Rom, for example, a medium which could have been invented for him, although he has been irritated by an insistence that his experiments within this non-linear, associative, encyclopaedic, hands-on mixture of text and image should be shackled by a demand for a story-board - an old solution for a new technology. Simply to suggest the key strands of his thought is to make clear both that several existing critical

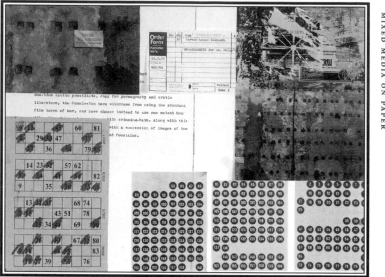

languages must be brought into play, and brought into play together, and that he is exploring areas for which no critical language has yet been developed.

But there is also the problem - related, but more mundane - of how to organise a study of an artist who has thematised and ironised organisation, classification, and who has done so even in his own case - should one call him a film director, a description with which he is often ill at ease, or an artist?

Order, in Greenaway's work - his films, his writings, his pictures, his exhibitions - is always linked to absurdity and human vanity. In the face of the ultimate interrelatedness of everything (there's no such thing as a red herring, he believes, 'everything is ultimately relatable'), of the infinite variety of things and bodies and events and the meanings we give to them, systems are merely pompous examples of chaos: evasive, manipulative, self-deluding myths. If his work is tirelessly systems-based, his systems - his games, lists, alphabets, countings, variously simple, intricate, playful, philosophical, comic - are above all ironic, self-referential, never in conflict with the surplus of material available for classification, a surplus which they display as much as they discipline. Order, in the world, is mocked by disorder and decay, counting is helpless in the face of the countless things to count; this is what we are reminded of by Greenaway's organising principles and counting games, because their arbitrary and whimsical nature is foregrounded.

The danger of systems is that they can appear natural. Greenaway suggests that we beware of their apparent inevitability in all areas by questioning the 'natural' systems of cinema (both narrative and documentary) and of exhibition display, the immediate contexts of his own practice. His

exhibitions flout normal categories of display and classification. His cinema often offers, in place of the norm of genre narratives, the 'natural' systems to get us from opening to final credits, a variety of skeletal structures, narratives only in the sense that 'anything that moves through time necessarily has some sort of narrative - 1-2-3-4-5-6-7-8-9-10 is a very minimal narrative'. This self-reference in Greenaway ultimately and necessarily relates - as does self-reference in the great early modernist works of art to which it may be compared, from cubism to Matisse to Duchamp - to the world 'outside' art. (A false spatial metaphor. If anything, each is 'inside' the other.) By exploring the narrow confines of an existing language or set of conventions, the properly self-referential artwork suggests how many new worlds might emerge into our consciousness - half-discovered, half-invented - if we expanded those languages and conventions. It is not just the particular narrowness of conventional or 'dominant' cinema that is exposed by Greenaway, the cosiness of its fictions and structures, but the more dangerous cosiness of those other systems and categories of value and belief which we do not regard as fictional, but live by.

This is clearest, most intellectually ruthless, in the rape scene at the end of *The Baby of Mâcon*, considered in detail below; but the film in which systems and countings are most explicitly present, informing every aspect of the form and content and articulated in the screenplay from the outset, is *Drowning by Numbers*. The film begins with a count to a hundred which anticipates that other count, with numbers present on the screen, or occasionally on the soundtrack, which carries us through the film, counting up to a hundred and down to the end of the movie. We see the Skipping Girl counting the stars - but any scientific element to this task is negated. She is, for one thing, not

Above, Left & Right: Drowning by Numbers

actually counting them - although it is a starry night - but counting them off her list, as an aid to her skipping game: she is not a cataloguer, unlike her hapless suitor, Smut, who registers deaths throughout the film; mostly of animals, but finally, in his last act before his suicide, his own. Furthermore - as becomes clear on reading *Fear of Drowning*, a text around and about the film divided into one hundred sections[16] - her list is not merely arbitrarily finite (when you've counted the first 100, she says, all the rest are the same - for her, 1-100 is like those primitive languages we hear about with a word meaning 'a lot' for anything after three or four) but filled with Greenaway's own jokes and references. 'At least a quarter will never appear on any accredited map of the Universe', he writes, although the principle behind these imaginary star names is identical to those behind the names of real stars: 'Name a star in homage to a friend, a lover or a teacher or a dog'. Or a hero - Kitaj is in there, along with other artists - (Barbara) Kruger, Bosch, Fabritius, Kneller. Or a character in another Greenaway film, past or future - Kracklite, from *The Belly of an Architect,* Spica from *The Cook, The Thief, His Wife and Her Lover*, and Tulse Luper, a fluid character, half alter-ego of Greenaway himself, slyly referred to in *Fear of Drowning* as a 'local hero', often referred to or present in earlier films, including *Vertical Features Remake, A Walk Through H* and *The Falls.* Zed, without two noughts, is star 67, and Castor and Pollux belong to that film's narratives of twinning as well as to the heavens, just as Groombridge is both 'a legitimate star' and 'a past favourite location'. The list is a labyrinth, a maze, in which we meet the artist and his world - and our own world, given a new twist.

It is tempting, therefore, to structure a book about Greenaway in a way which apes or echoes

the scaffolding of his ever-widening oeuvre. In a critical context, however, such homage or quotation too easily becomes parasitical, an empty repetition, a taking over of Greenaway's art as if from some higher position which both judges and appropriates - a kind of cannibalism, even, the kind which supposes that digestion involves a kind of identification with what is swallowed. 'As for critics,' Greenaway writes in his drawing/essay *Prospero's Six-Part Fool*,[17] 'one mediocre writer is more valuable than ten good critics. They are like haughty, barren spinsters lodged in a maternity ward.' The last thing one needs in such circumstances is a hysterical pregnancy.

'Losing Count', a working title since relegated to the present sub-section, is intended to suggest the inevitable failure of the viewer, of any viewer, to catch all the references - just as one never manages to get all of the numbers whilst viewing *Drowning by Numbers*. Such a failure is of course only a facet of the viewer's freedom; for every 'lost' meaning there is a new meaning - or association, or connection - which is the viewer's creative contribution. A work of art is not a crossword puzzle, to be solved, with only a single correct answer; it is better to have counted and lost count than never to have counted at all. This is a major part of Greenaway's message, but his own generation of explanatory material, through interviews, catalogues, documentary films about his feature films, books and exhibitions which rework material and images from his cinema, may paradoxically obscure this even as it considers it. In *Rosa* (the book) Greenaway (the author) notes, 'You can never be sure of communicating essentials, however hard you try', and that 'No phenomenon is free of personal associations, whatever the author wishes'.[18] This is in the course of inventing an audience for the opera the text describes, an invention which emphasises the corporeality of viewing a

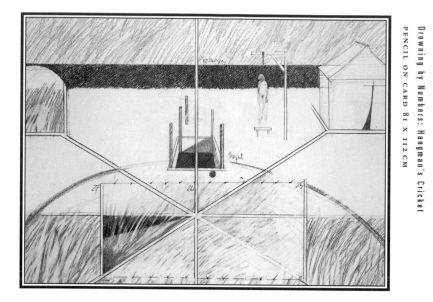

Drowning by Numbers: Hangman's Cricket

PENCIL ON CARD 81 X 112 CM

performance, the specifics of seating and of a particular view and absent-mindedness, which gives us permission for what we all do anyway: 'Don't be concerned, your imagination is inevitably going to wander'.[19]

One could easily accept all this explanatory material - which, fictionally at least, incorporates even our own subjectivity as viewers within its self-reflexivity - and look no further. Clearly, it must always constitute a starting point. But the title I have stolen from Greenaway's early film *A Walk Through H* for the present introductory chapter (it was another of my working titles) refers back to Greenaway's narrative of a journey guided by maps so imprecise that no two readings (or journeys) could be the same - a journey which is also a journey through an exhibition, for the maps are really paintings, not maps, and the walk is, on screen, a 'walk' through pictures at an exhibition - a walk ambiguously related to the narrative of the soundtrack. (Compare the journey through the scripts and strips of film shown within *Vertical Features Remake*, and both with Hollis Frampton's *Poetic Justice*: 'nothing but a table with a cup of coffee, a cactus, and in the middle a pile of sheets of paper; silently, the sheets follow one another to the top of the pile and we read - fragments seized at the whim of the succession - the scenario of a film; a rubber glove rests on the last page.')[20] What follows is not a chronological account of Greenaway's oeuvre, but treats it rather as if it were all at once visible in an exhibition space, simultaneously present and available so that any order results from the whims and interests of the viewers, following visual and conceptual echoes and reprises along with their trains of thought. This is utopian, and conceals the extent to which some of the work considered - the earliest films, some of the work for television, and, apart from *The Stairs*

Munich and Greenaway's contribution to *Spellbound,* the exhibitions - is only known at second hand, as well as the way in which an inevitable reliance on videos, with their 'small-scale miniaturisation of a film at much reduced quality levels',[21] can begin to eclipse the memory of seeing the films as they were meant to be seen, in the cinema. But it suits both the organisation and the texture of Greenaway's work, which is spatial, non-linear in its reprises and repeats, its remakings and remod-ellings, its cross-references between works, its encyclopaedic or musical rather than narrative-driven temporalities, and which, as one would expect from a painter, is extravagantly visual, and visual also in its thought processes, assumptions, terms of reference and demands. It is this quality which I hope to suggest, rather than replicate, in language - and in the structure of this book.

There is one structure, less playful and genuinely analytical, that might profitably have been used as a way into Greenaway's work: the remarks on cinema and its elements which preface the catalogue to the first part of his 'mega-cinematic' project, *The Stairs,* involving a series of ten exhibitions, documented on film and through publications, within and across major cities. I shall certainly be drawing heavily on aspects of the project, which is comparable to Eisenstein's attempts to relate film theory to film practice. (Comparable both generally, and in detail, for example in their shared interest in screen ratios, one of the structuring devices within *The Stairs Munich.*)

The exhibitions, which are largely 'held outside the confines and jurisdiction of the established or orthodox or conventional exhibition spaces', are disciplined by Greenaway's favourite device - poised between rationality and superstition, neatness and magic - of 1-100 (in Geneva, there were one hundred sites, one hundred days, and a catalogue which counts up to page 100 twice; and, in Munich, one hundred screens for one hundred years of cinema).[22] But the theoretical structure - which, it is already clear, will develop and shift with the actual exhibitions - isolates ten subject areas for consideration: Location, Audience, The Frame (already inseparably part of the Location and Projection exhibitions), Acting, Properties, Light, Text, Time, Scale and Illusion. Many of these areas will be discussed in some detail in what follows, and related - to admit the bias of the present study within the various contexts sketched above - in particular to the history of painting and contemporary art practice.

In the second chapter, 'Themes and Variations', I consider both recurrent ideas and recurrent images in Greenaway's work, and as I do so the impossibility of distinguishing form and content, image and idea, in his thought and visual thought should become clear. Any sequence, even any individual shot, simultaneously involves the relations of language to sight, of bodies to the body of language, of painting and cinema to literature, of viewers to artworks, of sound to vision. Sometimes the subjects of the segments in this section require a drawing of attention to, a cataloguing of, particular themes or images, rather than critical analysis; sometimes an exposition, an exploration of the wider contexts of the images and themes.

In the third chapter, 'Art Caught in the Act' (a title twisted from an early description of cinema as 'nature caught in the act'), I consider in some detail particular sequences both from Greenaway's features and from his opera/text *Rosa*, placing them in the narrow context of his own concerns and theories - aspects of which will already be familiar from Chapter 2 - and then widening the debates (about framing, or the viewer as voyeur) which they seek to join or establish.

In Chapter 4, 'Irony and Tragedy: Six Necessary Elements', I consider Greenaway through Aristotle's six elements of tragedy, outlined in the *Poetics*: plot, character, diction, thought, spectacle and music. Greenaway offers, often, an ironised, Darwinian tragedy, a tragedy without catharsis. This is Brechtian, in many ways; Brecht distinguished the 'Roundabout' type of spectator ('those who identify themselves with an incident like a child on a roundabout') from the 'Planetarium' types ('those who are confronted with a demonstration and observe it, like the spectators in a planetarium'). Another reason, perhaps, to have begun with a skipping girl counting the stars.

'Tulse Luper suggested my journey through H needed 92 maps, anticipating my question he suggested the time to decide what H stood for was at the end of the journey and by that time it scarcely mattered.'[23] In our present journey, G is obviously for Greenaway: Greenaway as author/artist/auteur, Greenaway as in 'have you seen the new Greenaway?' This is not a biographical study; it makes no attempt to explain the art in terms of the life (in the conventional sense of 'life', which increasingly excludes the consumption and practice of art, those excitements within the intellectual and imaginative life so central to any artist, in favour of 'traumas', moments of 'pure' feeling somehow imagined in advance of culture, those signifiers of the mythical 'true' self 'behind' the public image). This is, in part, a response to the nature of Greenaway's themes. Birth, copulation and death are themes so basic to any imaginable human culture that no particular biographical detail is necessary to explain their presence. It also respects Greenaway's own tendency to discuss his work in terms of the histories of ideas and of art, in terms of a cultural rather than a personal impetus, despite the almost unprecedented authorial presence of Greenaway in his cinema, to which he brings a dominance assumed in writing and the visual arts, but generally diluted in film-making. (*Rosa*, moreover, is perhaps the first opera not primarily associated with its composer, which raises the interesting question of whether or how it might survive, be revived and restaged, without Greenaway's involvement.)

Greenaway, it is true, offers occasional fragments of autobiography as triggers for his films. A psychosomatic illness in Rome led to *The Belly of an Architect*; a holiday in Wales and a day spent in a constantly interrupted attempt to draw a house inspired *The Draughtsman's Contract*; *Fear of Drowning* mentions the personal nostalgic associations with landscape which fuelled *Drowning by Numbers*. We know that his father was a keen ornithologist, and that Greenaway himself worked at the Central Office of Information, both facts of obvious relevance to his oeuvre, and above all to *The Falls*. But these anecdotes of creation are never offered as keys to particular recurring 'obsessive' images or particular films. (In revising the interview material for the present book, Greenaway added one purely autobiographical reference, linking *The Belly of an Architect* to the death of his father from stomach cancer, which Kracklite suffers from in the film; and removed another.) The Greenaway who offers a commentary on his own work can hardly be properly distinguished from this Greenaway-as-film-maker; his writing elaborates and joins his artistic practice rather than offering an origin for it, in the sense of an origin in Romantic creative anguish, rather than in the culture which it feeds and which it feeds on. This is also true in interviews, including the two extended interviews included here, extensively revised by Greenaway himself. The first was conducted as editing was continuing on *The Cook, The Thief, His Wife and Her Lover*, the second as editing began on *The Pillow Book* - and as work was continuing on a number of projects, including *The Stairs Munich* and the *Strasbourg Book of Allegories*.

EMPTY POOL MEETINGS EQUENCE 25 · Pg 89B/c/l

10ft

red ladder

faded light blue distemper.

faded dark blue lines

white flaking chairs.

dark evergreen topiary bushes.

Swimming Party

PENCIL ON PAPER

Themes
AND VARIATIONS
Being Clothed Naming
the art of Peter Gezza

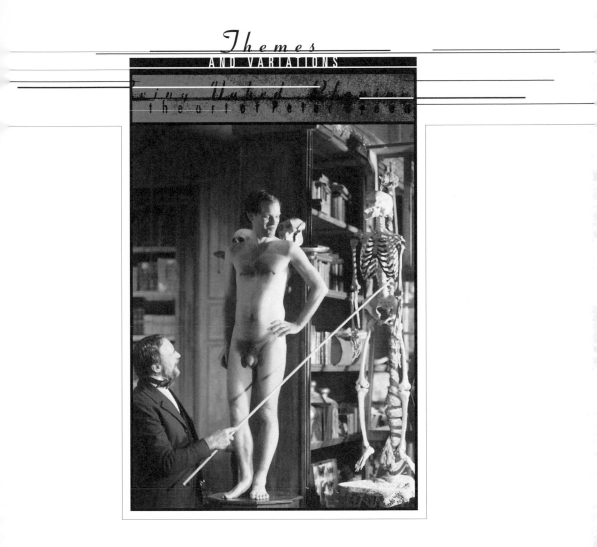

REPETITION TIME

Of course I repeat things - that's the way I learn.
ROBERT WILSON [1]

Repeated looking makes us see [things] in many ways. And repeated looking makes us see them many times in the same way.
Rosa [2]

It has been a curious condition of operatic convention that the same material is there to be legitimately repeated. Watching a static set organised to throw emphasis on what you are hearing as well as what you are seeing, forces a repetitive perception. I've seen that and I've seen that, and I've seen that again. Yet each repetition is not truly itself, but a continuing series of variations. And each one has to be different because it's older and more experienced than the last one. You will understand then that I repeat with variations. It's to be certain that I know what I am watching. Is that not as it should be? I think so. I enjoy a comprehension of things.
Rosa [3]

There are many favourite motifs that are repeated, but then who doesn't use a favourite motif repeatedly? And the major obsessions repeat because there is no end to the permutations and variations on a given theme, especially if that theme is sex and death. The painter Renoir said to the film-maker Renoir that artists have maybe one or two or three ideas and spend the whole of their lives repeating them. He hastily added that one or two ideas could be more than enough for a lifetime.

Theories of the sister arts and their relations swing between ludicrous over-identification and rigid separation, a history repeated as farce in the last hundred or so years with the new arts of photography and cinema. At the blunter edge of commonplace criticism and critical common-places, however, there is a tendency, almost involuntary, to swap and borrow critical terms, not least between painting and music.

Greenaway is much exercised by - and often, it seems, ambivalent about - such relationships, above all by marriages of text and image. His cinema looks back - and forward, since he feels that the potential of cinema has rarely been fully explored - to the Wagnerian theory of the *Gesamtkunstwerk*, the art work in which all the independent virtues of the various arts are brought together. Although he believes that opera itself is unfilmable, he also believes in an 'operatic' cinema which incorporates, to a far greater extent than conventional film has so far done, the virtues and possibilities of painting, theatre, architecture, music, dance and - despite his dissatisfaction with narrative cinema's reliance on adaptations of novels - literature.

'Themes and variations' is primarily a musical term, though there are obvious literary applications. Together with the notion of the 'reprise', it indicates the temporal freedoms which cinema gave (along with dialogue) to a painter to almost endlessly work and rework images - and without the consequences of such repetitions and alterations in painting, Picasso's 'series of destructions', the lost paintings covered over or scraped off in the pursuit of the final version. This succession - within individual films and within the oeuvre - is fused, still, with the painter's spatial sense of meanings as continuously present, overlapping, simultaneous, to be unpacked at leisure. The exhibitions are an attempt to put back into 'cinema' - the 'mega-cinema' of the exhibition - two things.

The first is the physicality of theatre or opera, and of the actual experience of filming: 'I feel that my experiences of making cinema will always be more stimulating, more fascinating and more exciting than your experience in watching it - you do not share the text, enjoy the preparations, see the manufacture of the sets and the props, feel the atmosphere of the architecture, be perplexedly stimulated by the range of choice possible in the casting, the location-finding, the editing of image, the selection of the sound and the development of the dialogue, and be party to the exacting decisions of scale and illusion.'[4] In his article on *The Cook, The Thief, His Wife and Her Lover*[5] Jonathan Romney noted:

> The first thing that hits me when I walk onto the set is just how hermetic a world has been created here. The usual gaps in illusion that you find on a film set - where a cocktail lounge wall abruptly breaks off to reveal an expanse of warehouse - aren't found here. This is a fully formed surrounding expanse of *trompe l'oeil*. The kitchen is an echoing Piranesi-like cavern in thick mildewed green, with arches, vaults, galleries, a warren of storerooms and passages behind, and towering frames hung with pigs' heads, pots and poultry. A long bench is stacked with cabbages, jars of fruit and pulses, wine bottles and assorted crustacea.

This was on the huge sound stage at Elstree; for *The Belly of an Architect*, the sets were set in and around major Roman buildings, notably the Victor Emmanuel Building, used for two months of filming 'after a great deal of very obscure negotiations'. In *The Stairs Geneva*, Greenaway writes of how he

had been much impressed by the Cine-Citta craftsmen [who worked on the film]. This small army of carpenters, painters and marblers, with their rags and broken chicken-feathers, easily and convincingly re-marbled the specially constructed wooden staircase each night, ready for the next morning's filming. To watch them was a delight at least equal to watching the actors perform - an occupation of equal purposeful deceit - on the very same painted steps the following day.[6]

The second is the viewer's control over temporality which the spatial arts share with reading. The image, in cinema, is always disappearing, always fluid, always in flight; it has no material substance, it can never be approached, considered. This allows the director almost unlimited control over what the viewer is physically capable of noticing. To take an avant-garde example, the William Burroughs cut-up films, the speed of the editing ensures that when the material is repeated, as it often is, the eye can never begin to explore the unnoticed details of a given shot, but only register that this, again, is what was fleetingly seen before - a remarkably aggressive use of boredom as a strategy. Watching the film is similar to a conversation with an Alzheimer's sufferer - it is not that very little is happening, or that a minimalist pattern unfolds through repetition, but that the same thing happens again and again, compulsively, but always as if for the first time. One never - to borrow a phrase of Stephen Heath's - 'sees more'. In dominant cinema, editing enforces involvement in the narrative, without pause for reflection (certainly not in its 'held notes', which do not invite analysis); the absorption of the aesthetic gaze, the interrogation of the image, is either disqualified

- overwhelmed - or relocated in a consideration of movement - of tracking shots, or of the editing itself. This can be resisted - in *Alexander Nevsky* one is constantly offered 'dynamic compositions' in the painterly, and perhaps Suprematist, sense, organisations of forms within the frame; and Greenaway constantly resists it, not least with his use of symmetrical compositions - but it cannot be overcome.

When painters or artists have approached the spatial arts over the last few decades, there has always been a special, a particular attitude to time. Warhol's, obviously, both with his real time, often linked to reel time, to the amount of film in the camera (so *Beauty No. 2* simply ends with the film running out), and his looped time, which Greenaway plays with and enlivens in *Rosa*, a very cinematic opera - 'a true description of *Rosa* would be film/opera, opera/film'. (A landscape, looped, suddenly has riders in it.) Wenders, also; his *Paris Texas* is referred to, though not by name, in the script of *The Cook, The Thief, His Wife and Her Lover*. Happenings; video; performance; there is a whole history to be written of non-narrative time in expansions of the visual arts, time which often involves boredom, repetition, ritualistic or compulsive behaviour. Perhaps there is a parallel history of music and space, in Cage, perhaps, or Stockhausen, in modern opera and music theatre - in which repetition in the work of Reich, Glass, Nyman might perhaps also be compared to and contrasted with Warhol. Greenaway's repetitions are more Baroque, more ornate. They are replete with meaning where other artists' repetitions are often emptied, drained of meaning, or exclusively self-reflexive (like many of the 'structural/materialist' films of the late sixties and early seventies discussed in Heath's 'Repetition Time'),[7] or even perhaps - since repetition in itself is a neutral device - in search of a transcendence very far from Greenaway's secular irony. But this broad tradition is a kind of frame for them.

There could have been far more sections in this chapter. Flashing lights (*A Zed and Two Noughts*; the photocopier in *The Belly of an Architect*; Tableau 17 in *Darwin*; Pflastersteine Max-Josephs-Platz in *The Stairs Munich*); lightning (the subject of *Act of God*; Biography 79 in *The Falls*; and, emphasising a Frankenstein reference, in *M is for Man, Music and Mozart*); female underwear (or the lack of it), one of the *100 Objects to Represent the World*, the subject of an early drunken joke in *Drowning by Numbers*, and featured in episode 3 of *Fear of Drowning*, a comic scene in *A Zed and Two Noughts*, a violent scene in *The Cook, The Thief, His Wife and Her Lover*, and a passage in *Rosa*. Other themes run across much of the discussion, throughout the whole book: corporeality, sexuality, theatricality, artifice, illusion, allusion. I have tried to suggest, through the looseness of the categories or examples - I make no initial organising distinction between the visual and the conceptual - how visual thought operates, in Greenaway in particular: through echoes and associations and reference at the same time as through what is immediate to the eye; through Baroque, emblematic, portmanteau images in which the pleasures of the text and the pleasures of the body - Greenaway's two inalienable delights - are simultaneously present, leading less to arguments that can be laboriously set out in order than to dense clusters of meaning, rhyme and metaphor. Often these themes can be seen to be overlapping at some level, whether through a parallel thought or a parallel image. Compare for example the similar use of red material - ribbons, a long thin flag - in otherwise very different scenes, the second drowning in *Drowning by Numbers* and Flavia's seduction of Kracklite in *The Belly of an Architect*. I have tried also to suggest the ways in which such overlappings work; Klee's invaluable phrase, 'the thinking eye', is useful here.

WATER

At the centre of the 'shot' in the first of the hundred viewing stages or platforms in *The Stairs* is the fountain in Lake Geneva: 'an eruption of white spume, a sexual motif for beginnings. All life starts with water.'

In Greenaway, many lives also end with water. Site 88 in *The Stairs Geneva* isolated a lakeside sculpture of a boy and his horse.[8] 'Near here in 1884 a young Italian rider got into difficulties whilst bathing his high-spirited horse, and despite heroic attempts to save him, he drowned. From this viewpoint of the sculpture, the boy's hand breaks the silhouette of his horse's back - it could be the waving hand of a drownee.' There are the drownings by numbers of the three husbands by the three Cissies, counted out as they go down for the third time, the first of which, in a bath, is 'rehearsed' by Kracklite in *The Belly of an Architect* - we see him experiment with suicide by drowning, and explain to his wife how impossible it is; the body overrides the will. In *The Draughtsman's Contract* - which begins with a woman's anecdote about making water - the bodies of both the draughtsman and the husband he cuckolds are dumped into the moat. *Death in the Seine*, a short film of 1988 (the same year as *Drowning by Numbers*), was inspired by Richard Cobb's book *Death in Paris*, based on a mortuary archive of bodies recovered from the Seine between 1790 and 1801. An unrealised project, *Massacre at the Baths*, concerns death by water in fact and fiction - Ophelia, Marat,[9] Woolf.

Prospero's Books restores water, shipwreck, drowning as the central metaphor of Shakespeare's *Tempest*, in which Ariel is also a water sprite, who walks on water. It is as watery a film as has ever been made, in which light, Greenaway's medium, is (as it were) diluted by water - as Prospero's ink is literally diluted. A famous scene in Orson Welles's *The Lady From Shanghai* compares cinema itself to an aquarium - a spectacle of light framed by dark - and the modern technologies with which Greenaway plays throughout the film allow tableaux which can be interpreted as variations on this metaphor; for example the early scene of Miranda's troubled sleep, where, behind her bed and framed by curtains, we see a tank full of nymphs swimming underwater, as the (toy) ship sinks. Greenaway has also used water tanks in his exhibitions, including *In The Dark*, the installation homaging cinema history which accompanied the projections for *The Stairs Munich*.[10]

Water, then, is associated with bodily functions and fluids, 'the fluids of my body, of my life' auctioned by the Church in *The Baby of Mâcon*; and with Greenaway's three stark themes, birth, copulation and death. In *The Cook, The Thief, His Wife and Her Lover* the lovers' first rendezvous is in a 'bathroom', the ladies' toilet. (There are plays within the script on 'john', WC, 'bathroom', and so on.) In *The Draughtsman's Contract*, the second contractual affair is consummated in a (real) bathroom.

In 1985, a twenty-five-minute film for Channel 4 recorded 26 bathrooms. Many of the shorter films are centred around water, including a documentary on synchronised swimming, *Making a Splash*. Two films made in 1975 have water in the title: *Water* and *Water Wrackets*. Five of the first six objects to represent the world are to do with water: A Cloud, Water, Snow, 100 Umbrellas and A Rainbow; number 49 is A Bath, number 64 is Ice, and number 87 is A Rowing Boat.

After the frequent use of streams and wide expanses of water in the films up to and including *The Falls*, two things are striking about the use of water in the feature films. The first is the extent to which water is shown as contained. The second drowning by numbers takes place at sea, certainly, but the first is in a tin bath (too small, it is noted, for a verdict of accidental death to be convincing) and the third in a swimming pool. (The sea, in the second drowning scene, is initially domesticated, framed in an interior shot, as the dialogue discusses baths - and the first drowning.) The conspirators are linked to the water tower. The sea itself - like the starry sky - is subject to ridiculous attempts to contain it, to reduce it to systems: the fish are numbered, there is a game of predicting the tides. In *Prospero's Books*, as has been noted above, there is a miniaturisation of the ocean, an ironic fore-grounding of the standard cinematic device of using tanks and models for sea scenes.

The second striking feature is the representation of water through light - light on walls, reflected from the surface of a body of water which we cannot see (though often we can see its container). *Watching Water*, an exhibition in Venice, included a basement which was 'a fantasy of artificial water created by light', and this, in addition to reworking *Intervals* (a short film shot in Venice in 1969 which shows no water), is a motif to be found even in *The Baby of Mâcon*, the least water-based of the features (on the back wall of the barracks during the extended rape scene). *The Belly of an Architect* is particularly rich in examples of this, starting with the water from the basin of the obelisk fountain in front of the Pantheon and continuing in the bathroom which is featured in Caspasian's first seduction attempt as well as Kracklite's experiments with drowning. (The light, in this instance, is greenish, in accord with the colour symbolism of the film.) It also appears in the bath-house sequence.

Watching Water (the text) and *Fear of Drowning* pursue the theme of water through lists and the kind of ironic references, narratives and narrative fragments familiar from Greenaway's early cinema. *Watching Water* ends with a list of films with water in the title, including *Boudu Sauvé des Eaux*. In *Fear of Drowning*, in addition to references to sailors, the sea, rivers, 'a ferryman without a boat', 'three old fishwives who chant' and 'a rhyme that contains every reference to water in the Old Testament - from Noah to Jonah to Moses', we find the following passage: 'Cissie Colpitts indeed did not drown - though her life saw many events associated with water. In fact she died in

Above: 100 Objects to Represent the World (1992)

Right: A Plumber's Universe: A First Version (1990)
MIXED MEDIUM ON CARD 81 X 107CM

her sleep, quietly haemorrhaging - the blood swelling up in her lap being the same colour as the red plush seat she sat in - in a cinema in Philadelphia. She had been watching a film by Jean Renoir called *Boudu Sauvé des Eaux*, which tells the story of a tramp saved from drowning against his will.' A Cissie Colpitts narrative is to be found in *The Falls* (Biography 27); it features a water tower which (as in *Vertical Features Remake*) becomes a film vault; one of the Cissies suffers from 'a new aversion to the darkness of cinemas'.

At the end of *Rosa*, rain falls.

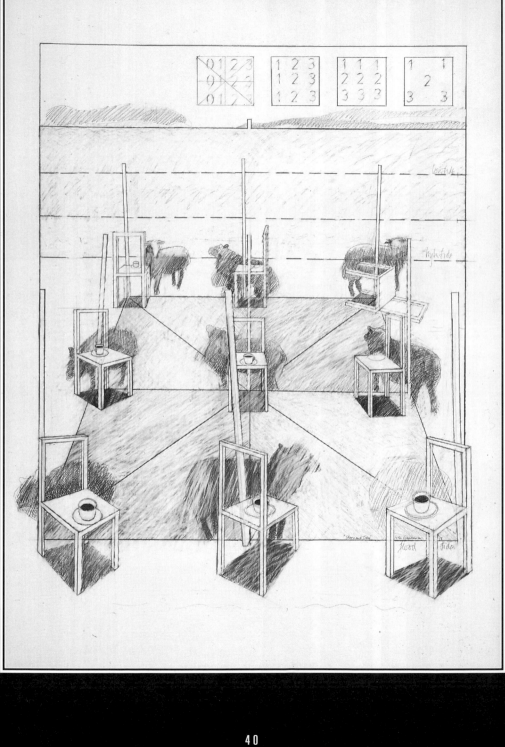

APPLAUSE

We are, shall we say, comfortably seated.

HOLLIS FRAMPTON [11]

Applause is a *leitmotiv* in *The Belly of an Architect*, linked to plot. There is applause at the end of the film, at the opening of the ill-fated exhibition, and from the drunken Kracklite. In the previous scene he has been given his death sentence by his doctor; now, running riot in an outdoor café before the Pantheon, he applauds the ancient building. This baffles the men who wait for a chance to control him, as the police eventually do; but we, the audience, know what he is doing. At the beginning of the film, at the outset of the exhibition project, the Pantheon, theatrically lit, has been applauded by the cast.

It is as if we ourselves were being applauded. Without breaking any 'rules' of cinema, the scene is subtly disruptive. A building is given a 'point of view' shot. The audience in the cinema is given a theatrical sight - actors facing them, applauding - uncomfortably close to the curtain call, the hinge between art and life which closes but is outside the drama itself.

Here is Greenaway's own gloss on this scene from *The Stairs Geneva*: [12]

In the film *The Belly of an Architect*, clapping the Pantheon was exhilarating. Not only was it required that the actors should clap that revered building seen under those auspicious moonlit circumstances, but the camera crew clapped also, as did the watching spectators.

The applause was not wasted. Maybe we were applauding the building's distant author or its long dead patron. Maybe the applause was for the building's history, its vicissitudes or its magnificent decay.

Maybe we were exhilarated to be clapping such a particular mixture of stone and shadow. Maybe the applause was to express a sheer exuberant delight in the canons of exhilarating architecture, in an exciting use of space and indeed in the performance of history that has both made and then swept around that building. We were undoubtedly clapping a performance, a performance, perhaps of history and time and sense of place, though that performance was not conventionally 'alive' or rehearsed or artificially provided for us as an officially attentive audience. But then why should it be?

The applause, then, acts in many ways like Christo's wrapping of the Pont Neuf or the Reichstag: it isolates, it frames; it redefines the relation of the crowd to a building as a relation between an audience and a performance. In Greenaway's choice of shot, in the press scaffolding in front of the wrapped Reichstag, it literally puts the building in perspective.

I have written 'redefines', but could have written 'rediscovers', since the architecture of power has traditionally used a rhetorical language to which the viewer is subject, as citizen, or believer. This legible spectacle has been rewritten, of late, by tourism. The modern ancient city is indeed 'artificially provided for us', through dramatic floodlighting, for example - but only in so far as we are consumers. The power relation has changed: the building is a supplicant, it offers up its past as a spectacle, a show, to visitors, rather than imposing a present power structure upon residents - who themselves become tourists at home, their civic pride related to how good their city is to visit rather than how good it is to live in. One could perhaps define tourism, the *son et lumière*, as a 'roundabout' consumption of the city, its view of the baubles and buildings of ancient power at the exact opposite pole to Eisenstein's revolutionary presentation of the palace and its contents in *October*; and works such as the wrapped Reichstag and *The Stairs Geneva*, which, not least in its catalogue and video documentation/exposition, elaborated and improvised around the city's history, as a 'planetarium' framing of that tourist viewing.

It is clear that this scene has inspired many later projects.

Since it has been said that a definition of a performance is any event witnessed by an audience, and delighting therefore in the axiom that audience and performance need one another as equals, my interest in the audience as 'the performance' has grown. I have begun to investigate the audience's participation in the performance they are witnessing in two recent film projects, *M is for Man, Music and Mozart* and *The Baby of Mâcon*. In both these projects, although the audience was present ostensibly to watch the event, in both cases they became involved with it, to such an extent in *The Baby of Mâcon* that the performance was dramatically realigned according to their intervention.

'Dramatically', here, carries its full weight, as we shall see. *Rosa*, the text, also fictionalises the audience; *The Stairs*, the exhibition, liberates it; 'the most important participant in *The Stairs Geneva* will be the audience - deliberately not a seated audience but one that can participate in an entirely perambulatory way, putting their attention to the frame and therefore to the framed event, in their own time and according to their own interest'. *The Stairs Munich* (which did not concern itself with the city's history, although that history often intersected one's actual experience of it) was also perambulatory, and ended with *In the Dark*, in which chairs were part of what one walked around; each screen in a hanging wall of screens was awarded its own light source and its own chair.

The Belly of an Architect was, in fact, the second film to use this device. The landscape is applauded in *The Draughtsman's Contract*. This was a way of emphasising the theatricality of the

view within an aristocratic estate, the artificiality which is also well established in the dialogue, and in the figure of the landscape architect from Holland. The garden is theatrical in advance of the draughtsman; and, indeed, his insistence on representing only what is before him is his downfall, for he misunderstands the extent to which his images - which record not nature but, in effect, a stage set filled with ambiguous properties - are, in any actual viewing, allegories, cryptic narratives of murder or adultery. There is a complex relation between draughtsman, patron and audience - he is often observed as he draws, so that his drawing becomes a kind of performance, and must also incorporate his audience when it enters into his frame - even if he leaves a face blank, with the aim of substituting the features of the absent husband (well represented by a blank, therefore) for those of his son-in-law, who becomes an ill-tempered stand-in. (The draughtsman cuckolds both halves of this composite figure.) This violent drama of the connections between the performance of a work of art and its audience is in many ways a rehearsal or anticipation of *The Baby of Mâcon*. (Both are also dramas of infertility.)

PHOTOGRAPHY

Photography and cinema share the camera.

STEPHEN HEATH [13]

In his essay 'Narrative Spaces' Stephen Heath notes how

> In so many senses, every film is a veritable drama of vision and this drama has thematically and symptomatically 'returned' in film since the very beginning: from the fascination of the magnifying glass in *Grandma's Reading Glass* to Lina's short-sightedness in *Suspicion* to the windscreen and rear-view mirror of *Taxi Driver*, from the keyhole of *A Search for Evidence* to the images that flicker reflected over Brody's glasses in *Jaws* as he turns the pages of a book on sharks, finding the images of the film to come and which he will close as he closes the book; not to mention the extended dramatizations such as *Rear Window* or *Peeping Tom*. [14]

Just as relevant to Greenaway's own 'extended dramatisation' of vision and representation is the longer roll-call of pictures about sight - there are narratives of blindness, from Duccio's blind man healed by Christ to David's *Belisarius*, narratives of not wanting to see, of averted gazes and hands held up to shield the face; narratives of voyeurism, of Diana and Susannah; there are the geometries of the glance which structure any composition with figures, and, differently, any portrait; there are the paintings about painting, from *Las Meninas* to Vermeer's realist allegory of allegorical painting, *Artist in His Studio*, to the teasing ironies of Magritte's easel series; and the painters' self-portraits; and the illusionist games of surface and frame in the genre of *trompe l'oeil*.

In *The Draughtsman's Contract* the draughtsman's perspective frame is explicitly compared to a camera: the film camera which both repeats and frames its view, in a series of shots poised between subjectivity and objectivity. [15] Subjectivity, since we have that rare thing in Greenaway's cinema, a 'point of view' shot, showing the action from the standpoint of one of the characters. (Compare the second drowning scene in *Drowning by Numbers*, Cissie 2 uses binoculars to view both her husband, in trouble in the sea and calling for help, and the runners on the shore. Binoculars are a common enough device in narrative cinema, but are rather startling in Greenaway; again, a point of view shot is drawing our attention to a device, a visual gadget, inviting us to compare the lenses of the binoculars with the camera lens.) [16] Objectivity, since that point of view is through a device which purportedly allows an objective record of the visual field; an objectitivity which is mocked

throughout the film, as the script explores the paradoxes and naturalised conventions involved in representing what 'is really there'. A drawing takes time to make, and despite the conditions which the draughtsman lays down to minimise change and enforce repetition, so that what is before him is increasingly a performance of what has been before him before, the visual field is full of events as well as objects as that time passes. He is vulnerable to inconsequential - but visually decisive - changes in the light or in the clouds, in the movements of people and animals, and is much mocked as a result. Ultimately, the conditions laid down in his contract offer him no more power over his subject than the game of predicting the tides offers over the sea in *Drowning by Numbers*.

The drawings claim a 'photographic' 'objectivity', then; but the camera which lines up behind the perspective frame is demonstrating the power of cinema as superior not just in realism - although it can record the sounds which (as is discussed) are absent from the drawing, and it can record the changing weather (which, at one moment, changed fortuitously in accord with the script) - but also in artifice. The story which is happening to the draughtsman (and the audience, left with a general idea of conspiracy) is told by the camera, to it, through it. Ultimately, any secure contrast between realism and artifice breaks down, because realism itself is artifice. We do not need to know that Greenaway's own attempts to draw a house inspired the film to make a connection between the draughtsman's attempt to control what comes before his perspective frame and Greenaway's need as a director to assemble his properties and his actors in a location in front of a camera. (The child who appears in the film, we learn from an interview, refused to be separated

The Draughtsman's Contract: Mr Talman in the Garden

PENCIL ON PAPER 77 X 52 CM

from his teddy bear, an anachronism running parallel to the draughtsman's problems with linen and clothing and ladders intruding themselves into his compositions.) The only contrast which does hold true will be explored below: it is between two kinds of perspective, one which records, as far as is possible, what can be seen by the artist from one viewpoint, so that the viewer as it were stands where the artist stood, a perspective of witnessed space; and one which uses the convention of perspective to construct a staged space on which an action is performed, set out, specifically for the benefit of a future audience, a perspective of narrative or allegorical space. The two are contrasted in the film. In addition to the drawings, into which meanings are smuggled against the artist's will, there is a painting, an intentional allegory; though both drawings and painting are subject to the endless and unavoidable ambiguities of interpretation. Both perspectives are also present in photography, whether still photography or cinema, though, again, both are ironised, mingled and thematised in Greenaway.

In *The Belly of an Architect*, a similar comparison/opposition is established (though it is less dominant in the structure of the film) between Greenaway's camera and Flavia's. In a sequence comparable to a scene with the guitarist/hero and the enigmatic neighbour/photographer/voyeur in Michel Deville's *Peril en la Demeure* (filmed two years earlier and released in Britain as *Death in a French Garden*, a nod towards the French title of *The Draughtsman's Contract, Meurtre dans un Jardin Anglais*), Flavia displays a sequence of photographs pinned to the wall, images which repeat or run parallel to the narrative of the film so far.

Often, when such devices are used in cinema, there is an unresolved confusion between the narrative camera, the camera as storyteller, and the still camera held and used by a character within the film, a confusion comparable to that in flashbacks or dream sequences that are purportedly subjective but, for narrative clarity and legibility, not filmed as if from the point of view of the character, but rather with the character clearly included in shot like any other. The two are fused in Edgar Reitz's *Heimat*, for example, with stills from the film presented within it as photographs taken and owned by the characters, as if they were snapshots. Nor, in the closing moments of Malle's *L'Ascenseur au l'Échafaud*, when we see the photos of the guilty couple (a brilliant conceit; it is the only image of them together in the whole film) are we supposed to wonder, *who took the photos?* - these photos that condemn them, that prove their illicit affair, these photos of them as lovers, *alone*. (Another common device, the freezing of a shot so it becomes a newspaper front page, is used at the outset of *A Zed and Two Noughts*. The newspaper also carries stories of a death in a bath, and the death of an architect.)

Such issues, as we have seen, are thematised in Greenaway, as they are, however differently, in any thriller/conspiracy/mystery genre, where photography can be used to suggest both a new subjective point of view - after the film has been centred on the hero's own, limited understanding of events - and evidence, objective proof of what really happened. Flavia has been shown taking many photographs - in the previous scene (with Kracklite's own camera), at the cutting of the cake before the Pantheon, in the Victor Emmanuel Building, at the tomb of Augustus, and, from a car, at St Peter's as Kracklite posts one of his postcards to Boullée. Sometimes, she is recording public events - a press photographer, in effect. Sometimes, she is closer to the private eye gathering evidence - here, of her brother's affair with Kracklite's wife, and of his habit of stealing postcards. One shot of Kracklite bending over a basin seems unmistakably a still from the narrative camera, but, in the scene from which it is taken, she does in fact enter the frame from much the same position; and she was at Hadrian's Villa, so another still, of Kracklite stooping to vomit, is at least possible; only a shot of Kracklite in a doctor's surgery seems demonstrably inconsistent.

But, in her studio, she also takes 'art' rather than documentary photographs: of the pregnant Louisa, and, in this scene, of Kracklite as Bronzino's *Andrea Doria as Neptune*[17] (Compare the juxtaposition in Antonioni's *Blow Up* of fashion photography and the photographs that blunderingly and impotently relate to, intervene in, real life.) The camera that she uses is framed by Greenaway's camera in a very similar way to the draughtsman's frame, though first we see it the other way round, pointing at us - Kracklite looks through it as he wanders round the studio. (The draughtsman is also shown looking through the grid at the camera. There are parallels with the use of projectors in *A Zed and Two Noughts* and the 'audience' clapping the audience in *The Belly of an Architect*.) Although installed, pointing at the conventional photographic studio dark paper backdrop, for a constructed environment, as the scene develops the camera is used to record 'evidence', like the photos pinned on the wall: as Kracklite and Flavia make love, visually split by the camera and tripod, Caspasian enters the frame - keys dangling from his hand, in a rhyme with Kracklite's own business with keys at the beginning and end of the film - approaches them, and takes their photograph. (In fact, he has only set off the flash, a false signifier of the photographic moment; there is no film in the camera.)

In *The Belly of an Architect* photography also takes its place in the history of human imagery:

The film debates whether immortality is possible through art. It starts with visual imagery in the Vittoriano that supports the concept of man reproducing himself in terms of sculpture and statuary - perhaps the most sophisticated mimetic three-dimensional art representation - the visual space around Kracklite is full of sculptural representations. The sculpture then gives way to Kracklite's image being associated with painting - more abstracted, more created, three dimensions into two. Then the preponderance of painted images of man on the walls of the baths where Kracklite goes to recuperate gives way to photographic representations, which in turn are replaced with the banalities of the photocopied representation. Sculpture then painting then photographs then photocopies.

In Flavia's studio fragments of antique sculpture, ancient heads, are elegantly assembled on a glass table, prominent in two shots. The scene includes all of the stages of representation mentioned here, since Flavia works from a photocopy of a painting.

The photograph joins the list of simulacra, representations, stand-ins, emblems in Greenaway, for whom everything is representational. What, I have suggested, gives his work its particular charge, individuality and excess is that, despite his inexhaustible interest in maps, models,[18] recreations, remakes, reconstructions, texts, even menus,[19] he does not simply divide the world (or the world of his cinema) into signifiers and signified; rather - and this is his particular Baroque sensibility - he invests all objects, all bodies, with intricate, inexhaustible meaning. But this investment - which might also be seen as a kind of negation of meaning, since such a free play clearly also destabilises meaning - includes a recognition that this is how human consciousness works. There are, however, biological priorities, constantly foregrounded by Greenaway, in the how and why of association and symbolism. The flesh will always involve sexuality, health and illness, mortality, whether at the level of esoteric reference or the subconscious - levels, since Freud, since Jung, in any case intricately related. As for Greenaway's own habits of thought, as one grows used to them, the bases touched become familiar through the very processes and repetitions which we are exploring here. This is the

sort of effort we are accustomed to making with a painter or writer; but the consumption of contemporary cinema has become a frighteningly passive experience, in which even character is established in advance of the viewing (through sequels, through the use of cartoon and TV characters, through stars, action heroes, essentially unchanged from film to film), and this has perhaps contributed to critical hostility to the kind of active viewing that Greenaway demands. Nor, despite such exhibition/texts as *The Audience of Mâcon*, is there in his work the kind of post-modern complicity between creation and criticism, a complacent 'irony' which neatly packages the appropriate pass-notes critique within the film itself while, crucially, leaving the pleasures of narrative largely undisturbed, that characterises much contemporary cinema, from *Exotica* to *The Last Action Hero*.

One consequence for photographs of (and within) a world in which everything is at once given an accentuated, highlighted, material presence and an alternative life, in the mind that encounters it, as a token, an instance (so that it is both its unique self and an example of all such selves), is that the photograph's claim to a privileged site between represention and reality, its status as a trace (and therefore, in some way, a truth) rather than a symbol, is simply erased; or, at the very least, held in suspension.

Photography is commonly and publicly regarded as being in some sort of extra possession of the truth. However, both practitioners and historians of the photograph know this to be barely sustainable. Like all other constructed images, photographs are taken by one subjectivity to be interpreted by others, and this present set of photographs is no exception. Indeed this collection revels in the unsustainability of photographic truth - but it does so not to deceive, but to delight in the contradictions and the confusions and in the multiplicity of interpretations that any single contemplation of a constructed image, photographic or otherwise, is prone to.

The problem, in fact, has been that there has been, in the commonplaces of our culture, a naive move from the fact that cameras can only record (there is a genuine question about whether cameras *represent*) something that is in front of them - so that Greenaway does need to assemble actors, sets, properties in front of his cameras, but can draw or paint images with the same content without any such necessity - to the belief that photographic images are 'true' in some unambiguous or philosophical sense, outside interpretation or, indeed, intent - the motive of the person who takes, prints, crops, frames, sets up the image. One can have a painting of a unicorn but not a photograph of a unicorn, since unicorns do not exist to be placed before a camera. Clearly, however, and most clearly in cinema, ficitions can be created for the camera; and it does make sense to say 'there is a unicorn in the film'. Fiction is so much part of our understanding of the word 'film' that it has to be qualified when fiction is (supposedly) absent: 'documentary film'. (Similarly, one could have a photo-collage of a unicorn. As photography begins to fuse completely with computer-generated imagery - as is happening in Greenaway's work both in 'film' and in 'stills' - this crucial distinction becomes increasingly irrelevant.) And of course, editing is always to do with a fiction or an argument, an intervention in the material reality of film to construct something new and particular to the viewing of the film. Pedro Meyer, a photographer who now works with computers, has beautifully severed the connection between trace and truth - always dubious, especially to practitioners - with his suggestion that we stop trusting the medium itself, that we trust the photographer, not photography, as we have always trusted the writer, and not writing. (Though our superstitious reverence for a Photography that mystically overrides any instance of this photograph taken by this photographer in this place, and processed in this darkroom, a Trace which erases the traces of its own material history, can perhaps be seen as parallel to the fundamentalist superstition of the Divine Text, writing without human origin and with an absolute authority and truth value.)

Had there been film in Flavia's camera, it would have recorded two naked actors on a sofa, as Greenaway's camera did. This, of course, is what we edit out of our account of narrative cinema, if we say 'Caspasian attempts to get evidence of Kracklite's infidelity with Flavia'. We do not, however, entirely edit it out of our experience of cinema. For all our talk of 'convincing' acting or 'ham' acting, we are always aware of performance. It is, to a greater or a lesser extent, what we have come to see, particularly in the star system. Brando is always Brando. This holds regardless of quality - Olivier is always Olivier, theatrically, in an intensely irritating, distracting way; De Niro is always De Niro, cinematically, not least in his admirable commitment to the character, his foregrounded 'invisibility'. Realism is a style of acting, not an escape from it. This awareness of acting and of individual actors or stars is increasingly true, not just because 'character', as something more than an alias for the star, is increasingly disappearing from dominant cinema, but also because actors and actresses are increasingly often naked on screen. Sean French has written how this disrupts narrative: 'For almost all [of *Don't Look Now*] you feel an intense identification with Laura's pain and her attempt to rebuild her life ... I say "almost" because, in the famous sex scene, your inner voice suddenly stops saying "Laura this" and "Laura that" and starts saying, "Oh, look, there's Julie Christie without any clothes on".[20]

In watching a Greenaway film, *The Baby of Mâcon* in particular, this doublethink is a part of the content, the argument, the structure of the film. It is not just experienced; it is considered. *The Baby of Mâcon* is constructed, in particular, about 'two phenomena I have never been able to suspend disbelief about in the cinema - copulation and death'. 'The present set of photographs' referred to in the passage above are the (inevitably 100) ambiguous portraits which constituted the exhibition *The Audience of Mâcon*.[21] The images are of the extras who constituted the audience within the film, wearing their costumes; and they are poised between their 'trace' existence as records of those extras and their fictional existence as pictures of characters, characters given an identity, an identity which they do not have in the film itself, by Greenaway's accompanying texts - captions and narratives which recall in many ways the voice-overs of *The Falls*, not least in their investigation of the relation between word and image, a relation so thoroughly questioned by Godard's cinema of the sixties.

Photographs cannot lie, because they involve, at their heart, a vacuum of meaning, a chemical reaction involving light. Captions lie; contexts lie; vision interprets, often without the intervention of reason, a reason which must begin by imagining a scene of photography in which the photographer, the camera are present. 'Uncaptioned or untitled photographs are strangely irritating often to a point of incompleteness', Greenaway notes; and he examines his image 55 at some length:

Image 55 is a photograph of a mature woman. She is standing and has her hands clasped. She is dressed in red, and her image is accompanied by a caption which reads *Lame Mother Of Three Daughters Who All Married Clerics.*

There is nothing whatsoever in the photograph that can substantiate the claims of the text, and nothing in it to deny them either. One certainty that text and image can apparently agree upon is that the subject is female. However, to be rigorously strict, knowing our current fascination for intersexuality and cross-dressing, even this fact could be argued as inconclusive. This of course may also be true in reality - the photograph cannot be held responsible for supporting or denying sexual ambiguity.

The vaguest knowledge of the period [1658] would suggest that this woman - as a mother - would almost certainly have to be married - though the text does not say so, and the ring on the woman's hand is not on the orthodox finger. There is no evidence that the woman is lame, for the picture crops her body at the waist - indeed if we were to reveal the whole figure, we might still have no evidence. Only when the woman moves - which she might well do in the film, might we be able to substantiate the text's claim - but then, being a fiction, the author might have asked the woman to act lame. Where do our beliefs start and end? As to having three daughters, it is impossible to verify such a fact from the picture, and as to the daughters marrying clerics, there is no opportunity of knowing this at all. The text imputes that her sons-in-law must have been Protestants, for Catholic clergy cannot marry, a fact which puts the woman in a different historical-social framework - for she would be an alien in the general Catholic community that we know is a characteristic of the film, and indeed of the other portraits.

We could travel further. It might be that certain literary and historical prejudices would suggest to us a superstitious connection between lameness and the production of daughters - not an ideal combination in a patriarchal society in which women had few rights. To the really pre-judicially imaginative, the combination of lameness and daughters might suggest spoiled or second-rate goods - and does that mean that marriage to a cleric is not a first-rate social contract? Looking at the evidence of the woman's age, the daughters must have been young brides. What narrative possibilities are presented here with a lame mother with three daughters swiftly - even brusquely - married off to Protestant clerics?

We could examine the image further and say that the woman's face betrays concern, even worry, or is the product perhaps of a life of continual anxiety. Building on the speculations already made, we could interpret the woman's anxiety in various combinations of social and religious justification. However lest we should become too enamoured of our speculations, it would be a useful commonplace of course, to suggest that these claims cannot be substantiated at all, because the apparent anxiety of the woman's expression could be a very temporary state - lasting no more than a few fractions of a second - brought on by the irritations of an over-zealous photographer or the boredom of working on a film set. It is this sort of refusal to rely on speculative factors tuned to the fiction portrayed, that the film *The Baby of Mâcon* hopes to address.

In some cases the caption-texts have been arranged so that both picture and text say exactly the same thing [Going through them to work out which those might be I discovered *Nun, Aristocrat,* and *Melancholic,* though this latter diagnosis might be seen as over-hasty. As one-word captions they rather weaken the following point, which is basically Lessing's. *A Jewess given employment as a confectioner* might - she holds a basket filled with bread - be seen as tautological by those confident in their ability to tell race at a glance. (Spica's anti-Semitism is made clear in *The Cook, The Thief, His Wife and Her Lover.*) *Archbishop who had achieved his position by preferment rather than merit* might be put forward by either a cynic or a student of seventeenth-century ecclesiastical history.] - that is within an eighteen words maximum - though this is where the image wins out for brevity, accuracy and economy, for to accurately describe an image in text is tedious, expensive on words and ultimately unsatisfactory, especially when read with the image close at hand as reference. Text can give specificity up to a point where image cannot, but there comes a time when the image always conquers the longevity and inaccuracy of textual description. All of which is curiously arbitrary in the face of our knowledge of this picture for we know that this woman is not living at all in 1658, she is a woman in her early forties living in 1992. [Now that the can of worms has been opened, this statement itself needs examination perhaps. We know that she does not live in 1658, for this is a photograph. Everything else - even, Greenaway himself has suggested, 'woman' - we have just been told; neither her age nor the year are visually present, though we can undoubtedly make guesses at ages and dates from visual clues within photographs. We are also told that 'the subject of the photograph ... is a milliner's wife from Cologne. She is certainly not lame, and she has two sons, and no daughters. Her religious preferences have not been investigated.'] And it is curious to note that already this photograph of a woman in the late twentieth century playing a woman of the mid seventeenth century has a history, for this image at the time of writing is one year old; the image has already developed its own history to compound all the other histories we might be deliberating.

The Baby of Mâcon itself, in its final sequence of applause and multiplied audiences - a sequence ending with ourselves, an unintended irony, given the hostile reception the film received - contains a reference not merely to theatricality in general, but specifically to one of the major figures in contemporary photography: Cindy Sherman. (Like many artists who are currently using photography, Sherman does not describe herself as a photographer; there are certain parallels with Greenaway's own hesitation about describing himself as a director.) The baby's mother is a cipher, a grotesque whose face is endlessly concealed, a character defined, through insult, as impossible: she is impossibly old, impossibly ugly even, to be the mother of either the play's baby, the doll, or the film's baby, to which the actress has apparently given birth (a birth as unbelievable as copulation or death). The actress who plays the actress playing this mother holds up her plastic body parts, precisely like those used by Sherman in her horror pictures and sex pictures.

It is worth drawing some parallels, less to pad out a reference, a quotation, than to chart some of the areas of contemporary art practice which Greenaway takes for granted. (The most exact comparison between Greenaway and Sherman is between Flavia's portrait of (Dennehy as) Kracklite as Andrea Doria (as Neptune) and Sherman's *History Portraits*, in which she appears as figures from actual or generic old paintings, most strikingly one by Caravaggio. Sherman's cibachromes, also made in Rome, date from 1988, the year after the release of *The Belly of an Architect*. *The Audience of Mâcon*'s juggling of past and present, trace and reference, is comparable to Sherman's.)

Many of the issues raised by Greenaway in the lengthy passage above are raised also by Sherman's first major sequence of work, the *Untitled Film Stills*, which relate, not to an actual film, but to (American) cinema generally. The kind of speculation that Greenaway elaborates and elaborates upon is a commonplace of Sherman criticism; or, rather, the possibility of such narrative extrapolation is endlessly asserted. Related in her early work to her own tirelessly disguised body - and through that body to gender as construct - artifice, fiction, story telling, and the archetype all lie at the heart of Sherman's work. Increasingly disturbing, violent, and bleak, and using increasingly obvious props to develop increasingly abhorrent scenarios - the possible critical connections with the rape scene in *The Baby of Mâcon* are clear - Sherman's images balance an emphasis on the body with an insistence on the artifice of the image and the means by which it has been created; a balance which is central also to Greenaway's practice.

The photographic forgery, or reconstruction, of Vermeer in *A Zed and Two Noughts* is, in fact, more than this; it also involves a recreation of Richard Polak's photographic reconstruction (1915) of Vermeer's *Artist in His Studio*. (This is less impossibly obscure than it may sound; it is reproduced in Scharf's classic text, *Art and Photography*.) [22] Recent years have seen an ironised return to an aspect of early photographic practice, the recreation of painting (whether genres of painting - portraiture, still life, the altarpiece, history paintings - or particular paintings) through photography - 'painterly' photography, or an early form of photo-collage, with multiple negatives brought together in much the same way as Constable's use of various sketches to construct a major landscape. The purity of Cartier-Bresson's development of photography as a distinct medium has been challenged theoretically, as we have seen, but has also simply lacked attraction for a number of artists unconcerned with the status of photography as a distinct, and distinctive, medium. (Initially, the new medium's lack of status, of history, was partly what prompted photographers to ape painting.) The absurdities of early photography could now be cherished in an age in love with quotation and parody; and the joke, somehow, could be seen to be on painting itself, a dead language buried by mocking homage. Paintings of the past could be used as a shorthand for 'culture', as images to be read off in much the same way as they would be used in an advertisement. The very gap between the source and the use made of it became the point, the subject. It is precisely here, however, that I would most carefully distinguish Greenaway from the post-modern; his love of art history has led him to question cinema rather than painting, and his knowledge of and commitment to the history of painting gives his work a depth, even - *especially* - as he quotes that history which is far removed from the easy pastiche of famous images which has dominated a cynical market.

The most extreme dislocation between fine art content and photography (though there is 'fine art' as past practice, the great tradition, and 'fine art' as the contemporary art scene, in which such art photography as we are discussing here has a major place) has come in the work of Joel-Peter Witkin, an artist in whom Greenaway is interested. (He wrote a short piece on one of Witkin's images for the Photographer's Gallery in London, and selected one of his photographs for his Sotheby's lecture.) Here the importance of the photograph as trace becomes crucial both for artist and audience. However artificial the image, however faked its antique appearance, its apparent history as a negative and print, the shock (or, for Witkin, a devout Catholic, the spiritual content) of its origin in a real corpse, or a real body with the defects of a classical sculpture (no arms, perhaps), is considerable. No painting could match it. Things are pushed a lot further in Witkin than in Sherman or Greenaway, producing a narrower, if sharper, impact. Witkin's 'stills' (as it were) approach the snuff movie as Mapplethorpe's approach the porno film, those areas where copulation and death are convincing because true. But Greenaway's artifice has been inflected by Witkin, notably in the amputation theme within *A Zed and Two Noughts*.

There is, however, an alternative source for this. Muybridge, who worked for medics as well as artists as he pursued his great project of photographing human and animal locomotion, took photographs of amputees to help doctors design artificial limbs. And Muybridge is the great reference point of *A Zed and Two Noughts*, as important as Vermeer, though never mentioned in the script. (Muybridge is also crucial to *Rosa*, in the treadmill movement of the horse, and in Esmerelda's grieving; as she crawls in circles on her hands and knees, she echoes Bacon echoing Muybridge.) [23] It is a curiosity of the shared history of photography and painting that it is precisely those stubborn, 'unaesthetic' aspects of the photograph, imposed by the camera as machine, that have most fascinated painters; a kind of clumsiness of space and time, the unwanted or unexpected details. Muybridge expected that his series of photographs of figures in motion - usually nude, to allow proper study of the body - would be used by artists as a kind of dictionary of form, from which a proper beauty, a product of synthesis rather than of copying any one image, could be created. It has been, however, the scaffolding which he expected artists to leave behind that has so fascinated them - not least the graph paper against which his models performed their athletic and genre activities, but even the descriptive titles that so amused Hockney. As the kind of painting for which they were designed as an aid was left behind by modernism, Muybridge's photographs seemed almost to bury it, mock it - prototypes of the post-modern images discussed above. (His most profound influence on his contemporaries was on painters and sculptors of horses, most famously Degas. His work, which had exposed the 'flying gallop' as bogus, created a terrible dilemma: what was true was not visually convincing, but what was visually convincing was now known to be false, and could no longer be used by a realist artist.)

For Greenaway, Muybridge has a double function. Firstly, *Animal Locomotion* becomes one more example of the vain cataloguing of infinity:

Again a project that mocks human effort - record all the movements of the human body and of most of Noah's ark as well - it could never be completed. Its purposes are so scientifically bogus - arguably Muybridge did all this work to help a horse-owner win a bet and provide us with a sexually charged catalogue.[24] It's as an unfinished and unfinishable catalogue of anecdotal ephemera that I like it the best - twenty-seven pictures from three angles of a naked woman throwing cold water over her naked female companion, forty-four pictures from four angles of a naked Muybridge walking a short plank, twenty-four pictures from three angles of an obese woman lifting her stomach off the ground. It's a telling example of all those highly equivocal human attempts - from Newton to Linnaeus, Messerschmitt to Darwin and every historian and scholar you can think of, to record, order and try to make sense of the variety of chaos.[25]

Secondly, Muybridge is 'a cinema prophet'. This is the link with Vermeer in *A Zed and Two Noughts*. Greenaway quotes Godard's remark that Vermeer was a proto-filmmaker because he was 'primarily interested in the two most important things in cinema - the world modelled entirely by light, and the split second. The woman's pouring of the jug didn't happen a second before, didn't happen a second later.' (One of the details that emerges in the irrational search for reasons for the crash which begins *A Zed and Two Noughts* - and, first, for clues that might lead to the reasons; Alba is, as it were, asked to remember any detail, no matter how insignificant it may seem, as if an act of God was a murder - is that Griselda, who died in the crash, had bought some china, including a milk jug. The milk jug is surely a reference to this same Vermeer painting of the woman pouring milk; and the china generally - which fragments reveal to be of poor quality - sounds as if it could be Delft. Vermeer is also known as Vermeer of Delft. So such details are important, do make sense, but to the artist and audience rather than to the characters.) But, for the purposes of the film, Vermeer is seen as a photography prophet, Muybridge as a cinema prophet. (Godard's remark fits still photography better, in any case.) This is more than metaphor; Vermeer seems to have used a *camera obscura* (though this has very recently been challenged), and Muybridge was indeed a pioneer of cinema, animating his photographs with his (happily named, in this context) Zoopraxiscope. Relics from this prehistory of cinema (also of interest to Bill Douglas, not a director one would immediately associate with Greenaway) were displayed in *In the Dark*.

In *A TV Dante*, Greenaway and Tom Phillips also animated them, including his hound and his (male) nude descending a staircase. 'We regarded Muybridge's figures as the timeless abstracts of being and moving.'[26] In using them within what is a kind of video history painting, a contemporary addition to a tradition of visualising Dante that stretches back to the Renaissance, Greenaway and Phillips were both using Muybridge in the way he would have envisaged, moving from his supposedly neutral 'abstract' of motion to a work of art in which it was given a new artistic meaning and context: so that the hound becomes Dante's wolf (and later in the same canto, the Great Hound of Virgil's prophecy) and the nude an angel descending, as Christ did, from heaven. They simultaneously acknowledged Muybridge's own status as an image-maker, even if it is a status largely conferred through just such appropriations.

In *A Zed and Two Noughts*, not only is Muybridge never mentioned in the screenplay, which is dominated by Vermeer; his images are never used. Rather, one of the dominating images of the film operates as a kind of homage to and turning of his great project. Movement is measured photo-graphically, against a graph, and animated from stills: but it is the movement of decaying corpses, revealed through time-lapse sequences (one of which is comically compromised by the disappearance of a prawn from a bowl during filming). Again, the movement is both animal and human: at the outset, all the animal bodies stand in for the human, for what is happening to the dead wives, killed in the car crash at the start of the film; and at the end, the widower twins commit suicide, lying down before the cameras so that their own decay can complete the evolutionary series of *natures mortes*. This plan is thwarted, however, by the snails which crawl all over the equipment and stop it working. (There is, perhaps, a reference here to Dali's *Mannequin Rotting in a Taxicab*, an installation in which three hundred Burgundy snails lived for a month with a wax mannequin in a 'rainy taxi'. There are certainly parallels to the final scene of *Peeping Tom*, as, like Smut, the central character attempts to record his own suicide. The ancient phonograph in the scene, and the music playing on it, also recalls *Les Carabiniers*.)

The graph against which the decay of the dead animals is measured is an echo of the bars and cages of the zoo. Also echoing those bars (another of Greenaway's 'visual tics'), as a line in Attenborough's commentary from *Life on Earth* included in the film suggests, are the stripes of the tiger and zebra. For Greenaway himself, at least, the claustrophobic figures of Bacon's paintings, often based on Muybridge, are associatively present as a tacit middle term.

The Falls makes frequent reference to and, in a documentary style, use of, photography, both still photography and film. Biography 11, Carlos Fallantly, includes a droll narrative (typical of the tone of most of Greenaway's early use of language in his films before the introduction of dialogue) which plays on the close metaphorical links between guns and cameras in Western culture:

A fowl-pest epidemic finally destroyed Carlos's poultry-stock, and two veterinary officials came to make sure he had burnt or buried all the corpses. Insisting that the one remaining turkey in the greenhouse should also be destroyed, the vet, a keen amateur photographer, promised to compensate Carlos with at least a set of photographs of his substitute wife.

Whilst the veterinary's assistant stalked the bird with a shotgun, the veterinary stalked the bird with a camera. When the mission had been accomplished, Carlos was not happy with the photographs of the turkey. He is now awaiting trial at Clichy for shooting the veterinary official, whose body was recently exhumed from the floor of the greenhouse.

The texts accompanying the photographs in *The Audience of Mâcon* and *Fear of Drowning* both represented, perhaps, an outlet for this kind of absurdist narrative surplus. Within *Fear of Drowning*, the book, is a proposal for *Fear of Drowning*, the TV series, a prequel to *Drowning by Numbers*. It contains, inextricably bound up with everything else that happens, including a great many games (one of which is a game derived from *Vertical Features Remake*), a kind of ironic parable, or series of emblematic images, of photography. One game is halted and the players ordered to 'freeze' to allow for satisfactory photographic exposures. The blind Sadie[27] has her daughter Cissie describe a photograph of the front of their house; Cissie invents 'elaborate and improbable detail because she wishes to conceal the fact that her own face is in the picture, scowling grumpily through the front window'.

Cissie then angrily throws the photograph away and demands that Tom[28] should take the photograph again so that she can be recorded in a better light. To match the improbable description of the house that she has given Sadie ... Cissie goes to great lengths to match her false description - with out-of-season sunflowers, a red bicycle, parasols, a laid meal on a wooden table and seagulls on the guttering.[29] Tom takes the photo but the resulting print is completely black - just like Sadie's blind vision of the world. However Cissie treasures it - for it represents her first photographic commission and was made especially for her. The blank photo[30] is still with her eight years later in a cinema in Philadelphia when she dies.

In a later episode, Sadie's husband, Cribb, has to describe a pile of Cissie's photographs to her in detail, which he does as best he can, although 'they are all a little mysterious - smudges, piles of bricks, black holes. Unknown to him but quietly anticipated by Sadie, there is a photograph at the bottom of the pile that shows Cissie with no clothes on.[31] [Meanwhile] Tom and Cissie are in the brightly-lit room of an empty house, tentatively exploring their sexuality by daring one another to take off more clothes for a succession of photographs.' (A kind of Muybridge striptease, perhaps.) Due to interruptions, Cribb never gets to the final incriminating photograph; later Sadie insists that Cissie herself describe the images. 'Cissie does so, explaining that each photo has an ingenious origin. Each one anticipates the various characteristics of the yet uninvented cinema: - the action shot, the time-lapse shot, the colour shot, the "ghost" shot, the chase. Sadie patiently waits for the description of the "nude shot" but Cissie ingeniously and convincingly invents instead a photograph of a bridge over the river in 1894.' (Premonitions of the unbuilt bridge have featured throughout, a variation on the running gag about the Eiffel Tower in *The Falls* - in biography 2, for example: 'This house was called "le nid" after the initials of Nathan Isole Dermontier, who threw himself from the Eiffel Tower in 1870. Melorder, Constance's husband, said the story was a fabrication, not least because the Eiffel Tower did not exist until 1889. Constance replied that Dermontier must have jumped from the roof of Les Invalides'.) 'Thus Cissie invents a characteristic for the cinema that still needs to be realised - the "Future Shot", the ability to film the future.' The final episode is full of photographic images (and watery ones; it ends with Sadie cursing the river in the rain), including the use of a camera's black cloth as a shroud.

But there is more to cinema than the camera. There is also the projector, its cone of light an echo of those neat, geometric, abstract cones that converge on the embodied or disembodied eyes of perspective diagrams. Light pours out of its lens, which does not receive, but projects appearance. *The Stairs Munich* was an exhibition celebrating projection, and its catalogue notes how often 'The cinema itself, with irony and amusement, plays the imitative game on itself, making cinematic references to its own passion for the power and illusion of the projected beam of light' including 'the cinema audiences rapt in attention beneath the smoke-filled projector-beam in more than one Fellini film', 'the shadow-play in Wenders' *Kings of the Road*', Tornatore's *Cinema Paradiso*, Michel Ange in *Les Carabiniers* (of which more later), and Woody Allen's *The Purple Rose of Cairo*. The list could be greatly extended - all those Hollywood studio movies about Hollywood studios, all the thrillers with briefings in rooms turned into little lecture theatres or cinemas, and *Peeping Tom*. In Greenaway's own cinema, *A Zed and Two Noughts* thematises projection, notably the projection of Attenborough's *Life on Earth,* viewed both by Oliver, who cannot properly put the death of his wife in perspective, and his brother Oswald. Both in a cinema auditorium and in an apartment we are shown projectors, or the light beams from a projector, shining straight at us. There are, as always, fine art parallels, or echoes: John Hilliard's grid of photographs of a camera taking its own photograph, moving from illegible whiteness to illegible blackness, *Camera Recording its own Condition (7*

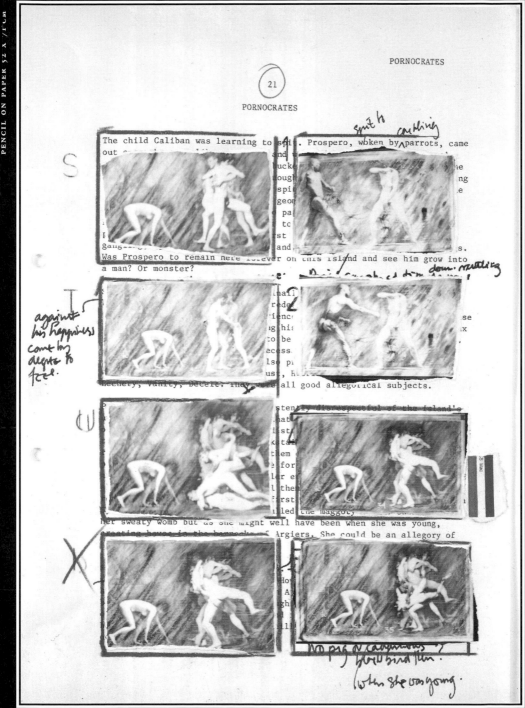

spit h *cackling*

The child Caliban was learning to spi... Prospero, woken by ∧parrots, came
out ... and ...
... ucke... ... he
... ough ... ng
... spi... ... e
... geon ...
... pa... to
... st
gaug... ... and ... s.
Was Prospero to remain here forever on this island and see him grow into
a man? Or monster?

down wrestling

*against
his happiness
came his
desire to
feel.*

... nall...
... rede...
... ienc... se
... g his ... x
... to be ...
... ecess...
... lso pu...
... ust, h...
... echery, vanity, deceit. They were all good allegorical subjects.

... stently disrespectful of the island's
... hat...
... list...
... tai...
... them ...
... e for ...
... er e...
... l then...
... irst...
... led the maggoty ...
... her sweaty womb but as she might well have been when she was young,
... ... Argiers. She could be an allegory of

... Ho...
... A...
gh...
d...
ll...

*No pig N (agnarous?)
you bird Mm?*

when she was young.

Apertures, 10 Speeds, 2 Mirrors), of 1971; and David Dye's *Mirror Film*, of the same year. 'The first image is of a cameraman behind his camera. It is not clear whether the image is of another cameraman or a reflection in a mirror. Gradually, a "hole" appears at the centre of the image, thus effacing the cameraman's head and shoulders and confirming the supposition that it is a mirror image. The image is gradually replaced by that of a person behind the mirror, scraping away the silvering. The original image is then reasserted by gradually moving another mirror into position behind the first.'

DARWIN

OR THE MISFORTUNES OF VIRTUE

The discovery of *DNA*, [Dawkins] says, means that Darwinism can be retold digitally; there is no need for any other explanation of the universe beyond that of the selfishness of the gene. There is 'no design, no purpose, no evil and good, nothing but blind pitiless indifference ... *DNA* neither knows nor cares. *DNA* just is. And we dance to its music.'

MEGAN TRESSIDER, INTERVIEW WITH RICHARD DAWKINS [32]

Darwin's evolutionary theories have dramatically obliged us to look at our animal origins and our physical selves with new eyes. Our ideas of corporeality and sexuality have to be adjusted with new sympathies. Now that we are no more or no less than a naked ape, our connections with our animal heritage make us severely doubt notions of there being any purpose to our existence other than that we can ascribe to animals, and since Darwin's theory suggests the individual is the insignificant servicer of the species then apparently the necessity to reproduce is our only pertinent function. Our programmed sexuality is the prime motivation of our existence. Each individual is only a suitcase for carrying and passing on the genetical code. Post-Darwin, it is not easy to successfully make any other human action, or behaviour, or achievement significant. In the light of this fact, we have been obliged to re-examine notions of the greatest sensitivity, to reconsider such dearly-held concepts as conscience, spirit and the soul, concepts which we pride ourselves on possessing to make us a superior animal, capable of communicating with even greater forms of intelligence, mortal or immortal. If we have not been able to ascribe our animal ancestors with these characteristics, how can we conceivably invent these characteristics for ourselves? The aims and ambitions that man has held important for so long, indeed which most of the last 2,000 years of western civilisation has been built upon, no longer have the same significance. There can be no validation for good and evil, no fixed moral code, no sacrosanct states of moral consciousness; there are no longer the same goals of moral perfection to aim for. The ethical imperatives that have seemed inviolate are now seen for what they are: constructs for the subjective comfort of a given people at a given time. Man-made constructs, not any given or universal prerogatives. By the final use of his thinking, Darwin was sure that despite any heartfelt wish for the contrary, man was not the sum and end of the evolutionary process, and that, in every likelihood, homo sapiens was, in evolutionary terms, no more than a link that would continue after him, and probably without relationship to him, since evolutionary

Peter Greenaway on the set of Darwin

progress had seen so many dead ends, cul de sacs, and abortive developments, especially in the highly developed species. Man could be described as a highly developed species.

Darwin has given man such a short communicable history and such a long uncommunicable prologue that looking back is no comfort either, because evolution apears so directionless, and so apparently purposeless. Darwin has finally put man irredeemably out on his own ... Darwin has given us a freedom that no social or religious programme has ever given us, for, if man is on his own, then all the checks we relied on to excuse or explain our own shortcomings and mediocrities have been removed. We are, at least, now free for what we want to be.

Darwin, TABLEAUX 16 AND 17.

It is unexpected to find a passage of text in Greenaway, especially in a documentary format, without any trace of irony. And indeed, irony is present as this passage from his television film of 1992 is read. Darwin is presented on screen as God, in a tableau based on Tintoretto; elsewhere in the film he is compared to Moses, to Noah. Darwin - as summarised above - is crucially important to any reading of Greenaway. If the young Eisenstein looked to disrupt bourgeois cinema from a Marxist-Leninist standpoint, Greenaway disrupts narrative and character from a Darwinian standpoint. For Eisenstein, history represents an overwhelming force; for Greenaway, natural history is equally overwhelming. Natural selection is a meta-narrative that leaves him sceptical about any conventional narrative, a meta-narrative that structures his own artifice. Death (was it Valéry who wrote this?)

is opposed to life only in the individual - an insight which strikes at the very heart of Western art, and particularly, perhaps, at the tragic. When Kracklite, the most 'sympathetic' of Greenaway's characters, dies, his death is not granted a space for conventional grieving. Instead, it coincides, schematically, with the birth of his child, a birth which, in a sense, renders him superfluous: he has fulfilled his biological destiny to reproduce. There is, in this, something of the toughness of Dylan's 'Ballad of Hollis Brown', with its sudden move away in the last verse from a close focus on the individual to a wide, unspecific world outside; there may be 'seven people dead on a South Dakota farm', but 'somewheres in the distance there's seven new people born'.

And yet these deaths are art deaths. Here is Greenaway talking in front of a slide of a plate from Vesalius's famous *De Humani Corporis Fabrica* of 1564, a plate which 'is also part of a series, where each figure is more flayed than the last, making a sequence that is almost cinematic and capable of animated life, like an awesome striptease where the discarded flesh reveals terrible vulnerability beneath':

> From *The Draughtsman's Contract* to *The Cook*, it's been pointed out that there have been fifteen
> violent deaths in five feature films, which of course is as nothing as regards human carnage in
> the complete works of, say, Hitchcock or Coppola, but I suspect that what may bring an audience
> up short is that in these deaths there are little or no condolences available, no sentimental gloss,
> and often what could be seen as no moral 'correctness', man, woman or child. Or indeed animal,
> for there have been many animals slaughtered.[33] This unsentimental boldness and open-eyed

forthrightness exists in these Vesalius drawings. Vesalius's purposes of course were to make plain his anatomical observations and in this regard their directness is a by-product of a scientific and very 'professional' desire to make teaching aids for medical students ... but they are attached also to the tradition of the heroic figure that is almost Michelangelesque and that makes them seem like pictures of great stoic and heroic suffering, where the pain is both displayed and detached, like a bold crucifixion with the caption 'forgive them for they know not what they do'.[34]

(*M is for Man, Music, and Mozart* is a kind of television opera/ballet, relatable also to the animation of the Brothers Quay. Centred around both creation myths ancient and modern and the evolution which, somehow, produced Mozart, it does indeed animate Vesalius, and in an optimistic direction. Vesalius's lost *Anatomy of Birth* is one of Prospero's books. Witkin has also spoken of his interest in working from Vesalius.)

Pain 'displayed and detached' - as it is to some extent in all art. Any confusion between art and life - the confusion at the heart of *The Baby of Mâcon* - and the experience of art becomes unbearable. Many people find too much detachment within art unbearable also, as if any refusal of consolation through art were itself a betrayal of art, and left it, however artificial, as an experience akin to actually witnessing suffering. Morality, as Nietzsche remarks in *Daybreak* (paragraph 3), is not demonstrated by nature and history, but continually contradicted by them; and this is why philosophy looks beyond them. Philosophy; and, we might add, narrative.

Art, in (so to speak) its nature, cannot simply repeat any message of absolute bleakness, although I would hesitate to categorise Greenaway's message as unambiguously bleak. 'To be free for what we want to be' is to be liberated; and to abandon hope is also to abandon despair, its shadow. Any kind of art involves, somehow, celebration, however 'depressing' its content. The sheer visual opulence of Greenaway's cinema is a celebration, and his emphasis on the corporeal involves the pleasures of the flesh as well as the thousand natural shocks that flesh is heir to. His use of quotation is (I have insisted) not a weary, helpless sign that all art can do is repeat what has gone before, but a consequence of a genuine delight in a thousand years of image-making. As for an art which uses Darwin - well, there is, in its very existence, some kind of question to be answered about the evolution of a language-using, art-making animal, an animal capable of developing the theory of evolution.

Art is an intellectual arena in which ideas can exist in a kind of suspension, a kind of play: art paints portraits of ideas. Given Greenaway's well-developed language across all categories, this is as true of his 'documentary' on Darwin as it is of *A Zed and Two Noughts*, in which evolution becomes a formal, structural element (even a basis for Nyman's initial approach to the music),[35] or of *Rosa.*

('This composer's name is Rosa - Juan Manuel de Rosa, almost the same as the General, Juan Manuel de Rosas, who slaughtered two million South American Indians in Brazil in 1857. Charles Darwin met Rosas and came to the conclusion that the General's policy of genocide exactly fulfilled the demands of Natural Selection.'[36] The political implications of Darwin's theories are considered in Tableau 4 of *Darwin*.)

Natural selection is, in Greenaway, at once: probably the right answer to the questions generally regarded as religious, Gauguin's questions; an idea with a history that can be considered, and a social context; and a creation myth to be equated as well as contrasted with Christian and Greek creation myths. Since Freud, the width of myth has been transformed to depth; it has been internalised, and its social context lost in consequence. The realities of power within a dynasty - Oedipus was a *king* - have been rewritten as fantasies of power within the bourgeois family. It is partly because of his reference points - the Baroque, Jacobean tragedy - that Greenaway can to some extent restore the political contexts and implications of myth, whether Christian or Darwinian. And Greenaway is an intensely political film-maker; a Machiavelli, even (which is not the same as saying he is Machiavellian). This use of myth also overrides character:

I would say no. [To the question 'would you see yourself in any sense as a religious film-maker?'] And yet. Although conventional moral values are not epoused in the films - rarely is there a satisfactory moral ending, the protagonists never walk happily and successfully into the sunset, good does not prevail and evil is not punished, there is much religious or specifically

Christian imagery. *The Cook* has much association with images of good and evil as symbols, white-haired androgynous angels and black-bearded satanic tyrants, naked Adam and Eve lovers, libraries of the tree of knowledge, descent into hell, the lover as sacrifice. I am strongly aware of the two huge mythological narrative systems that have created European culture - the Greek and Roman mythology and the Judeo-Christian heritage. Almost in my lifetime, these two memory banks of narrative and pictorial image have lost great influence and presence. I went to Methodist Sunday Schools as a child, high Anglican church as an adolescent, I enjoyed studying Latin and Divinity for four years, I was crammed with the usual classical literary canon. Contemporary educational methods probably mean that my children would not be taught who Jason or Joshua were. Whether this matters or not is forever arguable, but the legacy saturates a European cultural background. Certainly, it is necessary for a full comprehension of European imagery before 1850, and often after that date. The zoo of *A Zed and Two Noughts* is staffed with the gods of Mount Olympus, though you have to scratch the surface to find them. The go-between is the zoo prostitute, the Venus de Milo, the armless temptress to oppose the leg-less Juno mother-earth who is not required to walk. The figures of both these European traditions provide all the archetypes, all the allegorical figures; if you like, the complete encyclopædic set of the *theatro mundi* that you can move about the board - to temporarily dress them as Superman, or the Joker, or James Bond or Madonna or CP30 or Freddie Kruger, Joseph K or Bloom or Smiley, even as Einstein or Gandhi, Picasso, Mother Theresa, Saddam Hussein or Salman Rushdie can often almost seem merely anecdotal.[37]

Greenaway's Milo, after her erotic stories fail to divert or console the grieving brother as he plays with the snails that will ultimately bring the narrative to a halt, briefly takes on the role of Eve in an expulsion from paradise; the archetypes are radial, not rigid. Adam and Eve appear constantly throughout Greenaway, and they are there in *Darwin*, in Tableau 7; Darwin himself becomes a fluid archetype, connected not just to Jehovah and his servants and prophets, though Noah is a key figure generally, for his special relation to natural history, but to all the great bearded prophets of the nineteenth and early twentieth centuries. The staging of his study (and it is also, like the stage in *Rosa*, described as well as shown) specifically relates it to the studies of Prince Albert, Tolstoy, H. G. Wells, Shaw, Dickens, Ruskin, Marx and Freud (whose real study was raided in Vienna to provide exhibit 86 of *100 Objects to Represent the World*). There are further connections to be made with Prospero's study, and maybe Dante's, a key image in Phillips's original Dante prints.

Darwinism is linked, light-heartedly, to mythical creatures in *Flying Out of This World*. Greenaway imagines their fossils, wonders how man might evolve into a flying creature. ('Leda. A mating with swans. A dynastic move. "If I cannot fly myself then my offspring shall." ')[38] Bestiality,

notably in *Rosa* and *A Zed and Two Noughts* (Milo), is another recurring theme, poised equidistant between pornography, Greek myth, in which human couplings with beasts, or gods, or gods in the form of beasts, are commonplace, and a world view which emphasises the animal nature of man enough to question the reasoning behind that particular taboo. Felipe Arc-en-Ciel imagines a cross between a zebra and a woman; and also another, alternative zoo of mythical creatures - an equivalent of Borges's *Book of Imaginary Beings*.

A Zed and Two Noughts begins with a swan colliding with a car (a Mercury, another reference to the gods), causing the crash which turns the brothers into widowers; they promptly turn to evolution - specifically David Attenborough's *Life on Earth* - as if it were religion, capable of providing a personalised answer to the big questions. Reapplying the wonderful egotism of Christianity that imagines that the creator of the entire universe is actively interested in oneself, Oliver interprets natural selection as a process which has specifically evolved towards his own loss.

The author, of course, has also been pronounced dead, a god figure we have no need of. One could propose, to replace him, a natural history of meaning: from the work of art, ideas are expelled like seeds, carried on the wind or water, and, as in the parable, are often wasted, or are the origin of curious, unhealthy growths as well as sturdy ones. An artwork explodes like a dandelion head, but over and over again. Language, Burroughs has suggested, is a virus; so is art.

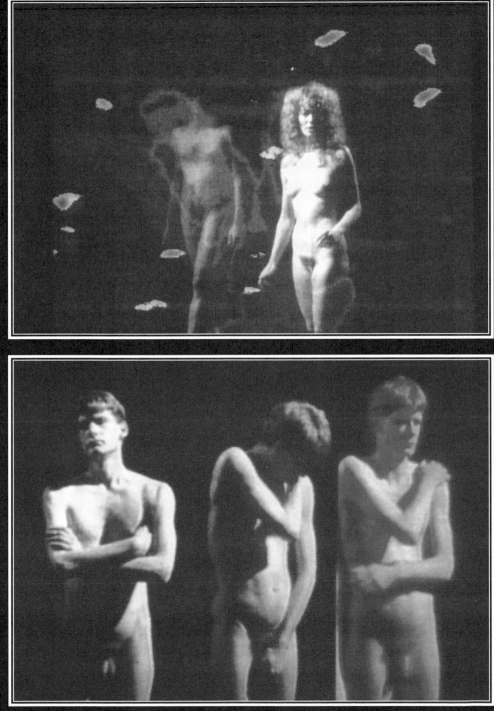

THE CURTAIN

The curtain, prominent in *Prospero's Books*, *The Cook, The Thief, His Wife and Her Lover*, *Darwin* and *The Baby of Mâcon*, is an effect of contrived theatricality. Since one of these films is based on Shakespeare, and another is centred on the performance of a play, albeit in a cathedral rather than a theatre, this is hardly to be wondered at.

But there is also a curtain, echoed by the flag and fancy sashes of the St George Civil Guard, in the painting by Hals that dominates *The Cook*. (It is included, at least in part, in most of the restaurant shots, and Albert's gang is a recreation, an interpretation of the picture, by Jean-Paul Gaultier as well as Greenaway.) If the curtain here is decorative, the curtain in art history has two major functions, both relatable to the use of curtains in Greenaway.

The curtain is often used in narrative painting (with what, on reflection, is often breathtaking artificiality; it is, perhaps, a device which strays into narrative from allegory, though both categories often co-exist within a single image) to suggest a transition, a movement from one state to another, a Rubicon. It is far more than a separation between two spaces, rather a spatial conceptualisation of before and after, of different realms. In Titian's *Diana and Actaeon* in the Scottish National Gallery, for example, it dramatises both the moment Actaeon sets eyes on Diana, and its consequences: he will soon be dead. In an allegory such as Bronzino's in the National Gallery, London, Truth is behind the curtain, and is revealed by Time. Often, these narratives and allegories involve nakedness, suddenly seen; this can either be a triumph, or a matter of taboo, of voyeurism, depending on whether the woman is a character or an emblem. A domestic, more realist variation on this theme involves the use of curtains around a bed; Rembrandt in particular employed this device, and reversed the direction of the gaze, so that the woman can look from behind the curtain.

'You should not have been surprised if the Hals characters were to leave the canvas and walk about the restaurant tables and the gang on the restaurant floor get up and pose in the picture frame.'[39] *Trompe l'oeil* is distinguished from representation, from conventional perspective realism, in its relation with the real space of the room, with the viewer's body. It proposes - instead of an alternative space, an elsewhere behind the picture plane explored purely through the eye, a space in which scale does not matter - an object or figure in front of the picture plane, life-size, related to the real space in which the viewer stands, which the viewer might reach out for, or speak to. It takes two main forms: great decorative schemes in palaces, where the entire space becomes theatrical, the walls unsolid; and domestic conversation pieces. Dutch still life and genre paintings were often hung with curtains across them; one variant painted half a normal picture (although

this inevitably involved a play, anticipating cubism, on the painting as itself an object in real space, thematising the knowledge that a painting is 'only' a painting which is required to 'use' it at all) with a painted curtain across the other half. The tease, here, went beyond any fooling of the eye, and involved deep plays on concealment and frustration, a sense that a painted curtain, too, must have something behind it.

In Pliny's founding anecdote of *trompe l'oeil*, Zeuxis demands that Parrhasius draw aside the curtain to reveal his painting; the curtain, however, *is* the painting. (Illusion, in the sense of delusion, can only be obtained by misdirection, by distracting the attention, by first removing the frame.)

These traditions (with which Hockney played in the sixties) inform Greenaway's use of curtains, though one need not strain for exact parallels. Cinema is, after all, a different medium. Any analysis of the opening of *The Belly of an Architect*, in which Kracklite and Louisa enter Italy on a train, make love (and conceive their child), and discuss architecture in relation to eating and bodies, would also have to relate the motif of the curtains, through which we see the landscape, to the editing. The montage here is perhaps the best example of what Greenaway has taken from Eisenstein, a confidence in openly schematic oppositions: it combines views from within the couple's sleeping compartment, views from the speeding train, and shots of the border town through which they pass and its station, linking fertility (the verdant landscape) and death (a tracking shot in a grave-yard). In one scene of *The Cook* only a curtain separates the thief from his wife and her lover. There is also Greenaway's painter's delight in stuff, in fabric, from Greek sculpture to Christo an ambiguous, half unconscious arena for richness, for abstraction, for an indefinable, almost musical exploration of emotional complexity, of protection, display, concealment, whether in curtains, table coverings or drapery. In *Rosa*, one sheet becomes a cinema screen; another becomes a shroud. There are canopies at Hadrian's Villa in *The Belly of an Architect*, in Tableau 9 of *Darwin* - a canopy which becomes a sail - and over Miranda, and her sheets, in *Prospero's Books*. So, in less theatrical films - *A Zed and Two Noughts*, *The Belly of an Architect*, *Drowning by Numbers* - the device of (often white) drapes moving in the wind at windows appears and reappears - in Alba's room, in Flavia's studio and Louisa's bathroom, the two seduction scenes, and in the remarkable building in which Cissie 2 lives - inflecting the climate, the ambience of the scenes.

For *Watching Water* the exterior of the Palazzo Fortuny, an architectural metaphor of the body, was hung, was clothed, with drapes in the Venetian tradition of Carpaccio.

SYMMETRY

Greenaway is not, emphatically not, a religious artist. 'And yet.'

The greatest indication of the profound influence of religious imagery on Greenaway is not the actual examples of tableaux which, as in *The Baby of Mâcon*, recreate altarpieces. It is rather the extent to which symmetry is so dominant a principle of his compositional style. Symmetry, not just in the Christian tradition but also in the most 'abstract' Eastern aids to meditation, is the organising principle of religious art. It is the secular that is off-centre, provisional, contingent, subjective, as intrigued by the frame as by what is being framed. It is partly because Greenaway's compositions are so habitually symmetrical that he has to introduce the frame as content, as it were, through curtains (themselves symmetrical), or doorways, or windows - or the draughtsman's perspective frame itself.

It is not that he is not aware of the edges of the frame - he complains that when films are actually shown, the edges of the shot are always compromised - but he does not use them to flatten the composition, to pull the eye back to the 'picture surface' (if the term holds good for a screen) as Degas might, or Barnett Newman, putting a 'zip' near the edge of one of his paintings. He is, for one thing, deeply interested in deep perspectives, a more secular device also tending to inspire symmetrical compositions, as in the Raphael Vatican frescoes which are echoed in the first scene at the Victor Emmanuel monument in *The Belly of an Architect*, although often in the Renaissance (as in Piero's *Flagellation*, a painting which structures much of the same film)[40] narrative or thematic complexity requires the division of the composition into clearly distinct, contrasted compartments: one in which a figure or figures are shown against a wall, close to and parallel with the picture surface, and one in which a corridor or a loggia or buildings drag space into the distance, towards the vanishing point. (Kitaj's later work, coincidentally, looks to very similar sources and devices.) A parallel cinematic source for such perspectives, which are linked with mortality in *A Zed and Two Noughts* (the brothers' conversation about decomposition), in *The Belly of an Architect* (the scene in which Kracklite learns of his approaching death) and in *The Cook, The Thief, His Wife and Her Lover* (the murder of Michael in the Book Depository, a location in which the camera's movements in and out of perspective contrast with the otherwise dominant frieze-like tracking shots across the restaurant, kitchen and car park), is *Last Year at Marienbad*, a key film for Greenaway, as we have seen.

But the symmetry operates at a number of levels, particular to each film. In *The Belly of an Architect*, all the buildings are shot in accordance with the strict rules of architectural photography,[41] until the suicide of Kracklite finally introduces a diagonal; but that first scene at the Victor Emmanuel monument is a particularly rich one to analyse in terms of verbal, conceptual and visual symmetries. Kracklite and Louisa have separate, but perfectly complementing, conversations, at

different levels of the building - the same two levels they will occupy as the film ends. (Louisa's exclamation, 'Christ!', as she is groped by a stranger - as Caspasian will later do, he puts his hand on her thigh - is also an echo of Kracklite's conversation.) Louisa's affair is already clearly signalled, and she talks to Caspasian on a red sofa; it is on another red sofa that Kracklite will make love to Flavia. Each successive shot is symmetrical, but two - one for Kracklite, one for Louisa - begin with a glaring imperfection which is then righted. Kracklite, on the balcony from which he will finally throw himself, is between two statues and two of his hosts: a *sacra conversazione*, of sorts. But as he leans against the window, one arm out, he is also half a crucifixion. (As the scene begins to sketch in the corruption that will plague the exhibition, he is also between two thieves, perhaps.) Finally, he stretches out the other arm, and is properly cruciform against the window, as he will be just before his suicide. Meanwhile, Louisa is sitting on the sofa with Caspasian in a way which requires another man to sit on her left to balance the shot; and this indeed happens.

In *A Zed and Two Noughts*, symmetry becomes associated with oppositions, twinnings, doublings, parallels, re-creations - all recurrent themes. What reproduction - copies, models, postcards - is to *The Belly of an Architect*, forgery is to *A Zed and Two Noughts*. Adam and Eve are here, as they are everywhere, the archetypal couple and the archetypal creation myth. (Evolution, it is suggested at one point, ends with a man and a woman; the photographic study of decay begins with an apple, with one bite taken from it.) Black and white - featured in the script of *A Walk Through H*,[42] and an important element of the costumes of most of the feature films, including *The Draughtsman's Contract*, a film about getting things down in black and white whether in a contract or a drawing

- provokes the question 'Is a zebra a white horse with black stripes or a black horse with white stripes?' Van Hoyten, a character also found in *A Walk Through H*, is stocking his zoo only with black and white creatures, because he is colour blind.

One scene may stand for the film as a whole. Alba is in bed, in a perfectly balanced symmetrical shot, a twin on either side of her. (The brothers move, in the course of the film, from being brothers to twins to Siamese twins; by getting a suit made that joins them together again, they are able to die together as they were born together. Alba sleeps with both of them; they both become the father of the child she carries, according to Alba if not biology. Pregnant women, in Greenaway, do not stay with the fathers.) Everything in the image is symmetrical; everything in the narrative, too. There is one blemish (soon addressed by Van Meegeren): we know that Alba only has one leg under the bedclothes. [43]

CELLULOID & MARBLE

PAINTING, SCULPTURE & ARCHITECTURE

I have often wondered if it were possible to talk about painting and cinema with the same language, as though cinema were an extension of the concerns of painting; to be able, without strain, to make a comparable and useful assessment between, say, Rembrandt's *Night Watch* and Welles's *Citizen Kane*. On the whole, there are few film-makers whose films debate and consider the processes of image-making that are considered normal and useful in discussing image-making in painting. Most so-called painterly referencing in cinema is limited to copying superficial resemblances in a spot-the-reference kind of way, and film appreciation, such as it is in this area, is usually confined to such adjectives as 'painterly' which, I suspect, is usually merely a lazy synonym for 'picturesque'. [44]

It is the premise of this book - elaborated throughout it - that the proper critical approach to Greenaway is to regard him as an artist who paints, makes films, and also operates within cities and buildings through the kind of temporary intervention which is a familiar aspect of contemporary art. Painting, sculpture and architecture are part of his context as well as his content, as the section on curtains indicated, but it is also useful to sketch in some of the more structurally dominant references and associations. The first of the two interviews included as an appendix offers a useful account of how intuitive the process can be, and how (as with Georges de La Tour and *The Draughtsman's Contract*) a painter can be a vast inspiration during film-making without the extent of that inspiration necessarily being obviously present in the final cut. It also is useful on the detail of influence, and on the limits imposed by the translations from paint to film. (I am writing 'film' or 'cinema' rather than adding 'or video, or high-definition television' to most of my sentences, but the differences between the media are profound. Tom Phillips has suggested a comparison between modelling and carving in sculpture. [45] One important aspect of the animated books in *Prospero's Books*, as the Omnibus documentary revealed, was how using the Quantel Paintbox allowed Greenaway to combine painting with 'film-making', and also to introduce the temporality of the act of painting.)

The passage from Greenaway himself with which this section begins indicates the extent to which he is concerned to escape mere pictorialism, a cinema as unambitiously dependent on painting as much cinema has been dependent on novels or plays. 'Once it has been explained to you that such and such a shot resembles a painting by Vermeer or Lautrec, you are quite at liberty to prefer

Vermeer or Lautrec, and you would be right', wrote Eric Rohmer in an essay from an uncompleted series, *Celluloid and Marble*. 'If the ambitions of the new art were confined to producing a skimped version of what its elders have brought to perfection, I wouldn't really give much for it ... What a film-maker worthy of the name wants to make us share is not his admiration for museums, but the fascination which objects themselves exert over him.' Greenaway's cinema is not a skimped version of painting, but a continuation of painting by other means; at its centre is both an admiration for museums and a fascination with objects.

I

The simplest way to include painting or sculpture within cinema is to recreate it through tableaux. (From the beginning, this has also been done in photography; Jeff Wall has recently created some remarkable, large-scale photographs, such as *After Hokusai*, through a painstaking contemporary version of the multiple negative.) This is a practice with a long history. Long before cinema, it was a theatrical device; David's paintings, particularly *The Oath of the Horatii* and *Brutus*, were enthusiastically recreated in revolutionary theatre. Tableaux were also performed as a kind of charade; Lady Hamilton, as Goethe's *Italian Journey* records, used to recreate the poses of ancient statues, while at the heart of his remarkable novel *Elective Affinities* are tableaux of famous paintings. Cinematic tableaux are common enough: in Buñuel's *Viridiana*, in Jarman's *Caravaggio*, in Godard's *Passion* (Godard never quite shows us an exact reproduction of the paintings recreated), in any popular artist biopic, which innocently assumes that any picture is a copy of what the artist saw in front of him. (It usually is *him*.)

As we have seen, in *A Zed and Two Noughts* the tableau is linked to forgery, and the history of photography. Generally, the presence or impact of individual pictures is complex and diffuse, and tied up with the intellectual atmosphere of the work as much as with the look of it, as Greenaway's mini-essay on Holman Hunt's *Hireling Shepherd* makes clear:[46] 'The painting is quoted by inference in *Drowning by Numbers* in affection for its marriage of superb surface and work-manship with public and private layering of meaning and metaphor.' It took Kitaj to rehabilitate such possibilities for modernist painting, Greenaway to explore their cinematic possibilities, and, as he was echoing their all-over complexity of content in a temporal medium, emphasise through what was lost in 'Pre-Raphaelite' cinema just what was specifically spatial and 'painterly' in a kind of painting long denounced as hopelessly literary.

But *Darwin*, a series of 'tableaux', remarkably reinvents the notion of the tableau within an inventive cinematic language. There is a freedom of invention in much of Greenaway's work for television which the financial restraints of feature film-making inhibit, particularly since the severity of the critical backlash against *The Baby of Mâcon*, amounting to a kind of unintended (one trusts) censorship through its commercial effects, undoubtedly affected Greenaway's bankability. *Prospero's Books*, which stretched the limits of what constitutes a feature film, saw the start of a new choreography of the moving camera and a dumb show, a parade, a dance before it. The performance of Michael Clark as Caliban suggested one direction in which to take this new language, pursued in *M is for Man, Music, and Mozart* through Ben Craft's choreography and performance. (The use of Vesalius and the anatomy tables of medical group paintings, particularly Rembrandt's *The Anatomy Lesson of Dr Tulp*, was also developed from the imagery around Prospero's *Book of Anatomy*.) A year later, *Darwin* developed a new painting-based language of cinema. Nothing could be further from the biopic, nothing could be closer to the spirit of paintings such as Raphael's *School of Athens* or *Disputa*, paintings which show thought, invent space as argument, than the tableau of nine-teenth-century thinkers through which the camera moves, tracking across, moving backwards and forwards, presenting images with intellectual connections, showing the actors-as-great-men performing thought, debate - but we do not hear these conversations, only the voice-over. One could find technical precedents in cinema; the elaborate choreography of Welles's bravura opening to *A Touch of Evil*, or the endless tracking shot down the road in Godard's *Weekend*, or the final seven-minute shot of Antonioni's *The Passenger*, quoted in *The Baby of Mâcon*, could all be compared to the increasingly complex long takes of *Darwin* (each tableau is one take) and *The Baby of Mâcon*. What is new is the particular, painterly kind of artifice, the detachment, the lack of (cinematic) 'purity', in a way; the insistence that we are witnessing a spectacle, a parade of a multi-layered theatrical

- not really cinematic - time which is being performed in the real time of the take. In a way, Greenaway has begun to dramatise the movement of an eye through a large picture - something which the documentary camera (parodied in *A Walk Through H*) has always done wretchedly with real paintings.

Another of the Raphael Vatican frescoes is *The Expulsion of Heliodorus*, a painting which combines a narrative acted out in two stages (its major group a riot of reference, invention and quotation, like any Renaissance *istoria*, so that the figure of Heliodorus, for example, is based on a river god) with a tripled audience - the Pope and his entourage; the widows and orphans, the victims revenged in the story, who point across the deep perspective to draw our attention to the expulsion; and ourselves, the viewers. (Initially there would have been a doubling, an audience looking at itself looking.) Modern art begins (with Manet) with an art that found itself unable to use the 'timeless' language of Renaissance painting without ironising it, mixing it with modern life, and this is the modernist irony central to Greenaway. Renaissance art, however, was not what the academies later made of it, but was itself a mixture: of the present day and the past, the past as parallel with an aspect of the present; of Christian and pagan languages; of innovation and homage; of narrative and allegory; of text and images out of and overwhelming text.

Such art - and Greenaway is attempting to create such an art for our times - has a double life, particularly as it shades into what was later called mannerism. It springs from, and allows, an infinite chain of association and esoteric reference; but also, at its core, is the human body and the limited range of archetypal narratives that spring from its frailties, glories and lusts. The intellectual micro-climate it creates is a way of holding at arm's length, like a severed head, the psychological truths on which it centres, distillations from a narrative which a spatial art cannot easily unfold. There is, for example, a painting by Bacchiacca in Berlin of the execution of John the Baptist. On the left are the women, on the right are the men; in the lower half of the picture the Baptist's body kneels defeated, in the female space. There is, unusually for the subject, no ejaculation of blood from the neck stump. Above the body, linking the sexes, are Salome and the executioner; a kind of dance is going on between them, around the severed head, which is not yet quite relinquished, not yet quite accepted, but already a prize. There is, in the audience around them, no exaggerated horror, least of all from the women. Some glance at the head, some at the body; all with an acceptance that sexual politics can claim such victims.

No human can be remote from such material. The distancing effect involved in the picture's treatment of the material - and, for us, in our own distance from the period in which it was painted - demands that it be considered, rather than consumed.

When you go to the National Gallery ... you don't stand in front of the painting and emote.

You don't cry, you don't shout, you don't scream. Why should we demand those sets of relationships in the cinema?[47]

II

Early influences on the early films were the 'land artists', mapping out landscape through new, conceptual forms of art and art language: Richard Long and Hamish Fulton, turning the walk into an art form, an art form ambiguously related to what was finally seen on the wall, a photograph, a minimal text, a map with notations of the journey; and Mark Boyle, combining random selection of a fragment of the earth's surface with a fanatical/ironic realism - initially documentary, ultimately hyperrealism. *Vertical Features Remake*, for example, shows the mapped square within which Tulse Luper was filming his vertical features, a parody or correction of Richard Long, who was walking round in circles first found and then displayed on maps.

The *Draughtsman's Contract*, of course, has an almost abstract debate about drawing at its heart, related to advice Greenaway received as an art student: draw what you see, not what you know.[48] The advice proves fatal, and in taking it the draughtsman becomes 'blind, in a way'.[49] Allegory, a more plausible category of image-making which draws on both what we see and what we know, is prominent as a balancing device, most particularly in the late scene between the draughtsman and Mrs Herbert in which, as the mythological associations of the pomegranates he has brought as a simple - and simple-minded - gift are explained to him, Mrs Herbert also becomes Eve, holding out the fruit (the French for 'apple' is buried, though not very deeply, in the English 'pomegranate') to him at arm's length. (There are hundreds of possible sources, clearly; but I suspect the precise source is Tintoretto.) The emphasis on candlelit scenes springs from the *ténébriste* tradition, especially Caravaggio and de La Tour. There has been a continuing interest in such dramatic lighting effects, notably in *Drowning by Numbers* (in night landscapes) and *The Belly of an Architect* (in dark interiors). Where the light sources are artificial, Joseph Wright of Derby - also important for *Darwin*, and mentioned in *The Stairs Munich*[50] - is an important source. 'The ratio of *The Draughtsman's Contract* was 1:1:66, which is exactly the same ratio that Claude uses in his *campagna* drawings.' The rococo is present in a picture from Mr Herbert's collection, which the draughtsman draws to Mrs Herbert's attention during one of their assignations, and in the living statue, a figure who anticipates Greenaway's later use of contemporary dance. (Compare also Bruce Nauman's *Self-Portrait as a Fountain*, 1966-67. Nauman is a spitting fountain; the statue in *The Draughtsman's Contract* is, at one point, a peeing fountain.)

Vermeer, Van Meegeren and Muybridge preside over *A Zed and Two Noughts*, as we have seen. There are, in addition to the many symmetrical compositions, a number of profiles, as there are in

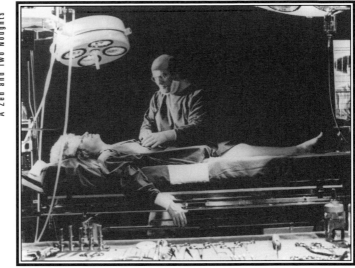

Vermeer; and, as befits a film structured around a great painter of interiors, it is - like *The Cook, The Thief, His Wife and Her Lover* - a film mostly of interiors, with night-time exteriors, lit by neon or artificial light. Oliver releases a number of insects, birds and animals - including a rhino, which Dali, for reasons of his own, linked to his obsession with Vermeer's *Lacemaker* - and this recalls Vasari's famous anecdote of Leonardo buying birds in the market to release them. The use of neon in an early interior shot with Oswald, in which a fluorescent light tube leans against a wall, recalls much contemporary art practice, Don Flavin's in particular. The more extravagant use of neon in the exterior shots of *A Zed and Two Noughts*, and in the abortive restaurant sign in *The Cook*, is perhaps a nod towards *Einstein on the Beach*.

In *The Belly of an Architect*, unsurprisingly, architecture is more important than painting, though sculpture is almost equally important. The use of sculpture is also indebted perhaps to Eisenstein's extraordinary use of sculpture in his cinema (the stone lion(s) in *Battleship Potemkin*, and the sculpture and *objets d'art* of the old regime in *October*), particularly in the sequence that leads from Louisa and Caspasian in bed to a matching figure from a Bernini fountain to Kracklite and Flavia at that fountain (also seen in a variety of postcard views which do not quite amount to a time-lapse view) to a head from the fountain to a close-up of the head in a reproduction of Bronzino's *Andrea Doria* to Kracklite before Flavia's camera as Doria (and then to the antique heads as Flavia seduces Kracklite). Bodies of stone and bodies of flesh are compared throughout; graffiti on statues echoes Kracklite's scrawlings onto photocopies of the belly of the Emperor Augustus, and anticipates the writings on the body in *Prospero's Books* and *The Pillow Book*. Both sculpture

and architecture often appear 'as themselves', as it were, shot on location, and the material effects of time are emphasised. As fragments and ruins, they are very Roman, linked to Piranesi's etchings, and contrasted to the mostly unbuilt neoclassical purity of Boullée, the subject of Kracklite's exhibition. (Kracklite denies that Boullée's designs anticipate the Fascist architecture that they influenced; Caspasian meanwhile is busy diverting funds from the exhibition budget to finance restoration of genuine Fascist architecture.) Apart from Bronzino's portrait of *Andrea Doria*, shown only in reproduction, and the murals at the baths which anticipate Kracklite's death, on the screen painting takes second place to printmaking - the engraving of a statue allegedly of Boullée, Piranesi (never shown, only quoted), architectural plans, and the Newton pound note. (We have already noted the importance of Piero's *Flagellation*, which is also never shown.)

The Stairs has changed our reading of this film: the connections between architecture, film-making and the exhibition have been multiplied and strengthened by it, and the viewing platforms in Geneva were clearly related to the structures which organise the 'theatrical' view of Rome from the top of the Victor Emmanuel monument.

For *Drowning by Numbers*, thanks to sections 17 to 23 of *Fear of Drowning*, we have the most complete, or at least most organised, of any of Greenaway's accounts of influence, quotation and association. Central to the film are the mid-Victorians who, like the seventeenth-century Dutch painters whose influence is constant, combine realism with allegory. (Impressionism, a curious realism of sensation rather than of matter - it represents the most extreme attempt to represent what is seen rather than known - is also unusual amongst realisms in its rejection, if not of content, at least of symbolism. Generally, realism seems to require some kind of quasi-allegorical self-justification for so painstaking an attention to the humble view or object.) Greenaway mentions particularly 'a group of paintings executed exactly between the years 1850 and 1860': Holman Hunt's *Hireling Shepherd* and *Our English Coasts*, Ford Madox Brown's *An English Autumn Afternoon, Walton-on-the-Naze* and the unfortunately named *The Pretty Baa-Lambs*, Millais's *Blind Girl, Autumn Leaves* and, inevitably, *Ophelia*, Arthur Hughes's *Home from the Sea* and *The Long Engagement*, John Brett's *Stonebreaker* and William Windus's *Too Late*. Added to these are illustrators of children's books: Arthur Rackham, Alfred Bestall (who drew Rupert Bear), Windsor McCay (who drew the dream adventures of Little Nemo) and Maurice Sendak. Vuillard proved impossible to include; Corot appeared fortuitously 'with a sudden break in thundery clouds and the use of artificial smoke that blew the wrong way'. A reproduction of Brueghel's *Children's Games*, a compendium painting of eighty-four games, 'rests on an easel beside Madgett's bed'. Rubens's *Samson and Delilah*, shown reproduced in a book, is an image, appropriately, of female power triumphing over male power, and, with a power of its own, helps to inspire Smut's self-circumcision. The Skipping Girl is dressed as a Velasquez *Infanta*. Still lifes are everywhere.

The Cook, The Thief, His Wife and Her Lover - another still life film - is, as we have seen, a dramatisation of a painting by Hals, in the manner of a Jacobean drama. It also involves 'the whole business of table painting - you know there's been almost a genre in table painting for years, Leonardo's *Last Supper*, and Frans Hals, Vermeer, even Van Gogh's *Potato Eaters* - the problems of what happens when you put people around a table'.

French film crews have a word for it, 'machicolations', as they do for a particular perspective shot, which they call a 'Mantegna', after Mantegna's *Dead Christ*. It is a favourite motif of Greenaway's, most closely related to the original painting in the second of the drownings by numbers, but also used for the death of Michael in *The Cook*. (*A Zed and Two Noughts* reverses it, showing the twins on their tilted platform - a motif later used for a *coup de théâtre* in *Rosa* - from above.) In *Prospero's Books* it is combined with the anatomy tradition for the *Book of Anatomy*. The link between corpse as Christ and corpse as dead meat is relatable to Bacon's crucifixions. Caliban's island is a recreation of eighteenth-century English Shakespeare illustrations. Again, however, it is architecture that is dominant, either recreated as sets or in model form, although the general splendour of the film recalls Venetian spectacle - Veronese's *Wedding Feast at Cana*, perhaps:

> This is a painting about crowds and architecture and people displayed in an architectural setting, something I have always enjoyed filming ... my great advantage over Veronese is that I can make people move and therefore invent a choreography that Veronese can only hint at. It is also a painting of great surface richness, light on stuffs, flesh, pots, dogs ... some may say it is a

reprehensible image of ostentation ostentatiously demonstrated.[51] I would agree with that and I still like it. It is a sort of painted encyclopedia of human movement, of the material satisfactions of life, where the subject matter is peripheralised ... I like its iconic strength - very frontal, very theatrically resented, almost arithmetical in its precise perspectives, a proscenium arch piece, strong verticals and horizontals, a grid painting, and an image that is very consciously framed.[52]

Because it has two texts, Greenaway's own account of the books and Shakespeare's script, there is a comparable peripheralisation in *Prospero's Books*. *The Tempest* (unlike the poem in *A TV Dante*) is lost, is like a lead vocal too far down in the mix, but not lost sufficiently to be replaced, a starting-point left behind. The happy ending, and the dumb show and masques, left the artifice (and the magic) uncharacteristically unrooted in - well, in cruelty, I suppose, in Darwinianism, in the dance between Salome and the executioner. If so, *The Baby of Mâcon* more than made up for this.

Greenaway, responding to his critics, referred often to opera (though a part of what he meant by opera was *Rosa* rather than *Madame Butterfly*, and *Rosa* would not have appeased them). I shall be discussing *The Baby of Mâcon* in relation to Brecht, mostly. In the present context, the references to altarpieces are self-evident; and I have mentioned Cindy Sherman. It is worth emphasising again that in the context of contemporary art *The Baby of Mâcon* appears as extreme, but not completely on the edge. Artists have gone further, particularly performance artists, whose explorations of corporeality - and the body is the big subject across a whole range of art of the last thirty years or so - have often involved real blood, real pain, real sex, even the risk of real death. Chris Burden had himself shot, and put himself in a sack on the highway, at the mercy of the traffic. Marina Abramovic's early performances were high risk, either because they involved knives or snakes within her own actions or because they set up situations of extreme, almost aggressive, passivity where the public could harm her. In the same edition of *Balcon* in which *Prospero's Six-Part Fool* is published there are photographs of Abramovic performing *Biography*, a reworking of her history as a performance artist in a theatrical context which plays on notions of the real and the theatrical; the audience is so accustomed to action in the theatre as staged that if finds it hard to believe that what it is seeing is a spectacle but not an illusion; that the blood is real. (Her current plans to recreate key performances by other artists - often male, and including Burden - take this dialogue between theatre and performance - and the visual arts - a step further. Is the new performance a 're-staging', as if of a play, or a tableau, like Sherman's often transvestite impersonations of paintings? In a repeated performance, we know how it ended, but not how it will end.) [53] Beuys, in a very famous performance, put himself in a cage with a coyote; in a somewhat perfunctory scene, Oliver (soon followed by Oswald) enters the tiger's cage, in one of a series of identifications - in addition to the grand Darwinian scheme - of the human with the animal. (There is a gorilla with one leg before Alba's amputation. 'That's what all we animals are here for - isn't it?', Milo asks - 'to be watched'.)

Contemporary art is poised between two poles: art as artifice, as representation; and art as trace, or performance, directly related to the body. Photography is able to suggest either, or both at once. Andres Serrano, for example, has moved from *The Morgue* series - large cibachromes of corpses, titled through the cause of death - to *Budapest*, a series of tableaux. Greenaway's cinema is self-referential, artificial, but it has real bodies moving through it (I shall consider this in detail later). What is unique - and yet at the same time places Greenaway as another contemporary artist operating between the two poles - is his increasing interest in finding ways of reconstructing for his audience the physical realities of the set, the props, the bodies which, in film, are traces still, but insubstantial traces, reduced to light.

Whether a critical language common to painting and cinema is possible is doubtful. (There is no longer, if there ever was, a common critical language even for painting itself.) What is certain is that Greenaway's cinema requires a critical analysis which is not restricted to cinema, but draws on terms and concepts and examples both from the history of Western painting since the Renaissance - and Greenaway is not just referencing that history, accessing it in some post-modern cyberspace; he is genuinely working within its languages - and from a base within the very different world of contemporary art practice. And this, although references are there to be spotted, involves a lot more than spot-the-reference.

All painting since Cézanne has been forced to address the picture surface. Outside 3-D fads, cinematic *trompe l'oeil*, cinema, surely, is doomed to a transparent picture plane, a window on its worlds?

Perhaps, although Le Grice's *White Field Duration* (1973; its title suggests both abstract painting - 'field' - and cinema - 'duration') projected light onto a screen, and only projected light onto a screen. Hollis Frampton's 'A Lecture' (1968) [54] is an exemplary exposition of the material/immaterial realities of cinema, placing its audience in the dark, 'this generic darkness', then offering 'the rectangle of white light' that 'is all films'. 'We can never see more within our rectangle, only less.' The rectangle is then modified, by a red filter, by a hand that blocks all light from the screen, by a pipe cleaner inserted into the projector's gate; so 'We have made four films' before the possibility of film - 'a ribbon of physical material, wound up in a roll: a row of small unmoving pictures' is considered by the commentary, which is tape-recorded and spoken by another film-maker, not Frampton himself. When it is considered, we are reminded that 'films are made out of footage, not out of the world at large', a reformulation of Mallarmé's advice to Degas, baffled that he could not write sonnets although he had plenty of ideas for them: poems are made out of words, not ideas. (*A TV Dante*'s reliance on a particular archive may serve as an example of the practical as well as theoretical implications of Frampton's remark.)

The links with *The Stairs Munich*, 'a manifestation of one hundred non-figurative projections', could hardly be clearer. The premise of the exhibition, which was not left buried in the catalogue, [55] but printed on the leaflets which mapped it out, in the press releases, on the scaffolding which carried the projectors, was stridently minimalist: 'Cinema is nothing if not a beam of projected light striking a surface with a framed rectangle of brightness into which shadows are introduced to simulate illusions of movement.'

'No attempt whatsoever [was] made to introduce figuration into the projections ... it would make the act of projection anecdotal'; rather, 'simulation of the actual movement of the moving image [was] undertaken by means that [are] associated with the mechanisms of camera and projector, with the notion of the colouring of shadows and a nod to those optical devices of wipe and mix that have long been employed by cinema'. [56] There were dates, the years counting up to 1995, sometimes within, sometimes beneath the screens; there were, occasionally, screens within screens; there were colour sequences and plain colours and moving coloured shadows.

What made a minimalist project maximalist was the city itself, although this may have cut across the conception of the project. 'The strong beam of projected light with its moving shadows is to be the predominant image of the screen-space, oblivious of the interruption of window and

cornice, brick, stone, tile or cement-rendering - creating a rectangle with pronounced edges. Inside the magic illuminated rectangle is cinema, outside is nothing and the night.'[57] But the night, in a major city, is hardly 'nothing', the 'generic darkness' of cinema into which all individual cinema buildings fade for the duration of projection. Apart from the interest precisely of the architectural details, illuminated by the projections onto some of the most dramatic buildings in Munich, or even the ivy growing on the Haus der Kunst, the projections were in constant dialogue with the city lights around them, with the 'projections' of car headlights, the 'figuration' of red and green pedestrian signals at traffic lights. (As I left Max-Josephs-Platz at the end of my second walk round the exhibition, the adjacent street was absurdly bright - a film was being shot there that night.) Any experience of the screens would encounter such dialogues; but any three-and-a-half-hour walk around a city involves mental as well as physical wanderings, driftings. My own projection onto the city full of 'emptied' screens - an unfamiliar city on a dramatically foggy night - was a fantasy that all the narratives of a hundred years of cinema so rigorously excluded from Greenaway's projections had bled out into the streets around them; instead of viewing a single story plucked from 'the million stories' of the city, I wandered through the million stories, picking up fragments of each: the city as montage, edited half at random.

The screen, as we have noted, can of course be thematised within cinema itself, as it has been often within comedy - Buster Keaton's *Sherlock Jnr*, and *Hellzapoppin'*, were as radical as Woody Allen's *The Purple Rose of Cairo*. The curtains that open and close at the start and finish of *The Cook, The Thief, His Wife and Her Lover* draw our attention perhaps not just to the theatricality of the film, but to the screen itself, and the curtains that reveal and conceal it. There is, again, the draughtsman's frame, a device for fetching what is distant to what is near, the surface of the paper, as much as for forcing distance behind that surface. The new technologies, animated photomontage/collage techniques, offer a new kind of multiple picture surface, created on a different kind of screen.

But in *Rosa*, which is about cinema and incorporates cinema but is not cinema, the cinema screen could become a property, could be represented; presented as a kind of action painting, a 'painting' of traces, a relic, a time-based work - or so it is described, but it is also, of course, really painted, part of a stage set. Film is projected onto a screen which is made from bed-sheets, the sordid history of which is considered in considerable detail; its stains are listed and analysed, catalogued: debauchery, debauchery, tears, blood, chocolate,[58] coffee, debauchery, orange juice, tears, blood, spittle, sweat, wax, debauchery, urine, shit, menstrual blood, beer, rectal blood, vomit, blood of defloration, male blood (from shaving or a nose-bleed or splinters), mould from fruit, wine.

A Zed and Two Noughts

STILL LIFE · FOOD · EATING · PROPERTIES

The author of this piece has a dubious attitude to people and to singers. Let's say he is as interested in things as he is interested in people.

Rosa [59]

This is not a confession, but a critical remark invented as a note which an invented member of the audience might, eventually, make. But it is a way in.

Nature morte; still life. If cinema and painting are to be considered together, there can be no better place to start.

> It is a Northern rather than a Southern art form ... after the Reformation, when religious painting virtually disappeared in the Protestant North, it became popular and was developed along various lines, the chief being the *vanitas* type, a collection of objects chosen and arranged to remind the spectator of the transience and uncertainty of life; the symbolic type, where the objects portrayed have a significance beyond their individual appearance, and one heightened by their association; into this latter category come many still-life subjects which at first sight appear no more than members of the third type - collections of objects arranged to display the painter's virtuosity. [60]

The virtuosity would primarily be Sacha Vierny's, but all three categories are present in Greenaway's still lifes, which are ubiquitous. Decay, often depicted in the leaves or fruit of a still life to suggest the *vanitas* theme (though also, of course, a practical problem for a slow painter such as Cézanne), is linked in Greenaway to meat and flesh: it is animated in *A Zed and Two Noughts*, and the two delivery vans in *The Cook, The Thief, His Wife and Her Lover* contain meat and fish, ostentatiously ordered by the thief, which are left to rot by the cook. With the extreme, almost medieval literalism which is a feature of Greenaway's work, the connection between decay and human mortality which an apple might imply in a Dutch painting is emphasised by having the two naked lovers escape in one of these vans, surrounded by decomposing carcasses. (In a contribution to an *Independent* article on Eisenstein, Greenaway described *Battleship Potemkin* as 'a brilliant story about a piece of stinking meat'.) [61] The still life in *Drowning by Numbers* combines Smut's numbered corpses with the fruit and insects appropriate to such sources as *The Hireling Shepherd*, a painting in which a death's-head moth is featured, along with the apples inevitably signalling the Fall; the

seduction of the Sunday-school teacher in the first scene involves tipping out a whole tin bath full of apples. *The Draughtsman's Contract*, as we have seen, is about meaning and sight, the pomegranate as a fruit and the pomegranate as a symbol. In *The Belly of an Architect*, we see an aphrodisiac - the figs first featured (in a heightened green, 'the colour of human decay')[62] in a splendid dish modelled on the Colosseum - associated, by Kracklite, with poison, a paranoid overruling of a common symbolic language with a private meaning. (This is later echoed, as Flavia talks to Kracklite at the fountain, by her false assumption that Kracklite's photographs have a sexual motivation.) *Prospero's Books*, a study picture, is a cinematic equivalent to those portraits of saints, scholars, diplomats, patrons in which still life details are attributes, indicators of outer and inner worlds. Darwin's initial interest in hunting and shooting allows the third tableau in *Darwin* to recreate the still lifes with game and guns of artists such as Weenix.

Decay, in the grain of the visual arts, has its attractions. The applause for the Pantheon, as we have seen, was partly for its 'magnificent decay'. The script of *The Belly of an Architect* considers how the ruin may be superior to, or more inspiring than, the complete building. At the outset of *The Stairs Geneva*, Greenaway writes:

> For me it is a frustration that cinema has no substance in the way that, for example, architecture and sculpture - even painting - have substance. And, as a consequence, I doubt whether cinema has any real history in the world. The passage of history effects inevitable material changes in an artefact. In that sense, cinema, or film, cannot profitably age, and it can have no intimacy with history. Even a

very short history permits an object to attain provenance, heritage and cultural power. Even attain cultural magic, certainly cultural currency and usage. The physical touch of history, which is not necessarily inimical to the well-being of a cultural artefact, can 'improve' its substance and enhance its significance. Without exception material changes in film are irredeemably disadvantageous. Film will not sustain ageing processes or be made profitably resonant by them.

A film cannot be photographed and rephotographed like a piece of architecture or sculpture [one of the constant activities within *The Belly of an Architect*, whether by the characters or by Greenaway himself], it cannot be re-interpreted like a piece of theatre or music, it cannot grow a patina or provenance like a painting, or be reproduced in its entirety as a painting can be reproduced; it is immediately fixed in a strange sort of present tense that will not profit by ageing.

࿊

Although the *Mona Lisa* is appreciated largely by proxy in miniaturised versions of itself, the original is material, physical and viewable; there is no original and viewable *Gone with the Wind*. It could be argued that film fails to satisfy the very particular demands of the five human senses, which should be ignored at peril, because a lack of unique presence leads to the dissatisfactions of banal cloning,[63] and a lack of material presence leads to the sort of disappointments and dismissiveness experienced by the thirsty in the presence of an oasis mirage.

Such analysis can easily enough be related to Benjamin's discussion of 'aura' in 'The Work of Art in the Age of Mechanical Reproduction'[64] but is more interesting in relation to the computer-generated imagery, still in its infancy, with which Greenaway is closely involved. Indeed, the section 'Materiality' in *The Stairs Munich*[65] develops the point in precisely this context, suggesting that 'it may not be coincidental that the representation of bodily contact through the depiction of physical violence and sex is multiplying, while the corporeality of our lives as both creators and spectators is decreasing'. His practice incorporates both ends of the spectrum, exploring corporeality, his overwhelming concern, both through immaterial, light-based media and through opera and the exhibition, both of which begin to offer the viewer some of the excitements of the film set itself. *Rosa* incorporates both aspects of his practice; and it is striking how the text[66] attempts to give to the scratched film of the loop (as well as to the screen) the kind of history and provenance that Greenaway feels cinema lacks. The material reality of celluloid - which, although it is rarely a conscious element of viewing film, has also been thematised often enough, even in 'dominant' cinema, through such films about or including projectionists as *Cinema Paradiso* - is now surely about to be completely superseded by electronic imagery.

⚝

In *The Baby of Mâcon*, of course, many of the objects are stage properties - and still life, in cinema, is related to properties, one of the subject areas to which, in the complete *Stairs* project, an entire exhibition is to be devoted.

Cinema, having its origins in theatre, literature and painting, has needed ... a wide variety of props or properties, significant objects that facilitate the action and in many cases are essential to its development and completion. These properties ... are, of course, multifarious, but it can be considered that there is a hard core of objects or artefacts that are constantly re-occurring, and constantly utilised in the action of constructed drama. [The proposed exhibition (clearly related to *100 Objects to Represent the World*, the objects of which, as the exhibition is turned into an opera, are to become properties themselves) is to consist of 100 installations, each with 100 examples of one of the 100 'most celebrated, most utilised, most essential properties', and would have an emphasis on cinema; but] many of these objects have been utilised for centuries in the dramatic exposition of events in literature, in the theatre and in painting. It was said that in every properties box in the Shakespearian theatre there was most certainly a severed head, a crown, a skull, a sword, a screen and a white handkerchief. In very many contemporary films there is sure to be a hand-gun, a car, cigarette-smoke and a telephone. In C19th melodrama you were certainly likely to find a clock, poison, and a coffin. In every age the properties of money, a mirror, a love letter, a key, alcohol and a door would certainly be familiar. Many of these properties - like the skull and the mirror - have been of enduring significance in traditions of Western painting, along with more particular objects used for their literal virtuosity and their metaphorical associations, like the peeled lemon and the soap bubble, the lute and the bunch of grapes [this latter was also an academic painting exercise for beginners], and the white napkin.[67]

This is the second passage headed 'Properties' in *The Stairs Geneva*;[68] the first takes the use of the pound note in *The Belly of an Architect* to suggest precisely how a property can operate in Greenaway's cinema:[69]

In *The Belly of an Architect* a great deal was invested in the property of an English one pound note ... now no longer valid currency [Kracklite mentions that they were 'dropping out of circulation',

9 5

which is precisely what happens to him], the English £1 note at the time that the film was made, in 1986, was a rectangle of green paper, light enough to be blown away in the wind, heavy enough in the film to assume great significance. It undoubtedly represents money, and by inference the exchange mechanism that turns art, exhibition and architecture into reality but, in Rome, certainly in the context of the film, it is the item of graft and bribery, coercion and persuasion that in many instances fuels the drama. It is foreign money, carrying alchemical notions of transference and conversion before it can be made valuable, and providing certain evidence of foreigners and foreignness. The note carries the image of Sir Isaac Newton, discoverer of gravity ... gravity is the method of death chosen by the architect in a spectacular suicidal drop from a high window to avoid the pain and humiliation of a cancerous death. The English bank-note is green - the architect's feared colour and emblem of his Roman enemies. With orange filters in the camera, the green and blue of the natural world in this film was purposefully reduced to emphasize the environment of a man-made city. The architect introduces his own nine-month decline into death by ominously flourishing the green note at the start of his demise, and it is the last thing he touches - blowing out of the grasp of his dead fingers as his body lies smashed across his enemy's green car.

Here is an inanimate ephemeral property asked to function in many complicated ways, carefully searched for by the camera as a counterweight to all the dominant images of the human contingent, and carrying the circumstances of the drama symbolically. [70]

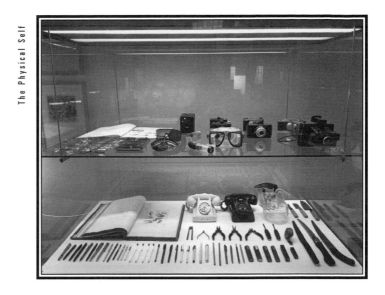

Much of this, in the viewing of the film itself, is clearer than one might imagine (or fear) from simply reading this account. The pound note is featured in the dialogue immediately after Kracklite's speech in the first Pantheon scene, and in eight shots, six of them close-ups; in the eighth, we see it burning, an echo of the final moments of *The Draughtsman's Contract*. (It burns in the cake, another prop which is made to work hard: it is based on Boullée's unbuilt monument to Newton, itself modelled on the Pantheon, before which the cake is placed; and, in addition to introducing architectural models, the unbuilt and the ruin, Newton, and the exhibition, the dialogue uses the cake to introduce Louisa's affair.) The apple-blossom on the note represents (laconically, being English, as Kracklite explains) Newton's apple; in the scene in which Kracklite is given his final diagnosis, he day-dreams of a death in old age (seventy-one, Boullée's age when he died), with his wife - (he pauses, he laughs) - his *second* wife picking orange-blossom. (In *Flying Out of This World* Greenaway links gravity to the Fall. 'Newton offered us a greater metaphor than he knew was possible when he sat under his apple tree and watched the fruit fall ... Think how the imagery would wither if he had witnessed, not the portentous fall of an apple, but the insignificant fall of a plum or pear'.) [71]

We have seen how the still life is linked to death. This is part of a whole complex of imagery linked to food. The still life is naturally a part of the sequence of meals, almost always out of doors, throughout the feature films, in examples of the 'table painting' shots. But food and eating are put through myriad sea changes of metaphors, reversals, associations and taboo-breakings.

The Belly of an Architect is a film about eating out of doors, and also about vomiting. (Compare

The Draughtsman's Contract, in which Mrs Herbert is sick after the first session of contractual sex; *Darwin*, Tableau 14, about Darwin's illnesses, and the scene in *A Zed and Two Noughts* in which Oliver coughs up the broken glass from the car smash which he has swallowed. Mitchel is sick at the table in *The Cook*, as is Albert before he eats Michael.) Vomiting is one of the first signs of Kracklite's stomach cancer. On the first occasion, Caspasian, as part of 'a history lesson - for foreigners', has been describing, and acting out, the poisoning of Augustus, ending by clumsily knocking glasses over as he imitates the emperor vomiting. Kracklite leaves the table; we see him disappear into the distance down a long curved perspective of columns, and then there is a sudden cut to a bathroom; he rushes into the shot from the left to throw up, in profile, into the basin. The final shot of the scene, in which, also, the corruption and plotting begins to become apparent, moves from this close-up to a middle view, from outside the bathroom, precisely the shot used in a parallel scene in which Kracklite, approaching the bathroom to be sick (apparently; he ends by only drinking from the basin), overhears a conversation, learning of the bleeding of funds away from his exhibition, and also of Caspasian's appointment with 'a lady who eats cake'. (This scene also parallels the 'voyeur' scene analysed below; there is even a reference to the model of Boullée's lighthouse which Caspasian will clown with. Flavia enters, saying 'we meet again, this time in a gentleman's toilet'; perhaps the germ of the lovemaking in *The Cook, The Thief, His Wife and Her Lover*.) The second occasion on which Kracklite is sick, this time in the open air, against a green-tinged wall, also involves a deep curving perspective.

A dog eats Kracklite's vomit, a Shakespearean image.[72] Dogs - often feral - could have a section of their own in this chapter. *A Zed and Two Noughts* begins with a Dalmation (a black and white dog, necessarily) straining at the leash. Dogs are there from the start, even before the curtains are opened on the action, in *The Cook, The Thief, His Wife and Her Lover*, the film in which eating is linked to sex, to torture and to cannibalism. The first 'meal' is the dog-shit which Albert is smearing across Roy's mouth. All his tortures involve eating; he wants to make Pup, the singing kitchen boy, eat his own belly button, after forcing buttons from his costume down his mouth; he force-feeds a customer whom he is throwing out of the restaurant to make room for the floorshow; Patricia gets a fork in her cheek. (A surrealist touch, as we see her afterwards in close-up with the fork still in place. There is a Dali painting of a composite body carving itself up - *Autumn Cannibalism*.) This use of food as torture recalls the scene in *A Zed and Two Noughts* in which Van Hoyten and Stephen Pipe force a rotting prawn into Joshua Plate's mouth, as punishment for his reluctance to join their coarse and blackly humorous conversation about the associations of its smell.

Albert mocks Mitchel's ignorance of what 'prairie oysters' are and, having explained that they are sheep's bollocks, adds, 'If you work for me Mitchel, one day I'll be expecting you to chew some-body's bollocks off ... on demand.' Much later, the joke rebounds on him, as they kill Michael, the lover:

ALBERT: Right Mitchel - this is where you're going to eat bollocks.

MITCHEL: No - I'm not going to. He's an old man. [He is the same age as Albert.] He might not have bathed recently ... Well - you know ... he must certainly ... He must have been with Georgina last night.

ALBERT: (hitting him) Shut up! Shut up! Shut up! Shut up! You worm! You little pissing worm!

There's a pause whilst Albert recovers from the prospect of Georgina and Michael being together. He's almost in tears.

ALBERT: (softly) Mitchel - you are an idiot. You can be guaranteed to always say the wrong thing at the right moment - can't you? I didn't mean you literally have to chew his bollocks off, you sad little whippet. I meant it metaphorically.

MITCHEL: What does that mean?

Albert was also talking metaphorically when he threatened Michael: 'I'll kill him and I'll bloody eat him.' It is a metaphor forced down his throat (as he has Michael's books forced down his throat in his murder) [73] when Georgina makes him eat his words - and Michael. In the scene in which she persuades Richard, the cook famed for his experimental dishes, to cook Michael's body for her revenge, she remembers the 'prairie oysters' joke. She also demands that he tell her what he saw the lovers do together. In dialogue linking voyeurism, the primal scene, fantasy and the cinema (Richard: 'and lovers in the cinema sometimes behave like that'. Georgina: 'That doesn't count'.) he admits 'I saw you take his penis in your mouth'. As Albert finally stands trembling above Michael's cooked body, Georgina says 'Try the cock Albert. It's a delicacy. And you know where it's been.'

⚜

There is a further category which Greenaway explores (primarily in *The Draughtsman's Contract* and *Rosa*, but also in *A Zed and Two Noughts*) but does not single out in his writing on still life and the property: the clue. The clue, a kissing cousin of the red herring, is an ordinary object with a hidden meaning peculiar to the plot, a meaning neither universal and symbolic nor purely subjective. In *Rosa*, the Investigatrix selects ten clues to the death of Rosa - 'Too many clues. Ten are enough.' - and they appear 'in massive excess', 'familiar objects grown huge'. The second clue, the (now enormous) pair of spectacles, recalls perhaps the huge prop glasses which Hitchcock had made to allow the reflection shot in *Strangers on a Train*; generally, the play on scale might also be compared to Magritte's *Les Valeurs Personelles*, an interior (with walls painted with skies) in which the bed and wardrobe are tiny in relation to the comb, the glass, the shaving brush, a match, a bar of soap. *Rosa*, the text, emphasises their physical existence as properties: 'They have been banged against the property-lift doors ... They have undoubtedly been used before ... They are the rehearsal props whose size is pure propaganda to intimidate us, a disbelieving audience.' As clues they are completely worthless, as clues tend to be in Greenaway - '6. Vegetation. At the time of death the composer was standing close to vegetation.' - and indeed they are also referred to as 'gloomy souvenirs of the murder'. The final 'clue' is 'A grieving widow'.[74]

The Belly of an Architect

BOOKS AND LANGUAGE

The book should be heavy with things and flesh.
ALBERT CAMUS, *The First Man*

I

Along with food, books are a still life subject. They pile up in studies, and they open up to reveal images and pop-up models of architecture, and in *Prospero's Books* they are magic, animated objects, in which the boundaries between words and images and the things that both words and images stand for or represent have been blurred or abolished. (There is a clear parallel in contemporary art, the work of Kiefer, whose *High Priestess* is a library, perhaps a re-imagined great lost library, of massive lead volumes, with words or images on every page, and objects also pressed between the pages; the *livre d'artiste* as sculpture. Borges was an early hero; Dante's *Divine Comedy* is a book as the universe.) Books are also, since this is Greenaway's world, a cause of death; Michael (doubly so, since books lent to Pup lead Albert to him), but also Alcan, one of the ten composers to die a violent death listed in *Rosa*, who gives his name to a character; he was suffocated by falling books. They are also, since this is Greenaway's world, related to the body. The script of *The Belly of an Architect*, from the start, relates architecture to bodies, mostly metaphorically, though architecture has often used proportions related to the (usually male) body not merely practically - the obvious need for buildings to reflect (or consciously dwarf) the human figure - but at abstract, esoteric levels of mathematics as mysticism. (The metaphorical associations of the Palazzo Fortuny are considered in paragraph 8 of *Watching Water*. 'The Palazzo Fortuny can be appreciated as a building of female architecture, and it is our intention to clothe it, being aware of the femaleness of its anatomy, front and back, vulva, anus, navel and the heraldic architectural clitoris above the front door. Such architectural anthropomorphism can conceivably be extended to the interior anatomy. Vesalius, the anatomist, who, as a student in Venice, was allowed to dissect the human body without persecution, said that 'the body is like a palace set in water and kept alive by air'.) *The Pillow Book* makes the (perhaps less intuitive) connection between book and flesh:[75]

> I am certain that there are two sure and dependable excitements in the world - the pleasures of the flesh and the pleasures of literature. It may be a commendable ambition to bring both these enduring stimulations together - so close together in fact that they can be considered - at least

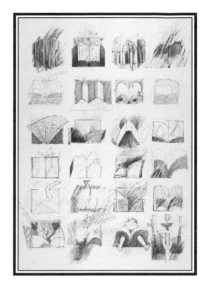

Above: The Pillow Book

Right: Prospero's Books: A Catalogue
PENCIL ON CARD

for a time - perhaps for the length of a film - as inseparable. Imagine the body as a book, the book as flesh. Consider text as physical ecstasy. (unpublished proposal)

The Pillow Book follows on from 'Ex Libris Prospero', a brief text for *Parkett* No. 26 (1990) in which the connection between bodies and books is made in an episode of extreme violence:

The Neapolitan soldiers made a book-marker out of the gate-keeper's tongue and put it in his bible where it says 'give me the keys to the kingdom of heaven.' Then they caught the gate-keeper's wife and they stripped her. One soldier put a knife into her mouth and cut downwards and another soldier put his knife into her vagina and cut upwards and the two cuts met between the breasts and then they opened her like a book - pulling back the white skin pages that turned to red skin pages. And you could see her ribs and understand - perhaps - how her breasts could give milk and what little impression the navel has on the body's anatomy once the top skin has gone. Then they caught the gate-keeper's daughter and stripped her and held a knife at each of her nipples intending to make a book that opened the other way. The gate-keeper capitulated and gave them the keys that they were asking for and they ransacked the palace rooms. They lanced the scribes in the library, spitting them alternately with venerable books; one scribe, one book, one scribe, one book, one scribe. Then they went into the nursery and searched the cots and found the small child Miranda, and each Neapolitan soldier picked her up and kissed her. Then they went to find the Duke who was fast asleep with a large book open on his chest. They tumbled him off his bed and, laughing, dressed him in the wrong clothes so that he looked like an idiot and not a duke. They wrapped his protesting head in a stained and tattered dressing-robe. Then, since he continued to resist, they dragged him by his feet across the marble floors and they bounced him down the great staircase.

Antonio finally stopped them as they tried to drown the Duke in a horse-trough. He cut at their backsides as they bent over the choking Prospero. He sliced their buttocks sideways, adding a horizontal slit to their mother-given vertical one. 'Buttock-books - to be read horizontally in the occident, and vertically in the orient,' said Antonio. He too had browsed in Prospero's library. Sebastian promptly had the soldiers hung. They died, their feet soaked in blood and their mouths full of the only words they had ever read - *ave Maria* - not out of a book but off an altar cloth.

Books are everywhere, but there are few readers - though we, the audience, have a lot of reading to do, certainly in *Rosa* (the opera) and all the short and feature-length works using the new technologies which are loaded, sometimes over-loaded, with calligraphy, enforcing a connection between body, speech and text. One could imagine a Derridean reading, considering primacy and privileging, and it would not be a reading arbitrarily imposed; but it would have to focus on the key set of ambiguities for an image-maker (particularly one who writes film scripts which draw on paintings which themselves drew on texts which - and so on *ad infinitum*): what is the nature of the translations, the movements, from texts to images? As with Kitaj and Hockney, the source of Greenaway's take on this particular problem was an art school orthodoxy, at a period of abstract, formalist triumphalism, and his discussion of Millais's *Ferdinand Lured by Ariel* suggests a continuing ambivalence:

> I was told when I was at art school in the late fifties to avoid those rooms in the Tate Gallery that had red flock wallpaper and exhibited the Victorians. There has been a considerable movement since the mid-sixties towards a greater appreciation of nineteenth-century English painting, though its reputation still does not travel well outside the UK. It is not easy to find a Frenchman who has heard of Brett or Dyce. This painting ... illustrates *The Tempest* and sets up arguments about illustration of literature and the English disease of literary painting ... the success of this painting to Millais' contemporaries may very well lie in the faithfulness to the text, putting pictorial image very much at the service of literature, a place where the Renaissance world put it, but if you believe in the primacy and independence of the visual image, the autonomy of painting is not negotiable, and should not be a slave to literature. In making

Prospero's Books: Semiramis's Husband PENCIL ON PAPER 32 X 44 CM

A TV Dante with Tom Phillips, concepts of illustration and even the euphemism, 'illumination' were uncomfortable to me. I criticise dominant cinema a great deal because of its slavish dependence on literature - most films are still illustrated novels. So much so that a whole branch of the literary effort seems now devised entirely in the hope and prospect of being filmed.[76]

The same (Sotheby's) lecture describes the impact of seeing Kitaj's first Marlborough show, a crucial early influence:

I have the catalogue with my enthusiasms still scribbled - embarrassingly - in the back. No doubt it came exactly at the right time for me. I was at art school and didn't really know what I was doing - I was repeatedly told my paintings were too literary, I was not interested in observational work or being a dispassionate documentor, or even a passionate one. Art schools are so successful at breaking your confidence. [Greenaway ended up as a mural painter at college, which he has since related (in *Anatomy of a Filmmaker*) to the scale of the cinema screen.] And I suddenly saw this body of work that legitimised all I had hopes of one day doing. Kitaj legitimised text, he legitimised arcane and elitist information, he drew and painted as many as ten different ways on the same canvas, he threw ideas around like confetti, ideas that were both pure painterliness and direct Warburg quotation [Kitaj was using material from the *Journal of the Warburg and Courtauld Institutes*, an academic journal devoted to the study of iconography, the relation of text and image so central to Renaissance *istoria*, portraits and allegories, of which

so much modernism was so suspicious.]; there was unashamed political passion and extravagantly bold sexual imagery. His ideas were international, far from English timidity and English
jokiness [Kitaj is an American exile], and that English timid and jokey pop art. He didn't seem
to follow anyone - Degas draughtsmanship excepted - I envied him and still do. As in much
twentieth-century painting from Mondrian to Le Wit, here [*Specimen Musings of a Democrat*]
is the grid again, a hard background discipline directly related to the picture's rectangular framing
and ratio and flat surface - a space for organising and filling with disparate information - to suggest
a legitimate homogenous whole. I think both the device of the grid for picture-making, and the
list for text, are essential to my cinema practice - naked demonstrative ways of organising information
in some sort of coherence. I often walk around the film-set with a book of Kitaj's paintings
under my arm, whether we are shooting seventeenth-century melodrama or twentieth-century
architecture - he is a painter in whom I have not a single misgiving and I could not say that
about any film-maker.

Unlike Kitaj himself, Greenaway continues to regularly use the grid, that favourite modernist
device, as an organising device for his own painting. Here, he clearly relates it to strict formal concerns,
to the physical existence of the painting as object. (Precisely the same concern for a strong human
content expressed through a stress on artifice - or, put differently, a 'realist' stress on the actual
means and conditions of making art - can be found in Hockney, not otherwise an obvious artist to
relate to Greenaway.) This is one of the areas which distinguish Kitaj from Millais; the others are
collage - a simultaneous, spatial, organisation of verbal material, which also creates a new 'text' of
its own, through free association, rather than following an existing narrative - and, crucially also
for Greenaway, the insistence on text as image: one can paint language - as painters have done since
it became a visible, even dominant part of the urban scene - or film it.
   Language as image has not only become a part of painting; there is an entire gallery/installation
tradition of text works (Wiener, say, or Baumgarten), which Greenaway has acknowledged and
joined within his exhibitions, for example *Watching Water*:

Behind the television monitor playing a section of ... *Drowning by Numbers* is the text that
structured and disciplined and gave birth to the film. The text is hung in some two hundred
frames on the wall, covering perhaps some thirty square metres. This text is the physical background to the small screen that shows the film on a monitor which is less than a metre square. The
origin of the project is text - the result is image. Derrida said that the image always has the last word
- but since the word is an image - the statement is more than the paradox intended. Most images
are illustrations, slaves to text. Before literacy, could this have been true?[77]

Prospero has his books, but he has mastered them, and he is an author rather than a reader. Michael is characterised as a reader - and he is mostly silent, in contrast to Albert and his gang, who are crudely vocal but have problems with readers and reading. Mitchel is practically illiterate; Albert is actively hostile to Michael's books - which he throws to the floor - and stumbles over the menu. (It is in French, and is a running gag, or running sore, throughout the dialogue, as Albert makes a meal of his pronunciation. Michael, meanwhile, is reading books on the French Revolution; the title page of one of them is recovered from his mouth by Georgina after his murder.) [78] Both *Prospero's Books* and *The Cook* have complex confrontations between language and silence; confrontations relatable, perhaps, to those between poetry (speaking painting, in the old debates) and painting (mute poetry). One reason for moving from painting to film is to escape silence.

Michael and Georgina conduct their affair (at Georgina's insistence) in silence, setting up assignations through dumb show and glances. The public silence of a woman abused beyond belief and the private silence of a man who sits and eats and reads alone come together in a wordless, physical affair. It is Albert who makes them talk to each other; at first he is forced to put words into Georgina's mouth; she just repeats everything he says. Even afterwards their dialogue is sparse - about silence, about reading. (Albert thinks Georgina is a reader - she reads in bed and even on the john (the site of Albert's sexual activity and fantasies, which complicates things) - but her first question on entering the Depository - have you read all these books? - is the classic remark of the non-reader.

Readers, like Pup, simply head straight for the shelves in such a situation. When she says 'What good are all these books to you? You can't eat them!' she is not just prefiguring Michael's death, but echoing Albert's attitude.) Finally there is a monologue, from Georgina to Michael's corpse, about how Albert has treated her, in part an answer to the question left unanswered when they first spoke together alone.

In the restaurant, Michael's books are out of place; Albert's remark that it isn't a library does have some point to it. The Book Depository is one of Greenaway's most resonant locations. It is, in a way, the restaurant reversed: a building full of books in which the kitchen, bathroom and bed are out of place. But it is also a kind of Eden. There is much expulsion imagery at this point in the film (the lovers, to overegg the pudding, are hosed down by a character called Eden), visually stunning but indecisive. The expulsion of the lovers from the restaurant, fleeing Albert's anger still naked from their lovemaking, is undoubtedly into a hellish world of mortality, the meat-van filled with rotting meat, but they emerge from it into the Depository as if into paradise - a paradise in which knowledge and carnality are central. Such 'indecisiveness' might be welcomed as a break in a practice in which even whimsy is rigorous, with any number of reasons queuing up to justify and thicken every image; in a scene such as this, one is forced back to the characteristic visual richness of the images themselves. This is also a film in which time, or period, is delicately and beautifully poised, through intense theatricality. It is modern, but since it is an artificial environment, without the location shots of *The Belly of an Architect* or *Drowning by Numbers*, and since it is modelled on Hals and Jacobean drama without attempting to be a history film (as are, in their very different ways,

The Draughtsman's Contract, *Prospero's Books* and *The Baby of Mâcon*), it occupies a strange imaginative space, not so much ahistorical as multihistorical. (There is also something Dickensian about the Depository; perhaps the space itself, the kind of fantasy room related entirely to individual desire - sex and books! - that tends to surround Dickens's characters; perhaps the view, mostly implied, of the London (? - the script says only 'city') rooftops; perhaps the strange figure of Pup, whose name, moreover, is close to 'Pip'. His capture may even be a faint echo of Pip's famous encounter with Magwitch in Lean's *Great Expectations*.) The closest comparison is with *A Zed and Two Noughts* (recalled at the outset by the neon letters in the kitchen), another film of elaborate costumes, interiors, night-lit exteriors, and rotting meat.

The second narrative/image of language and silence, the first scene between Prospero, Miranda and Caliban, plays a series of imaginative variations on Shakespeare's text, suggesting what might have been had the original been higher up in the mix throughout.

Some books have pictures, Kitaj famously remarked, and some pictures have books; *Prospero's Books* is a moving picture with moving books, in which writing - the calligraphic hand that travels across the 'picture surface' - doubles the emphasis on authorship, on origin, already foregrounded by the device of having Gielgud speak all the parts (a muting of the other actors further pursued, as we have seen, in *Darwin*) as if he were a poet speaking paintings.

Miranda's dialogue has hitherto been spoken over her sleeping form (though her sleep has been troubled - adding to her erotic charge as sleeping beauty); this is the first time she has left her bed. She walks, from another deep perspective, approaching the camera as it approaches her, through a sedate version of the flashing lights motif, to join her father, identified again with a quill dipped in watery ink - his 'Awake' is both sound and vision - at his pool. Now they move left to right, the 'positive' direction,[79] to enter, through a cinematic/theatrical change of scene comparable to those in *The Cook*, Caliban's space. This is a grotto, where the nudity, contrasted with Miranda's dress and Prospero's robe, is no longer an allegorical flourish, framing the central characters, but darkly Dionysiac: a Nature punished, held in check. One youth walks another as if he were a wheelbarrow, with his hands the wheel and his legs the handles. Within the *Gesamtkunstwerk* we have entered the world of contemporary dance, of eloquent bodies; and this silent world of speaking bodies, in which the sexuality of the medium (the dancer's own body) is fully exploited (it is certain, Greenaway remarks in *Rosa*,[80] that audiences watch dance with sexual desire), gives an ambiguous edge to what follows: for Caliban, Michael Clark, is the most beautiful creature in the film: beauty as the beast. The procession towards him has been intercut with the rude descent of liquids (including shit and piss; the first stream of piss in the film represents the tempest itself - Prospero's responsibility - and lands on the ship) onto the open pages of a book - a Spica-like desecration immediately

qualified by the description of the book, the *Book of the Earth*, which is 'impregnated' with 'minerals, acids, alkalines, gums, balms and aphrodisiacs of the earth'. (There is surely an echo here of Pliny's *Natural History*, encyclopaedic, anecdotal, ranging across mineralogy, medicine, and even art history - since the arts of painting and sculpture use pigments, metals, stones.)

Caliban is earth; he has been addressed as such already:

Slave! Caliban!
Thou earth, thou! Speak.

Here of course, in this film, he cannot speak. All he can do is put his tongue out, not like the pedant in *Prospero's Six-Part Fool* who can write with his tongue, but combining crude insult with crude sexual invitation (as the comic actors do in *The Baby of Mâcon*). As Prospero describes how he 'would gabble like a thing most brutish', Clark first sticks out his tongue and then contemptuously flicks it with his fingers.

His entrance, responding to Prospero's summons, is dramatic. We have just seen his birth enacted, Mâcon-like; now, visually, he is born again, emerging (a back to front birth) out of light into water, diving into a pool very unlike Prospero's and climbing onto a central rock on which he stands.

And dances; Clark displays, on his prison/rock, the entire island which was once his own, then shared with Prospero, before he was banished for attempting to violate Miranda. (A modern reading in terms of colonialism is irresistible.) He does not regret his attempted rape:

> O ho, o ho! - would that it had been done!
> Thou didst prevent me; I had peopled else
> The isle with Calibans

but clutches his penis as the words are spoken, turning his back on Prospero and Miranda but looking over his shoulder at them as he does so.

Again, in the context of Greenaway's cinema, this is ambiguous: fertility in Greenaway is, if not exactly morally good, the central drive of natural selection. Sex in his films is linked to fertility in ways unimaginable in contemporary 'dominant' cinema, where sex is associated exclusively with immediate pleasure, and pregnancy, where it is considered at all, is likely to be a disaster for at least one of the partners. *The Cook* is a film which deals with infertility; that is a part of its bleakness. The affairs in *The Cook* and *The Belly of an Architect* are both accompanied by brutal lines about the need for contraception (or lack of it): Caspasian, having discovered Kracklite with Flavia, remarks that Louisa and Kracklite's baby has been the perfect contraceptive; and as Georgina finally begins to talk for herself in her first conversation with Michael she outrages Albert by announcing (apparently to a stranger) that 'Being infertile makes me a safe bet for a screw'.

Any representation of Nature, then, is framed by Darwin. But there are two spectacles of Nature in *Prospero's Books*: that which surrounds Caliban, a rhetorical wildness and wilderness, Salvator Rosa-like, a Nature which, like Caliban himself, is visited as if an inmate of an asylum, for the frisson and the contrast; and the almost absurd mock-pastoral setting against which we see Miranda's approved suitor - and then Miranda with him - in the next scene. (Both versions of Nature are framed, contained by Alhambra-like architecture.)

In that scene Ferdinand/Gielgud speaks to Miranda, asking her 'If you be maid or no?', and when she replies he exclaims

> My language! Heavens!
> I am the best of them that speak this speech,
> Were I but where 'tis spoken.

Nothing could more clearly distinguish him from Caliban, the subject who curses kings and language (quite apart from his own attitude to her maidenhead).

With Gielgud speaking all the lines, certain aspects of the text become clearer, others more

31

THE PAST

*Looking for Caliban, Prospero searched the island for a week. He wandered
it restlessly for a further month. Miranda had ___ climbing the three
hundred and ___ five steps to the flat lead ___ the library roof
and calling ___ time, ___ the necessity ___ ories no longer
exclusively ___ the soon ___ of the ___ ered hills ___ an
unofficial ___ party. ___ expect ___ day to come ___
Caliban's body, maybe ly___ among ___ cropping sheep
in a grassy gulley ___*

*Or washed up on a distant ___ wrack hiding his fac___
giant starfish ___ ng acro___ his ge___ olled in ___ and
like dough ___ in b___ for ___ caugh___
low bough___ the ___ g___ h of ___
hamstring ___ ng ___ aw___ the
Would ___ alib___ of ___ o___ ? Or
bones? ___ ie ___ ith ___ hor___
the razor-___ n. ___ he ___ the ___ bone___
hands with the curled ___ nail on ___ ttle ___ er. All ___
was Caliban's mirror, ___ lid to a metal ___ t was left lying ___
flat warm rock in ___ field, its shining ___ catching the ___
sun and ideal ___ ___*

*the ___ by Cal___ appearance ___
___ ght BC ___ aliban.*

*___ ook an i___ Prospero ___ Miranda
___ ef___ education ___ isation, ___ ___ ___
___ the self-am___ ng p___ ng Sycorax ___ ___
___ she ___ ented M___ id so with som___ ___ ___ and
___ ple ___ perplex ___ so used to ___ ___ that
___ tched ___ stood beside ___ would have thought ___ ___ ___
___ symbol of Old Age.*

complex. Prospero, certainly, curses Caliban as much as Caliban curses him. When Caliban - and this is also written, word by word, across the screen - 'says' that Prospero taught him language, 'and my profit on't is, I know how to curse', it seems less an instance of a savage and ungrateful inability to use reason, a deliberate squandering of a gift, than it does a literal truth. Prospero has done nothing but curse him throughout the scene.

Dramatically, one reason for the scene is to fill in the audience on the history of the characters; we get information in between the curses, a narrative of power and language which is also another narrative of naming a world, and expulsion from it. Caliban was his own king before he became Prospero's only subject; there was, specifically, an exchange of language for reality, of knowledge of names (a faint echo of the real power of naming) for dominion over what was hitherto unnamed, with Prospero teaching Caliban language and Caliban showing Prospero 'all the qualities of the isle'. But Caliban was offered language without power: his curses, his attacks on the written word (he hurls a book away, he throws up pages into the air (- another image associated with Prospero elsewhere in the film),[81] are his helpless response to Prospero's access to language as magic. (At the end of the film, Prospero echoes Caliban's gesture, burning and drowning his books, a renunciation of his magic.) Prospero's curses are also commands. 'I must obey: his art is of such power.'

Power might be defined as the ability to match the world to one's words. This is a large part of the way words and things, words and actions, are laid side by side in Greenaway's cinema. It is a visual habit he has, to set an image of a word beside an image of what it names (the still lifes that are set on the menus in *The Cook*, for example), but his narratives of power are narratives of the word and its power, or lack of it, over chaos. The Prince, in *The Baby of Mâcon*, has a power which he cannot yet understand or control - his words can be quoted as commandments, yet he cannot overrule them. The draughtsman's contract gives him power over Mrs Herbert's person, but not over the world - human or natural - in front of his perspective frame. Spica, who dies carrying out his own curse, is halfway between Prospero and Caliban. Brute force can enforce anything he says. Both his strength and his weaknesses are transparent in his language (not least with regard to his sexuality).[82] Spica's language is a signifier both of his power over (for example) Roy and of his blustering social inadequacy. It is only when language is a form of violent action, of physical power, that he has any power over language; and even then there is a fatal confusion, even within his power, between curse and order, the literal and the metaphorical.

More generally, the word/image play in Greenaway can be connected with Magritte ('another great favourite of mine, I particularly like him when he plays with the words that do not relate to the image') and Godard's fractures between image and soundtrack. The connections with Magritte in particular are worth exploring, for they are both conceptual and visual. I suspect that the look of the twilight exteriors in *A Zed and Two Noughts* owes something to Magritte's night/day painting,

L'Empire des Lumières, a clearer link are those paintings in which a painting stands on an easel before a view which it at once conceals - the canvas blocks the view - and reveals - the painting is of the view and exactly matches the rest of the view (also painted, of course) that we can see around it. (If the retrospective shown at the Hayward Gallery had been held before 1982, and not in 1992, the catalogue illustrations taken from Cassagne's *Traité Pratique de Perspectif*, used by Magritte as a student, could have been triumphantly flourished as sources for *The Draughtsman's Contract* as well as *La Belle Captive*.) There are other links: Magritte is another artist who uses grids, often of boxes containing objects linked only through dreams, as in *Le Musée d'une Nuit*. (The fourth box, here, through a *trompe l'oeil* paper cut-out, is closed off, another variation on Magritte's favourite play between showing and concealing.) Magritte, as a surrealist cataloguer, has it both ways: catalogues, museums, are absurd, but the objects are connected - by his own dream, by Freudian theory, by the viewer - or by any combination of the three. *Le Pont d'Héraclite* - an incomplete bridge with a complete reflection, though it may only be a cloud which makes the bridge seem incomplete - appears to be a direct source for the reflections and photographs of the as yet unbuilt bridge in the *Fear of Drowning* scripts. Most pertinent to the present section, however, are the three paintings entitled *La Clef des Songes*: grids again, window like - indeed, like Duchamp's *Fresh Widow* - with each 'pane' showing an image with a word beneath it. The third version (in English) has a horse and the words 'the door'; a clock and the words 'the wind'; a jug and the words 'the bird' and a valise and the words 'the valise'. The final image is tautological, although, this being Magritte, he might equally well have pointed out 'ceci n'est pas un valise'. The horse is not a door, but one shuts a stable door after the horse has bolted. The clock is not the wind, but time flies like the wind. The jug is not a bird, but it looks a little like one, at least after we read the caption. I have related Greenaway's insistence on artifice, on the fact that what we are considering is first and foremost a work of art, and its coupling also not with formalist minimalism but with a maximalist content, to Kitaj and Hockney, and in the fifties and early sixties these are the artists who doubled up language and the languages of painting in this way; but Magritte is an artist whose interest in artifice and illusion, in catalogues, in metaphor and literalism, in word games, is clearly of crucial importance for Greenaway.

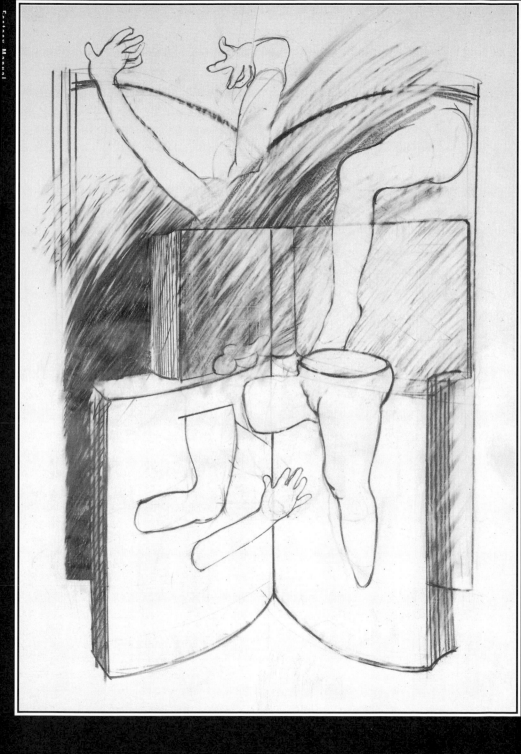

MAPS

Maps are both texts and images. They also have an intimate relation with reality, as we use them to get around: we generally read them in direct relation to our surroundings. This relationship is fictionalised in *A Walk Through H*; some of the maps fade as the narrator is using them, but later he discovers 'the correct walking pace'. *The Stairs Geneva* includes a still from *The Belly of an Architect,* captioned 'The architect stands on the map of Rome'. The map is the floor Kracklite stands on; behind him are the viewing platforms which isolate, and name, the most famous sites, and behind them is Rome itself. The deliberate narrowing of the gaps between symbols, words and things which I have suggested is a constant feature of Greenaway's art operates neatly enough in this instance.

Key texts regarding maps are the script *A Walk Through H* and the catalogues to *The Stairs*, itself a project to be followed by using maps. *The Stairs* involves three-dimensional interventions into real spaces, applying the wit and whimsy of the two-dimensional walk through H - and Greenaway's delight in inexhaustible connections - to real places and histories. In *The Stairs Geneva*, one platform, 'chosen in irony', framed a military statue together with a sign which read PAIX. Another framed the Laura Ashley shop; Greenaway noting that Ashley's death was caused by falling downstairs (a rather callous detail to be added to his grand scheme), and also (Geneva being Calvin's city) that she was 'successful in the only occupation permitted to women by Calvinists - knitting and needlework'. There were many framings of statues, a further connection with *The Belly of an Architect,* as was the interest in framing framings: 'Site 91. Mont Blanc framed by an arm and a breast'. (The bronze breast, thus framed, itself became an inverted mountain.) Each site, in the catalogue, has its own fragment of map, often amounting to a plan of a building.

In the theoretical part of the catalogue, the section on 'location' is valuable for the insights it offers into Greenaway's sense of the relations between two and three dimensions:

Cinema can only offer limited illusionary three-dimensional space which must be made significant within the rigid confines of a rectangular frame, and it can conventionally only offer one viewpoint at a time. [Ever since *A TV Dante*, Greenaway has used new technologies to counteract this.] Consider working the situation backwards and attempt to recreate a 'real' location solely with the information given by the film; very rapidly that real landscape would be full of voids and blanks, and grossly ill-fitting details. It has long been cinema practice to accept this misalignment of real space - and cinema audiences have well learnt to accept this great spatial deception with extraordinary equanimity.

(This is hardly unique to cinema, since most attempts to recreate the space of paintings using perspective as a loose convention rather than a diagram of space would discover similar voids and blanks. Greenaway's use of Piero's *Flagellation* and Vermeer - a painting and an artist whose spaces have been successfully recreated - takes on a new significance in this context.)

In *The Draughtsman's Contract* great efforts were made to complement the nature of the demands for veracity that were integral to the plot by filming a location that would be fully comprehensible. More than one enthusiastic viewer, without assistance from extra-frame sources, and without visiting the place of filming, has been able to recreate the location in geographical exactness solely from information taken from the film-frame.

(Compare the way that architecture is framed in *The Belly of an Architect* - including such scenes set in interiors as the keyhole scene discussed below, which, although related to point of view shots, is extraordinarily precise in its presentation of space.)

I have always been fascinated by the particular excitements aroused by a sense of place, the distinction of a particular *genius loci*. This is true if the place, space or location is indeed a real one but is certainly also true if the location has been invented in words, in a painting or in the cinema.

Since familiarity erodes anxiety [a clue, perhaps, to Greenaway's use of repetition], the strongest memories I have as a child were the unfamiliar places of summer vacations. If possible I was the last to leave the beach, shut the door, close the curtains, never certain I would see the world outside again just as I had left it. I was hesitant about travel because of the unlikelihood of being able to repeat an experience of place, and I especially disliked travelling fast in case I failed to understand the connections between places. I slept on trains to avoid consequent misalignment, and I was happy that there were superstitions enough to legitimise my fear of not seeing a place again. I threw coins into every available fountain. I still feel uncomfortable in an unknown place, but a map will usually combat the discomfort, for at least a map will offer a spurious sense of capture and therefore some sense of understanding, and will situate the details and continuity of a place even if it personally cannot be experienced. I need to see the back of buildings.

Irony is always spatial. To say one thing and mean another (the crudest definition of irony, too close to a definition merely of sarcasm, and unsatisfactory because irony-free) does not involve a move from what is said to what is meant. Irony involves never leaving behind the surface meaning, never quite not meaning it, never simply meaning the opposite of what is said. So ironised cataloguings, mappings, retain still some superstitious meaning.

A Walk Through H can be seen as a fiction exploring the superstitious penumbra of our use of maps - and our interpretation of paintings. It contains Greenaway's best joke, also by chance a prophecy if related to a film-maker eventually more comfortable with a French (or Dutch, or German) audience:

This is a map made by an exiled pianist as a directive to the members of his band. He could not foresee that his musical and topographical instructions should be used backwards. As a cartographer he was not appreciated in his own country.

FAMILY RELATIONS

- Thy father was the Duke of Milan, and
A prince of power.
                         - Sir, are you not my father?
- Thy mother was a piece of virtue,
She said - thou wast my daughter.

Miranda's momentary confusion is of a piece with Greenaway's own scripts. Family relations are always important, but often confusing. The draughtsman spends some time trying to establish their legal consequences in particular. The brothers in *A Zed and Two Noughts* are revealed as twins, and then as Siamese twins, and then as a single father (of twins), though there is always, with paternity, the possibility of deceit, of fakery, and indeed Alba decides that Arc-en-Ciel should be the father instead. (By this time, her nickname is Leda, and paternity, in the case of Leda, was a very complex business indeed.) In *Drowning by Numbers* the Cissies are grandmother, daughter and niece,[83] although Cissie, as *Fear of Drowning* sets out in some detail, is a multiple character of infinite complexity across Greenaway's work as a whole. Smut has no mother; the Skipping Girl has no father. The affairs of Kracklite and Louisa with Flavia and Caspasian are poised between incest and wife-swapping, without quite being either.

The Baby of Mâcon revolves around a real but impossible mother, her daughter's claim to be a Virgin mother - and the mother church. There is also a priest's son, which ought to be impossible. This is not the first miraculous birth in Greenaway:

Paulo had died at the age of 83 over a telephone arrangement he had with a night-club owner whose girls continued to give Paulo excitement over the phone. The giving of pleasure had apparently been reciprocal, for Paulo's favourite girl had borne a son some nine months after Paulo's death. (*Dear Phone*)

CONTRACTS, DEALS AND BLACKMAILS

There is *The Draughtsman's Contract*, of course; an adulterer's parody of the marriage contract which is itself parodied in a second contract, in a film much concerned with property and bodies as property which ends, in another example of language related to action, with a verbal, ironic contract with the draughtsman as he is stripped, blinded and murdered. *A Zed and Two Noughts* is full of deals, mostly for the possession of bodies. Milo attempts to barter her sexual favours for a publisher for her erotic animal stories. The dead, or about to be dead, bodies of animals or women - Milo's again, ten weeks pregnant and with both Van Meegeren and Van Hoyten believing themselves to be the father; and Alba's - are subject for negotiation over their use, or potential use, in the 'experiment' (more akin to the installation work of an artist like Damien Hirst, which may be indebted to it) investigating decay. Prospero has a contract with Ariel. In *The Baby of Mâcon*, the daughter/virgin mother, at the height of her power, makes a series of ruthless deals with the petitioners who seek aid from the miraculous powers of the child. Simple greed - demanding a lifetime's honey rather than three years, although three years would in fact have been a better deal - escalates until it reaches the contemptuous claiming of one of an old man's daughters for prostitution to pay for the baby's father's sustenance, of another to lay with him to keep him amused, and, even more cynically, of a third daughter for a nunnery - to placate Cosimo.

The Belly of an Architect is full of corrupt deals as the exhibition is taken out of Kracklite's control. Caspasian's photo that never was suggests blackmail rather than his sister's voyeurism. Kracklite cannot even post one of his cards to Boullée without a deal: we see him sitting on the pavement, framed by two doorways, a red mailbox behind him (red is an important colour in the film). He writes his postcard. A man approaches, and stands near the mailbox. Cut to a car from which Flavia takes photographs; we see, through the car, Kracklite approach the mailbox to post his card, but the stranger is stopping him; we now see the two of them in close-up, the stranger's hand resting on and blocking the mailbox slit (the perspective of the first shot is now on the left, within it another red detail, a street sign: No Entry). Kracklite hands the card to the man, who waits. Kracklite pays him. The man posts the card. We return to the car, and hear 'he's learning'.

His next and final bribe is to allow him into the Victor Emmanuel building for the exhibition he is supposed to be opening. Inadvertently, it contains a pound note, which is returned to him - the same note he holds as he falls. A pound note, if you read it and believe it, is also a contract, between the bearer and the Governor of the Bank of England.

CLASSIFICATIONS AND SYSTEMS

Order and method. As our officer always said.
He was still saying it when he died.
How did he die?
He exploded.

JEAN-LUC GODARD, *Les Carabiniers*

The term species thus comes to be a mere useless abstraction, implying and assuming a separate act of creation. It is certain that many forms, considered by highly-competent judges to be varieties, resemble species so completely in character, that they have been thus ranked by other highly-competent judges. But to discuss whether they ought to be called species or varieties, before any definition of these terms has been generally accepted, is vainly to beat the air.

CHARLES DARWIN [84]

Painters create spatial meaning: meaning as it is apparent in an image, in which nothing disappears from view, and the associations filtered through the thinking, the embodied eye - iconographical, sexual, religious, cultural, formal - do not succeed each other, but co-exist, in an experience of duration without linearity or coherent sequence. Only in the weary succession or desperate rush of writing do these meanings and associations follow on from one another, prioritised, stacked like aircraft waiting to land.

Linear meaning entering such a system is transformed by it. To demonstrate, for example, a causal link between Herod and the Massacre of the Innocents, early Renaissance painters invented a kind of moral space in which the massacre takes place at Herod's feet, as if ordering and witnessing were a single act.

Eisenstein's montage is comparable to this supposedly 'primitive' narrative in many ways, but already it is relying on memory, on sequence, rather than simultaneity. What, in a painting, is a formal rhyme, in cinema can only be premonition and reprise, theme and variation. Two pulses flow through cinema: narrative, and the continuous present, the immediacy of what is before us. It was this immediacy which allowed Buñuel to alternate two actresses, radically different in appearance, within the same part in *That Obscure Object of Desire*; not everybody notices. Hitchcock made shameless and conscious use of this cinematic present in his editing, for example at the end of *The Lady Vanishes*, which makes no logical sense at all, and in the cut in *The Thirty-*

Nine Steps which carries his hero from a precarious position halfway across the Forth Bridge to the Highlands. Greenaway does something similar in *A Zed and Two Noughts*, cutting away from Milo's scream as the twins are in the tiger's cage to the twins, naked but unharmed, talking to Van Meegeren. The tiger's roar follows them from one scene to the next, but no explanation accompanies it. Cinema operates simultaneously through *and next, and next, and next* - and through *now*.

We have seen how Greenaway is both determined to exploit and expand the possibilities of cinema as *Gesamtkunstwerk*, to play with words and music as well as images, and concerned at what is lost in the move from painting. He retains as much simultaneous, spatial meaning as possible, and he reinvents it for a temporal medium; and he also surrounds his practice of cinema with a parallel practice of painting and still photography and exhibition/installation. His cinema clearly demands an attention comparable to that before painting - perhaps before (or within) the vast Baroque and Renaissance schemes to which the initial idea for *The Stairs* paid explicit homage, architectural schemes not graspable in a single glance.

It also often organises itself around structures, 'narratives', that are imaginable as diagrams - spatially, at a thought's glance, as it were. There are the two graph lines of *The Belly of an Architect*, the gestations of Kracklite's child and of his cancer. There is the simple counting of *Drowning by Numbers*, 1-100, the sequence which is also a cycle, a skipping game; and the triple drowning. (One sign of female superiority in this film is in the contrast between male and female attitudes to counting. Had the Skipping Girl been a boy, her counting would have kept going, to reach a record - or keep a record, like Smut's record of deaths, open-ended. It is the women who win the equally circular catching game, a dance to the music of time; and when the three Cissies count, their counting in threes, although a potentially infinite sequence, is really a way of saying three every time, a mantra of their power.) *The Baby of Mâcon* is a kind of Russian doll of time: within the present, the seventeenth century, within the seventeenth century the time of the miracle play which is being performed, within the miracle play the 'original' Christian story.

Systems of classification are always present in the films, even if they do not structure them. (Works may also be parts of wider systems stretching across the oeuvre; *Rosa* is part of a far wider project on the deaths of ten composers.) Some systems repeat. We have already considered the basic 1-100; there is also 1-92, a number taken (in error, as Greenaway explained in *Anatomy of a Filmmaker*) from John Cage. There are ninety-two maps in *A Walk Through H*, ninety-two case histories in *The Falls*. What distinguishes Greenaway from many of his sources is perhaps his foregrounding and thematisation of his systems. *Vertical Features Remake*, for example, uses narrative to frame, to make visible (and audible), systems related to the material of film itself, to the number of individual frames in a sequence, which otherwise would be completely invisible.

Letters are as important as numbers; the alphabet runs through *A Zed and Two Noughts* like the

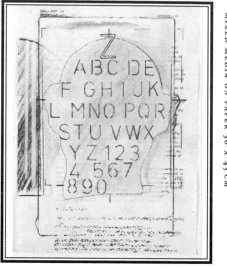

Head Text Series : Z

MIXED MEDIA ON PAPER 36 × 45 CM

countdown in *Drowning by Numbers*, elsewhere it halts at a particular letter - *H is for House*, *M is for Man, Music, and Mozart*. There have been many literary works based on the alphabet - Barthes used alphabetical order to determine the order of the sections of *A Lover's Discourse*; Flaubert had his *Dictionary of Received Ideas*, which in translation loses its order by maintaining its structure - but anyone who has enjoyed the juxtapositions and unlikely pairings upon an alphabetically arranged library shelf or within an index, or read the surrealist poems entitled Index of First Lines ,has already begun to understand the chaotic possibilities of alphabetical order, a kind of 'objective' method of collage. *Rosa* ends, after the singers have taken their bows, with an 'index': an index of the performance and its component parts, but one which gives definitions also, becoming a kind of dictionary. 'Grief. An emotional experience often brought about by a great sense of loss. The subject of this loss is completely immaterial.'[85] (In performance, this index lasted over twenty minutes, riding an unexpected James Brown groove, and included, even more unexpectedly, a quotation from Rod Stewart's 'Do You Think I'm Sexy?', which itself (folk, blues and pop traditions are systems of echo and quotation as labyrinthine as any work by Greenaway) is based on a Bobby Womack riff.)

In *A Zed and Two Noughts*, as in *Drowning by Numbers*, there is a close association between systems (and naming) and childhood. The alphabet is recited alongside animals' names by Beta, who is named, by Alba, after the second letter of the Greek alphabet. (Alba wants to have twenty-six children, though it is pointed out to her that there are only twenty-three letters in the Greek alphabet, in a conversation mirrored shortly afterwards by the remark that 'Vermeer only painted twenty-six paintings, and three of those are dubious'.)

The interest in encyclopaedic systems - non-linear in the way they are used, with their own kind of simultaneity - is clearly linked to this interest in alphabetical order. *The Falls* presents itself as an extract from a directory 'published every ten years by the Committee investigating the Violent Unknown Event': ninety-two case histories, in alphabetical order, taken from nineteen million, all the names beginning with the letters Fall, in itself an important word for Greenaway, involving both loss of Eden and a failure to fly.

Some films are structured more individually. *A Zed and Two Noughts* has a Kitaj-like associationist structure difficult to grasp; the film at least partly originated with a collagist association between a number of disparate images, 'the three most conveniently recognisable ones [being] a tape, an ape, and a borrowed photograph':

The tape was a three-minute time-lapse film of the decay of a common mouse first shown on the BBC *Horizon* programme in 1981. Thanks to the speeding up of the time-lapse material, it was seen that maggots acted in unison on a corpse, devouring it systematically in a pack. It was the camera-operator's ambitious hope one day to film the decay of an elephant.

The ape lived in Rotterdam Zoo and had only one leg. The animal had been chained in a back-yard. The chain had bitten into the leg and the spread of infection was only to be prevented by amputation. When the animal climbed and swung about in its cage there were times when it seemed that the missing leg was no impediment at all. Its incapacity had, it seemed, been victoriously overcome.

And the photograph had been a generous loan to me in 1978 for use in an encyclopædic film called *The Falls*. It showed a confidently smiling woman standing between the elegant, enigmatic, identically twinned Quay brothers, puppeteers and film-makers whose methods of film-animation were not so very different from the concepts of squeezing time that had made it possible to see how the maggots had devoured the mouse carcase. [86]

Nevertheless, it is organised around the eight stages of evolution - and the eight episodes of *Life on Earth* - which are repeated in the decay experiment. (The zoo itself classifies, although eccentrically, as we have seen.)

There are also references, or quotations, which amount to systems, such as the use of Vermeer in *A Zed and Two Noughts*. Such one-off 'systems' can be used, as they were in much avant-garde music and painting of the sixties, to organise the making of an artwork, so that the 'rules' that have been 'deduced' from them operate as an anti-intuitive programme for creation, with nothing or little in the final artwork itself to indicate to the viewer that they are present. But they can also be clearly on the surface; in the riot of systems that is *Drowning by Numbers*, Brueghel's *Children's Games* implies that the film itself is a comparable compendium of (in this case often fictional) games, the rules of which are often explained through voice-overs.

Smut's jumping game, 'Flights of Fancy or Reverse Strip Jump', has (blasphemous) biblical associations, and uses the familiar and magical number three, a recurring theme and system in itself. The game is recorded in Muybridge fashion at every leap; Smut is another of Greenaway's photographers, as is Madgett. (No doubt the fact that the strip is in reverse - it is a very complicated way of getting dressed in the morning - is lost on the policemen who (in one of Greenaway's fragments of plot, signalling rather than developing narrative) see these and the other Polaroids taken for Madgett's book of cricketing injuries as possible evidence of sexual abuse.) 'Flights of Fancy' also recalls the early film *Windows*, the script of which is worth quoting in full:

In 1973 in the parish of W, 37 people were killed as a result of falling out of windows. Of the 37 people who fell, 7 were children under 11, 11 were adolescents under 18 and the remaining adults were all under 71 save for a man believed by some to be 103.

Five of the 7 children fell from bedroom windows as did 4 of the 11 adolescents and 3 of the 19 adults. Of the 7 children who fell all cases were of misadventure save one of infanticide.

Of the 11 adolescents, 3 committed suicide for reasons of the heart, 2 fell through misadventure, 2 were drunk, one was pushed, one was accredited insane, one jumped for a bet and one was experimenting with a parachute.

Of the 18 men, 2 jumped deliberately, 4 were pushed, 5 were cases of misadventure and one, under the influence of an unknown drug, thought he could fly.

Of the 11 adolescents who fell, 2 were clerks, 2 were unemployed, 1 was married, 1 was a window cleaner and 5 were students of aeronautics, one of whom played a harpsichord.

Among the 19 adults who fell were an air-stewardess, 2 politicians, an ornithologist, a glazier and a seamstress.[87]

Of the 37 people, 19 fell in summer before midday, 8 fell on summer afternoons and 3 fell into

Drowning by Numbers Series : Night Cricket

PENCIL, PASTEL & INK ON CARD 81 X 112 CM

snow. The ornithologist, the adolescent experimenting with the parachute and the man who thought he could fly all fell or were pushed on spring evenings. At sunset on the 14th of April 1973 the seamstress and the student of aeronautics who played the harpsichord jumped into a plum tree from the window in this house.

Windows was inspired by the deaths of prisoners of the South African police; Smut's own death by hanging is recorded within his counting 'game', and is itself described as a game, with Smut's own final voice-over. (We may begin to wonder - as we do in *Sunset Boulevard* - what, exactly, is the site of such a voice-over, what is the nature of its relation to what is shown, and begin to notice the artifice in one of the most basic of cinema's narrative conventions.) One of the film's own games names characters after famous last words. Just as *trompe l'oeil* breaks the contract between art and life by removing the frame, in *Drowning by Numbers* the contract between what is life (and death) and what is 'only a game' is broken, at least within the play of the film itself.

In *The Cook, The Thief, His Wife and Her Lover*, *Prospero's Books* and *The Baby of Mâcon*, all based on drama in different ways - *The Cook* is a kind of Jacobean revenge tragedy (and has since been staged as a play), *Prospero's Books* incorporates *The Tempest*, and *The Baby of Mâcon* is about the staging of a play - the confusion between the space of life and the symbolic space of the playing field, the dissolving of boundaries between them, becomes a series of meditations on theatricality; all the world becomes a stage, within a film. But of course, other systems intrude: Prospero's books are also a system cutting into Shakespeare's text; and *The Baby of Mâcon* has the rape scene, based on a coldly Sadeian mathematics, a one-off and perverse countdown to mortality.

The early films often mock or parody documentary film-making, not least its authoritative (authoritarian?) tone of voice, presenting false material in a 'convincing', or at least fairly conventional, way (*The Falls*, a film about characters who have been struck by the Violent Unexplained Event) and true material in a more avant-garde way (*Act of God*, a film about people who have been struck by lightning). (There is a tantalising glimpse in *Anatomy of a Filmmaker* of a film Greenaway made for the Central Office of Information, a documentary which seems easily relatable to the rest of his work; how did it appear in its original context?)

Some of the consequences of system-based 'narrative' will be considered below. Here, it is worth mentioning how ideal a collaborator Tom Phillips was; his practice had been running parallel with Greenaway's for years before they came together for *A TV Dante*. (Indeed, Greenaway has suggested he was an early influence.) Both artists operate through systems, though one might distinguish them schematically. Phillips often uses systems to generate material in a series of open-ended projects. *20 Sites, n Years*, an infinite documentary project, comparable to Long's circular walks, but encyclopaeic rather than minimal (no wonder Phillips's favourite Greenaway film is *Vertical Features Remake*), chronicles twenty sites around a circle centred on Phillips's (now former) studio, and is to be continued after Phillips's death. *Terminal Greys*, a series of abstract paintings, mixes the unused paint left at the end of every working day and paints a strip with it. Greenaway generally uses systems to organise material, in a series of ironised closures. Both artists, however, have intricate oeuvres in which characters and ideas repeat and echo through and across any individual work, creating a complex web of coincidence and association, with shadowy or fluid characters. Phillips has invented a surrealist writer whose name is an anagram of W. H. Mallock, the author of *A Human Document*, a novel chosen at random for deconstruction. His collage/novel treatment of that book, *A Humument*, includes - besides Irma, the heroine - Toge, a figure who can only appear on pages including the words 'together' or 'altogether'. Greenaway, of course, has recurring 'characters' - or subjects of impossibly contradictory narratives - such as Cissie Colpitts and Tulse Luper. Both are interested - and involved - in contemporary music, itself often systems-based, and indeed both have been librettists of operas: out of the endless material generated from his mining and undermining of *A Human Document* Phillips created a print/libretto for *Irma*, a 'lost' opera that has now been 'recreated' by several composers. Both are highly literary artists; much of Phillips's work includes language. Both are interested in postcards. Greenaway's fourth film was *5 Postcards from Capital Cities*, and the published script for *The Belly of an Architect* includes the script for a supplementary project based on the postcards Kracklite sends to Boullée. Phillips based a whole series of paintings, notably *Benches*, on postcards. His notes on 'The Postcard Vision' rework the Mallarmé remark that everything exists to be put into a book, which Greenaway himself reworks in paragraph 34 of *Watching Water*. 'We could amend this provocation to suggest that everything exists to be put into a film ... Or further - everything exists to be put into an exhibition - including every book and every film.'[88]

Greenaway's longest collaboration, of course, was with Michael Nyman. It began with *1-100* in 1978, and continued until *Prospero's Books* in 1991. The interview with Nyman in *Peter Greenaway*[89] is invaluable for his detailed account of how his own systems dovetailed with Greenaway's, in *1-100*, *A Walk Through H*, *Vertical Features Remake*, *The Falls*, *The Draughtsman's Contract* and *A Zed and Two Noughts*. *Drowning by Numbers* was made after the interview, but *Fear of Drowning* explains[90] how its score is related to *The Falls* - in which Cissie Colpitts appears. Nyman's attitude to melody appears comparable to Greenaway's to narrative. 'Christian Wolff disait, à une époque où Cage travaillait sur les fragments d'atomes musicaux - où tout était séparé - que *tout à la fin devient mélodie*'. He uses mathematical structures, initially independent of the piece, and develops them musically. He works with fragments of existing music: in *The Falls* and *Drowning by Numbers*, Mozart's Concertante for Violin, Viola and Orchestra (specifically in the recording which was part of a job-lot of 78s bought by Greenaway in 1964, a lucky dip which also inspired the use of animal songs in *A Zed and Two Noughts*); in *The Draughtsman's Contract*, Mozart again, initially, and Purcell. (The music always began as an independent piece, with a continuing history and life of its own, whatever the negotiations with the images it accompanies - images often still unfilmed when the writing of the music began.) Nyman's comments on his use of Mozart suggest the time games to come in *The Baby of Mâcon*, and more generally Greenaway's own use of quotation, and indicate both the sympathy between their approaches and the mutual influence of their ideas:

Pour Peter, l'idée initiale de *The Draughtsman's Contract* a pu être un de mes morceaux de musique intitulé *In Re Don Giovanni*. Quand j'ai recommencé a ecrire en 1976-1977... j'ai découvert seize mesures de l'ouverture de Madamina de *Don Giovanni*. J'ai repris ces seize mesures et j'en ai fait un nouveau morceau. Non pas un morceau qui utilisait la musique de Mozart, mais un musique littéralement sortie de celle de Mozart, utilisait d'autres informations et les redistribuant. Voici un exemple de morceau musical qui est d'une part de xviiie siécle, et d'autre part de la fin de xxe; une sorte d'intégration des deux. Vous ne pouvez pas dire que c'est du Mozart, vous ne pouvez pas dire que c'est de Nyman: mais c'est évidemment Mozart et c'est évidemment Nyman. C'est Mozart vu à travers mon regard, mon expérience de la musique minimale, de la pensée structuraliste, un certain sens de la musique analytique et une certaine familiarité avec la musique des Beatles, de Jerry Lee Lewis, Steve Reich, etc. Je pense que ce morceau qui existait déjà dans les toutes premières versions de scénario a dû donner une idée a Peter, dans le sens où il pouvait faire un drame quie prenait ses racines au xviiie siècle mais qui était aussi concernée par les idées artisiques, philosophiques, théoriques et politiques fondées en 1982.[91]

BIRDS AND FLYING

This chapter began with water; it ends with air.

100 Objects includes a crashed aircraft. Another exhibition, *Flying Out of This World*, was entirely devoted to flight, human flight. *Prospero's Books* ends with Ariel's take-off, but then Ariel is a spirit, 'an airy Spirit' (although he enters the first scene with Caliban 'like a water nymph'); human attempts to fly are closely related to gravity. The exhibition of drawings from the Louvre links them through a commentary, 'animates' them like frames from a narrative, and they become part of Greenaway's image-system. When we see a sphere - two drawings by Redon, one each by Annibale Carracci and Giulio Pippi - we are not surprised to find Boullée in the text, hailed (as a substitute for Newton himself) as 'master of the heavy mass, guardian of gravitational spirit'. A year before the exhibition, *Prospero's Books* had borrowed (for Ferdinand's first meeting with Miranda) the figure balancing on a ball in Coppola's *One from the Heart*, a romance of exemplary artifice; Coppola had borrowed it from Picasso. Another set of drawings, one by Mondella, one by Mantegna and two after Mantegna, shows gravity represented by a ball again (in Giovanni Da Brescia's engraving) but mostly by a fat man, almost too heavy to lift - Silenus, in the Mondella, the Mantegna and the Rubens copy after it, his dead drunk dead weight an echo of (or inspiration for?) the fat part of a fool in the *Balcon* sequence, and the fat shipwreck victim in *Prospero's Books* who is raised to the surface by nymphs (all we see is the upward movement underwater).

Air is connected very often with water, conceptually, but also visually - in *The Falls*, and in *Prospero's Books*, where the primer of small stars is rhymed with light on water; one overlaid on the other. This is often true even with the birds, so common in the early films especially. Many of them are water birds: geese, seagulls, the swan which (in Swan's Way) crashes into a Ford Mercury full of pregnant women at the start of *A Zed and Two Noughts*. 'More than a few incidents of dramatic danger', Greenaway remarks in his commentary to Vleughel's *Studies of Wings*,[92] 'have been caused by low-flying swans unable to change course without much foresight, unable to gain much height without a forward plan. And the beating wings make a noise like a creaking row boat allied to heavy breathing.'

Flying Out of This World itself is a return to the imagery of *The Falls* and *A Walk Through H*, in its constant linking of real and mythical creatures, and its emphasis on the erotic - often, again, between humans, birds, and gods in the shape of birds, as well as in its major theme of human flight. (See the commentary on Gannymede, pp 102-5; or on the drawing after Primaticcio, p 114: 'if we cannot fly, if we cannot take flight, we reserve its unexperienced delights for

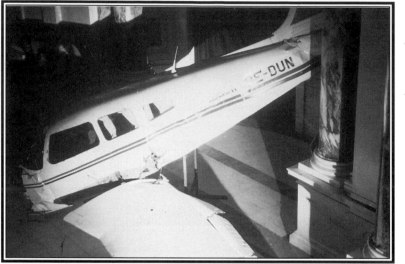

metaphors of sexual desire'. This is surely related to water and drowning (*Drowning by Numbers*), and being saved from drowning (*Prospero's Books*). The first drowning is a punishment for sexual infidelity; the second a punishment for lack of sexual interest; the third, with underwater shots which anticipate and contrast with the nymphs in *Prospero's Books*, begins as a seduction.) *A Walk Through H* indeed suggests how early the idea for *Flying Out of This World* - if not its final, ambitious form - was present: 'This ostensibly is the floorplan of a gallery where I had once arranged an exhibition on the subject of flight.' Another commentary reads:

> The next three maps had been the property of Canton Remadel, an ornithologist and a pioneer aviator. He designed kites based on his observations of seagulls. The kites were often made of wastepaper which came from his work room. Paper, which sometimes bore his designs and drawings. This is such a strip. I'm told it is a re-working of a flight plan of a much earlier conceptual aviator. I took the route of the third alternative. When first asked about the likelihood of making an aircraft, Remadel was reputed to have said that it would be easier to breed giant seagulls and then ride the offspring. Tulse Luper said that the maps Remadel had collected together for his final flight had been taken from the most brilliant aeronautical drawings of the time. Remadel crashed his last plane into a cliff at Hastings knocking my great grandfather into the sea. My great grandfather had been collecting seagull eggs.

The third biography from *The Falls*, longer than most, can be quoted in full (the film itself has

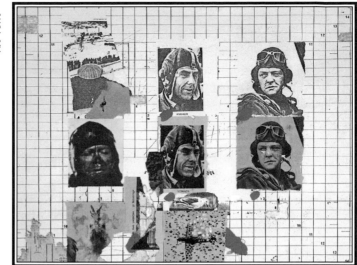

a slightly longer text than the published script used here) to give a flavour of a major work. The aspects of continuing relevance need no gloss. Kavan is one of the many languages invented for the biographies, which also often have diseases invented for them, the best of which involves a recurrence of all the previous diseases and wounds suffered by the victim. In Biography 81 there is the following exchange, of relevance here: 'Interviewer: Did you fly too near the sun? Armeror: No. My hero is Daedalus.'

Melorder Fallabur, the registered husband of Constance Ortuist Fallabur, is a comparative-flight-historian. With a fine disregard for the almost inevitable humility of failure, Melorder persisted in advertising his unassisted flights from London's tall buildings, always making himself available for interviews. He speaks Katan which may or not explain his nonchalance, his insouciance and his equivocal grasp on the realities of gravity. The following interview was recorded on the roof of the Shell oil company sky-scraper beside the river Thames in London.

INTERVIEWER: What number, Melorder, is this building on your list?

MELORDER: It's in the top twenty in London, but there is some trouble getting a permit to land.

INTERVIEWER: Is it high enough?

MELORDER: It's a possibility, though the draughts are inauspicious. I don't want to end up in the Thames. I can't swim, even if I can fly.

INTERVIEWER: Your researches have surely told you that the likelihood of success is very limited?

MELORDER: We all know there has been a conspiracy. Only the failures have been recorded. We are all too interested in Icarus and not enough in his father.

Melorder had been employed as an official witness of the violent unknown event, and because of what he saw, he had himself sterilised as a precaution against making his wife pregnant. He need not have worried, for it soon became apparent that a high proportion of those affected by the vue, male and female alike, became sterile anyway. Melorder's brother-in-law, Rapper-Begol, had remarked flippantly that a true vue mutant could only satisfactorily reproduce itself with the aid of a placenta that had developed an egg-shell. Melorder and his wife rarely lived together after he had been sterilised.

INTERVIEWER: Is it true you were married in a DC-10 flying over the Eiffel tower?

MELORDER: That was the intention. But by the time the chaplain recovered from air-sickness, we were flying over Les Invalides.

INTERVIEWER: Is your wife going to watch the flight?

MELORDER: No. She said 'too much entertainment, and not enough research'.

INTERVIEWER: What about the timing?

MELORDER: For the inaugural flight, I intend to use lights, so the most auspicious time would be in the evening. I'll make it down into the shadow of the building when the shadow is at its longest.

INTERVIEWER: That shadow is important to you?

MELORDER: Consider the times that shadow has rotated around this building. I was born down

there in the Lambeth general maternity hospital. My mother started labour in that shadow, and had to wait until it came around again before she was finished.

When his duties as official observer of the vue were over, Melorder had turned his attention to publishing an encyclopaedic history of flight, and to the formation of an aircraft museum at Rishangles.

INTERVIEWER: It's been said that having started your life in the shadow, that's the way it's going to end for you?

MELORDER: I have no intention of fulfilling that particular forecast.

The vue had affected Melorder's sight for the better and his hearing for the worse, and the muscles along his arms, and across his chest and back had become enlarged, engorged and strengthened. His doctor referred to the phenomenon as 'Patagium Fellitis' or 'Skin-Wing Aggrievement'. It was this useful characteristic that eventually persuaded Melorder that his historical and theoretical knowledge of human-flight should be put to practical use.

INTERVIEWER: I hear that Armeror Fallstag [biography 81] has sent you a wreath?

MELORDER: He should save his money - I'm not dying by gravity.

Water, for Greenaway, is what you drown in; air is what you fall out of. Similarly, swimming is related to flying, as in the instructions for rehearsing flying in *Flying Out of This World*: 'Air will drive itself into your mouth and nostrils at speed. Just like water'.[93]

The draughtsman cannot paint birdsong (nor Talmann's whistling - another simulacrum?). Nor can he stop the clouds moving. A cloud is the second of the *100 Objects to Represent the World*. There are ten cloud studies in *Flying Out of This World*. A cloud is water in flight.

Art Caught

IN THE ACT

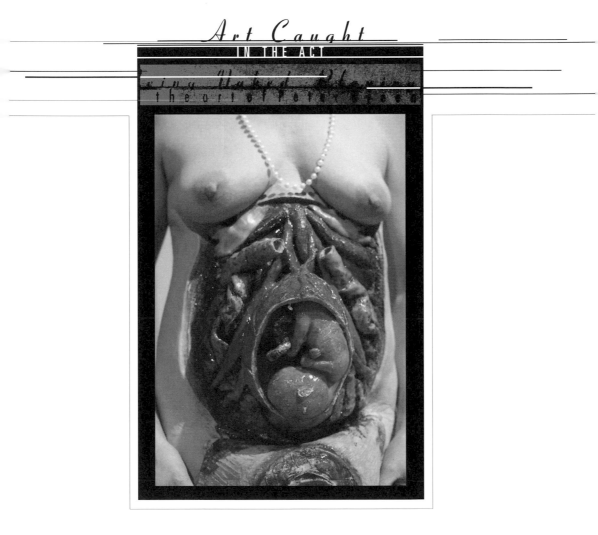

FRAMES OF MIND

(And which art is not close to cinema?)
SERGEI EISENSTEIN

53.]M[ ]D[= A dream of seeing through one eye only.
HOLLIS FRAMPTON [1]

Cinema has incorporated, stolen from, translated other arts, defined itself in relation and opposition to them. Greenaway's cinema is a particularly complex example of this: in its simultaneous fascination with text and hostility to a dominant cinema 'slavishly dependent' on literature (though recently this dependence seems to have been supplanted by an equally slavish dependence on cartoons, comics and old television programmes); in its (operatic) theatricality; and in its relations with art history and the contemporary art world. It is also a cinema linked to an unprecedented degree with Greenaway's own related but non- or mega-cinematic projects, so that his films have the kind of visible penumbra of 'sketches' and preparatory works once routine in painting. Literally, they have drawings and paintings and collages around them, but also exhibitions, books, and documentary or supplementary films or programmes. Equivalences, and differences, between the arts are thereby highlighted as particular images and interests are carried from text to stage to paper to film to computer generated image, inflected by the medium, its grain, its history, its formal constraints and opportunities and properties. How does a picture frame compare to the frame - if that is what it is - of a cinema screen, and how do they both compare to the 'frame' of a stage? Is there a continuum of narrative, or of 'voyeurism', across the media? Or a set of family relationships? Should we see the projects themselves as single entities which overwhelm any differences, with every local lack compensated for elsewhere?

Certainly, such considerations structure films which are so often about other art forms. It is quite possible, for example, to consider *The Draughtsman's Contract* and *The Baby of Mâcon* as parallel narratives of life and art inextricably linked and, more specifically, as narratives of 'off-stage' - or outside the frame.

Consider two clusters, or families, of narrative, imagery and metaphor across the range of Greenaway's oeuvre. The first is to do with devices and spaces to do with looking and representation and performance, with viewing and image-making, and it includes the draughtsman's grid; Flavia's camera; the projectors in *A Zed and Two Noughts*; the Polaroids taken by Smut and Madgett; the

prequel narratives in *Fear of Drowning*; the binoculars in *Drowning by Numbers*; the exhibition and the viewing platforms and the keyhole (of which more later) in *The Belly of an Architect*; the viewing platforms in *The Stairs Geneva*; the fields of play in *Vertical Features Remake*, *A Walk Through H* and *Drowning by Numbers*; the screens in *Rosa*, *The Stairs Munich* and *The Baby of Mâcon*; and the motif of the table in the operating theatre, an operating theatre with unavoidable echoes of Rembrandt and Eakins which, in *M is for Man, Music and Mozart*, explicitly becomes a theatre, but is also closely related to the mortuary slab, and the dissecting table. The bodies on those tables belong to the second family of narratives, the images of the body as symbol, flesh as emblem, allegory, diagram - the continuing use of Vesalius and related skeletons, models and flayed corpses, of (so to speak) educational bodies; the decaying bodies in *A Zed and Two Noughts*, and Alba's body, dressed up and operated upon by Van Meegeren; the allegorical figures in *Prospero's Books* and the *Strasbourg Book of Allegories*; the bizarre identities taken on by the players in 'Hangman's Cricket', and Smut's appearance as a compendium of cricketing injuries; the Baby of Mâcon itself, as symbolic child and as mutilated sequence of fluids and relics; Esmerelda's inking up of herself to resemble a horse in *Rosa*, and Rosa's posthumous appearance as a 'Christ for centaurs', in an opera explicitly concerned with 're-creations', with actings-out. This is parallel to the interest, already considered, in film sets, in clues, still lifes and properties, in the 100 objects that can represent the world.

There are distinctions to be made within these groupings between representation *of* bodies and objects, and representations *by* and *through* bodies and objects; cinema is strangely poised between the two. What is constant throughout is a double emphasis: on the material realities of image-making, and acting, and the media employed by the artwork; and on the ambiguities, paradoxes, but above all the physical conditions of being a viewer or a member of an audience, or a visitor to an exhibition; or, indeed, a reader.

The present section is to do specifically with images and stagings of sex and death, the most telling and acute occasions of Greenaway's explorations of the limits of representation. I will focus in turn on the central metaphor of a film about drawing, a sequence in a film about an architect, a sequence in a film about a performance of a play (fictional, existing only in the film), and images from an opera which had its first public 'performance' as a text - a novel about a particular performance of an opera. This section draws on, or sketches out, areas of criticism developed in relation to painting and theatre, as well as referring to other films. Just as, within those old films based, too closely, not closely enough, on novels, films which begin by clumsily moving to a 'dramatised' cinematic narrative from the pages of the book 'itself' - or rather a property version of it, a leather-bound 'classic', a signifier of literature that at once dramatises and conceals that literature is not what we are witnessing - there is here, in both criticism and artistic practice, a problem, or at least an issue, of digestion, of rejection (as in a transplant), of transposition. What is literally true of painting may be only metaphorically true of cinema. A precise term may, related to a sister art, become imprecise or misleading. It is within this territory of transferred and translated ambitions that Greenaway's own frustration with cinema clearly lies. Above all, what frustrates him is the flight, in cinema, from the physical (the body on stage; the film set; the property; the location; the paint on the canvas) to the trace of the physical, the physical become immaterial, coloured flickering light. He finds in cinema a doubled poverty of matter. Neither the medium nor what is represented by it are palpable; and the viewer can neither enter into its space nor control its time: 'We cannot inch a little to the left, to see the dining-table from the south side. If the director wishes us to see the table from the south side, then he will instruct his cine-matographer to show us the table from the south side ... this is a deeply impoverished situation, when we know that tables can be viewed from north, west and east as well. We must endeavour to correct this sad state of affairs. An exhibition may help. We could use a contemplation of the phenomenon of the exhibition to improve the status of cinema.'[2]

At the heart of this critique there seems to be a Platonic dissatisfaction not just with cinema, but with the image as image; as if Vermeer's studio were inherently more interesting than Vermeer's *Artist in His Studio.* Or a dissatisfaction comparable to the young Eisenstein's, wondering (viewing the audience's satisfaction with fictitious actions in the theatre) 'why strive for reality, if for a small sum of money you can satisfy yourself in your imagination without moving from your comfortable theatre seat?'[3] It can be set beside Bazin's contrast between seeing the world and watching a movie:

[In life] It is we who decide to choose such and such aspect, to pick this rather than that one according to the demands of action, of feeling or of reflection, but someone else would perhaps choose differently. Whatever the circumstances we are free to do our own *mise en scène*: there is always another possible choice which can radically modify the subjective aspect of reality. Now, the director who chooses for us, exercises, in our place, the discrimination with which we are faced in real life. We unconsciously accept his analysis because it is consistent with the laws of attention; but it deprives us of the privilege, no less grounded in psychology, which we abandon without realising it, and which is, at least virtually, the freedom to modify our method of selection at every moment.[4]

But Greenaway also seems to be identifying himself with Michel Ange in *Les Carabiniers*, who, in the great comic scene which is also a parable and even a history of cinema, visits a cinema for the first time. First, he is frightened, like the legendary first viewers of cinema, by a train approaching the camera. ('The Lumière brothers' passenger train, sailing into the sensorium straight out of the vanishing point of perspective, punctures the frontal picture plane against which painting had gradually flattened itself during nearly a century.')[5] Then, having enjoyed a comedy, he gets excited by the short erotic film *La Bain de la Femme de Monde*. Attempting to get a better view of the society lady in her bath by moving from side to side, he approaches the screen and jumps up and down in front of it; eventually, baffled by his inability to touch anything in the projected image, he brings down the screen itself, only to find the woman still bathing, still inaccessible, on the wall behind the ruined screen.

Les Carabiniers contains another famous dramatisation of the dealings between the world and images of the world. The cinema scene itself is presented, in a conventional though ironised conceit, as a postcard home, with Michel Ange's voice and handwriting introducing, slipping into, the narrative. When the two soldiers return home to their girls they bring home spoils of war which are all postcards. Carefully but absurdly catalogued, one of many connecting points between this sequence and Greenaway's cinema (including not just the use of postcards, but even their subjects; we see the Victor Emmanuel monument, and the fountain in Lake Geneva), these postcards are slammed down in triumph one by one on the table, as if ownership of an image and ownership of the thing 'itself' (the category of 'women', chosen by the heroes to 'continue their line for ever-more', makes no distinction between reproductions of paintings, erotic postcards, and pin-ups of actresses) were identical. 'These are our title deeds', says Ulysse.

The grid's mythic power is that it makes us able to think we are dealing with materialism (or some-times, science, or logic) while at the same time it provides us with a release into belief (or illusion, or fiction).

ROSALIND KRAUSS [6]

It is possible to view *The Draughtsman's Contract* as a kind of oblique gloss on this second scene. All the films made by Greenaway in advance of this first feature film had mocked systems by using systems, mocked documentary 'truths' by parodying documentary conventions; now perspective itself was ironised by focusing on it as a system.

We have already noted the framing of the perspective grid by the cinema camera. One of the major differences between grid and camera is that the camera/photograph interprets/records the visual field as light (as did Vermeer's *camera obscura*), while the grid/drawing interprets/records it as an accumulation of discrete things, represented by lines. There are the diagrammatic perspective lines and squaring-up lines that create the space but do not appear in it (in *Rosa*, as performed, they appear in the space but do not create it); and there are outlines. There is therefore already a paradox, if the grid is seen as a way of painting what is seen and not what is known, since outline follows knowledge of what a form is; the object as outline is a visual noun, derived from drawing as naming. (In advance of drawing this tree is the category of trees, which inflects the eye's discrimination within the view; and 'view' itself, of course, is another category.) In the psychology and controversy of centuries of Western painting, line is knowledge about what underlies appearances, colour is

'mere' appearance, the look of things and not the truth about them.

The draughtsman comes to grief because, well aware of the relations between property and image, he remains satisfied with drawings in which objects are represented as if in an inventory. (Berger's *Ways of Seeing* may have influenced the intellectual framework of the film.) Within the spaces which he records are, however, objects as symbols, clues regarding murder or adultery. He is drawing stage sets, filled not with property, but with properties, but he will not or cannot recognise this; for him, a pomegranate is merely an exotic fruit.

We should not, however, complacently regard 'the draughtsman' as a stable figure. The drawings are Greenaway's, and we are never intended to lose sight of their dual authorship (as we are intended to ignore the obvious fact that the half-finished picture on the actor's easel in a biopic is not a genuine work-in-progress by Van Gogh). They can be placed, as images, in relation to the rest of his work: the drawings for *Vertical Features Remake*, itself comparable as a film to *The Draughtsman's Contract*; the fascination with an accurate mapping of location and buildings systematically expressed in *The Draughtsman's Contract* itself and *The Belly of an Architect*; the interest in clues. The shot through the grid involves five pairs of eyes - the draughtsman's; the actor who plays the draughtsman's; Greenaway's; the cameraman's; the viewer's.

⚜

From the standpoint of dynamics, a work of art is the process of the birth of an image in the

The Draughtsman's Contract 'The Yew Walk'
PENCIL ON PAPER 77 X 52 CM

spectator's senses and mind ... this dynamic principle underlies all true-to-life images [even] in the seemingly static art of painting ... similarly, true-to-life acting is not copying the results of feelings, but calling feelings to life, compelling them to develop and overgrow into other feelings, in a word, to live before the spectator.

EISENSTEIN [7]

Perspective - (re)discovered for the Renaissance by an architect - is, as used in Western painting, a loose set of overlapping conventions, devices, techniques and indeed assumptions shared by artist and viewer. It has, broadly, two fictions of space and the viewer's relation to space. The first, theatrical space, creates a stage space, explicitly addressed to and created for an audience, within which the action is (equally explicitly) performed, perhaps (as Alberti suggests) with at least one figure mediating between action and audience through glance and gesture. The action - historical, mythical, allegorical, literary, explanatory even - is imagined, 'recreated', not presented as if witnessed, somehow 'prior' to the painting, set down. Legibility is all, and often overrides logic, or reconstructible realism, in order to further understanding. (Compare the shot in *The Belly of an Architect* in which Kracklite puts an image into the photocopier face up; such flourishes for the sake of the viewer are commonplace in painting.) The second, witnessed space, proposes that an artist has been in a particular location at a particular time and represented it so that viewers, before the finished canvas, identify themselves with that viewpoint as the source of a narrative, or an account, of something seen in the world and represented; the artist has been *there*, and done *this*. Theatrical space presents; witnessed space selects, crops, literally or metaphorically. Degas, the subtlest inventor of witnessed spaces - who well understood, as his sayings all attest, the artifice involved in realism - knowingly painted theatricality itself, showing actual theatrical spectacles, notably the ballet, as a series of restricted and particular views, as incomplete, witnessed spaces seen from particular seats in the theatre. Dancers are shown addressing the best seats in the house, but are shown from the wings or from a less good seat; backdrops are shown close-up, as illegible pigment. We become viewers looking at an audience looking at a spectacle, viewers whose gaze is merged with both an artist and an audience, the audience we are looking at. The audience as an abstraction addressed by an image has been visualised, thematised, deconstructed, broken down into a fragmented mass of individual and partial views. Manet's *Déjeuner sur l'Herbe,* unresolvably, includes or suggests both witnessed and theatrical spaces, as it includes or suggests both mythical/pastoral and modern times.

In theatrical space, then, the viewers are, so to speak, simultaneous with a space (and time) created for them. In witnessed space, there is an implied succession; the viewers are somehow after the event, are metaphorically 'standing where the artist stood' and, therefore, no longer in the gallery, in a sense; in a sense, they are no longer themselves. There is again a doubled view, like the strange mix, in reading a first-person novel, between the reading and the narrating 'I's. One fiction comes to us; the other drags us in. There is an imbalance, however, rather than a symmetry: witnessed space can be - indeed, since art is defined ultimately by an audience rather than by an artist, it *must* be - a subset of theatrical space. And here succession may be overwhelmed by a rhetoric of immediacy.

This becomes even clearer in cinema, where the witnessed, or point of view, shot is related to a character and not an artist; what would a director's point of view shot look like, what would distinguish it? It surely requires, to be imaginable, an erasure of narrative, of narrative at least as that which involves us. It requires, surely, *every* shot to be a director's point of view shot, not merely 'characteristic', but, as it were, signed - and distanced, and distancing. What is unimaginable in dominant cinema is ever-present in Greenaway.

In painting, the perspective grid can be used as an aid to the creation of both spaces, although, again, to frame is never merely to witness, and always also to dramatise what is chosen or assembled for representation. Perhaps the most famous visual account of it is Dürer's woodcut *An Artist Drawing a Woman Using an Optical Frame,* showing the artist using his perspective frame to draw his model. The artist is getting a view of her which is a sort of eroticised Mantegna, or (although the model is clothed) a premonition of Courbet's pornographic *The Origin of the World.* (The foreshortening in Mantegna's *Dead Christ,* as already noted a key image for Greenaway, still appears remarkably bold, original, even perverse; it is certainly a *coup de théâtre* in its sudden questioning of our detached role and viewpoint as viewers, its suggestion that we are somehow witnesses, and not an audience. The distinction between the theatrical and the witnessed is subject to all manner of theological blendings and nuances when the body in question is Christ's.) But the real reason why the artist's view of the model is depicted as it is (is there such an image in Dürer?) is that the woodcut itself is conceived within a theatrical perspective. As in many other images which are also narratives of looking (of the Judgement of Paris, for example) the model's pose is coherent, legible, not from the artist's viewpoint represented within the picture space, but from ours. Do we, are we invited to, imagine a studio in which Dürer set up a perspective frame, and in front of it placed what we see: another artist (or model pretending to be an artist), another perspective frame, the model whose skirt the other artist looks up? Hardly; the system *used*, rather than the one *demonstrated*, places no artist's eye in advance of the viewer's. ('Eye', rather than 'eyes', in common usage. Greenaway reproduces the woodcut in *The Stairs Munich*[8] and notes that though 'Dürer and Canaletto certainly used a drawing frame, which could be defined as an invisible screen employing the use of a back projection supplied by nature ... it is not quite the useful apparatus it appears to be. Human vision is binocular, and the head moves'.)

This is one reason why we are so unaware, generally, of the narrative camera of which the grid which it frames in *The Draughtsman's Contract* reminds us; it is borrowing (along with the novelist's omniscience and omnipresence) an ancient convention of painting, although to do so the director must create an artificial world in front of it, a world which he may wish to share with us.

There is a third term or possibility within (perhaps only just within) perspective: illusionistic space, by which I mean, strictly, *trompe l'oeil* - whether in the domestic Dutch and nineteenth-century American traditions (*trompe l'oeil* of witnessed space taken to extremes) or in the vast, all-encompassing schemes which decorate palaces or overwhelm the worshipper in Baroque churches (*trompe l'oeil* of theatrical space taken to extremes). It involves (sometimes after a genuine mistake, or an uncertainty which is, if possible, tested) a thematised, unstable split between what *appears* to be so, to be 'there', and what we *know* to be there. It is representation without a coherent space or site of representation, without a frame or with a frame itself destabilised, a blurred and uncertain boundary. The importance for Greenaway of its flickering ambiguities, its simultaneous artifice and naturalism, and not least its taking of a metaphor (art is like life) literally, will be considered in the next section.

But perspective has recently been analysed primarily in terms of the male gaze, of voyeurism; and I want to move away from the draughtsman's drawings, in which bodies and sex and death are merely implied, away from the draughtsman's grid, to a keyhole, the keyhole through which Kracklite watches his wife's adultery.

KRACKLITE AT THE KEYHOLE

I like to understand what I am shown.
Peeping Tom

If painted narrative is generally performed for an audience, for the viewers, if it is condensed and made explicit within and out of a fictional space, if it is a space sandwiched (as Lessing suggested it must be) between the artist's and the audience's common knowledge of the narrative time from which it is derived, then there are consequences for the representation of bodies within narrative. They will always be open to the viewer's gaze, even if their own glance does not meet it; the coherence of their poses is not internal (as it were) to the space of the 'stage', to the represented space, but to the wider space of the 'theatre', to the space of representation. They are not *spied on*.

This is one way of defining the difference between the nude and the naked. The nude is a display of nakedness; the naked is witnessed nakedness. (Witnessed not necessarily by a voyeur; perhaps by a husband, a lover.) Defined this way, the difference between male and female nudes is delayed; it becomes a matter of what manner of narrative they respectively perform. The male nude has a far greater repertoire, is far more often far more active, but even within passivity there is a gap: all those female nudes waiting for their men, all those male nudes waiting for their death.

In the history of the nude and its relation to the viewer it is surely crucial to consider very precisely the roles of ownership, commissioning, the spaces in which the image is viewed, the audience - is it a commissioned wedding picture, or a painting initiated by the artist and seeking a buyer amongst the crowded walls of the Salon or Academy?

This is not the occasion to write such a history; but perhaps there is, within it, a transition. In Pliny, there is an intriguing dialogue between artists and kingship, not least in depiction of the nude. In one anecdote, the king commissions an image of his mistress; a sight of her is granted to Apelles in order that he can return that sight, immortalised, made permanent, to its rightful owner. When the king realises that Apelles has fallen in love with his model, he gives her to him. Nowhere, in such a story, is there anonymity; nowhere (although complete power over the woman is assumed) is there voyeurism, in any narrow sense. When a *petit maître* paints, for an unknown future purchaser at the Salon, an image of Venus, a model unknown to that purchaser, real power has been transposed into fantasy. The ownership is only of the image; the bourgeois (who, of course, has his own real power over real women in his own society) is offered an image before which he can stand as if he were a king.

Societies with no taboo on images of naked women (or which, rather, distinguish between pornography and the nude) will still have taboos on voyeurism. In Western painting there are frequent images taken from narratives of voyeurism, a subset of all painted narratives about looking. The taboo which is pictured as breached is that of men looking at naked women (mostly as they bathe), not men looking at pictures of naked women (often shown as 'bathers'); so it is possible that such subjects might become occasions to gratify the male viewer's pleasure (generally unchallenged) in the image rather than to question or consider the practice of voyeurism, or compare it to the viewing of a painting. Boucher, for example, paints Diana bathing, but not Actaeon, and the subject - of a youth who is turned into a stag and killed by his own hounds as punishment for accidentally seeing the goddess bathing - is overwhelmed. But the waters, generally, are surely muddied by the incorporation of, say, the elders, two dirty old men, into a picture of Susannah bathing. Diderot certainly thought so, though his analysis of a picture in the Salon in which she turned away from the elders and towards the viewer - thereby at once concealing and revealing what were generally called her 'charms' - centred on whether she had not, by thus offering herself to the viewer, ceased to represent, embody, virtue. Had she known we were there - had she been an odalisque, meeting and welcoming our gaze - she certainly would have ceased to be Susannah.

But if we look at her without her knowledge, are we not like the elders? Are we not - although our sympathies must surely be with her? - represented in the painting (if we are men) by their gaze? Male desire is represented in a most unflattering light - it is opposed to the clearly virtuous characters before us - yet the point of view of the image is precisely that of the amoral desire, which is presented as our own. What we are shown defies us to deny that we are shown what we want to see.

This can only happen in painting when (alongside parallel changes in theatrical convention) it uses perspective to suggest, not a performance of a narrative before an audience which acknowledges that audience, but a performance of a narrative as if each individual member of that audience, now an isolated individual, involved subjectively, not collectively, somehow 'witnessed' it - identified with it.

The experience, in painting or in theatre, does not become less theatrical; just *differently* theatrical. It is not, in fact, at all like being 'there'. But it encourages precisely the kind of involvement with the narrative which Brecht hated in theatre. In painting - in the work of Greuze, for example, or many of the Victorians - it did not *discourage* the aesthetic gaze, detached, formal; it *provoked it into being*. Whistler hated painting which demanded to be read as literature, and proposed a new way of looking at painting, which suggested that it might be heard as music. But the painting of Whistler's time also pursued a kind of painting which genuinely explored the idea of witnessed space, as space and not as narrative. Cézanne investigated perspective before the landscape motif or the still life, dissatisfied both with its denial of binocular vision, the second eye of the painter, and perspective's inability to properly deal with time - the time in which the artist moves and paints, and in which the motif, and the light which plays upon and within the motif, constantly alters. Degas investigated urban space and time, and, where Cézanne accumulated time within the final image, Degas invented what Cartier-Bresson was later to call the significant moment. He also transformed the motif of the bather from the nude to the naked - or, one could also say, moved from a narrative of voyeurism to an approximation of voyeurism.

Degas explicitly referred to his pastels as voyeuristic, keyhole pictures. They were, of course, fictions, drawn from models in the studio - nothing could be more conventional - but what their fiction did was to transform the relation between the figure and the viewer. Nothing about the figure - though everything in the formal invention of the image - admits, acknowledges, is aware of or, crucially, is *organised* for the sake of a viewer, and this is not an acted out ignorance. Bathing, for the first time, has something to do with washing and nothing to do with display. Degas's nudes were denounced as ugly; but then the voyeur (unlike the bourgeois collector of nudes, who could buy strange fantasies of voyeurism, odalisques, images of spaces forbidden to the male gaze) must take what he can find. As Georgina suggests to Albert in *The Cook, The Thief, His Wife and Her Lover*, in a scene which is a kind of mirror image, a negative, of the scene of Kracklite at the keyhole (she has been with Michael for the first time, and he is still hiding in the cubicle), men who hang around ladies' lavatories - or watch them washing and drying themselves, perhaps - are asking to have their illusions shattered. Degas gave women a reason to be naked distinct from being looked at by men, and the fact that men were looking at them immediately became problematic.

There is a quotation from Picasso pinned up in Greenaway's office: 'I paint what I think, not what I see'. There is also a cartoon by Jacot, a response to *The Stairs Geneva*.

A bourgeois on one of Greenaway's viewing platforms - in his suit, his hat - looks through the viewing circle at a young woman, at a 'girl', a 'blonde', in her bra and panties as she stands at her open window. Holding up a restraining hand to his wife - he does not stop looking at the young woman, he just holds his hand up to the face of his wife, who is old - his age - with dark hair, a sensible handbag, a double chin; who stands in the street and waits, who looks at him - he says, 'reste où tu es ... Tu n'y comprendrais rien!' ('Stay where you are - you wouldn't understand a thing!'). There is also a caption: 'Stairs' à Genève ... Une question de point de vue!'

It is a version, in a way, of Doisneau's famous photograph of a husband taking a sly glance - as he stands next to his wife - at the nude in the shop window, unaware that he is part of an elaborate set-up. Doisneau knew he would get some such photograph; 'human nature' is like that.

The cartoon is a neat enough expression of the two views of art: art is sex, and therefore clear enough in itself, however much it is wrapped in irrelevant theory; or art is baffling, not to be understood at all. In neither case is it suitable for the wife, of course, though the joke is that she would understand what is going on here all too well.

The relationships within the drawing can be analysed easily enough. It is essential to the joke that the young woman at the window - framed twice, by her window, by the viewing platform - is, like a Boucher nude, happy to be looked at. This first relationship, entirely visual, between the bourgeois and the girl, is, although loosely voyeuristic - he stands as if at a keyhole - authorised, doubly authorised: by the way she looks towards him (though he is hidden from her, the anonymous viewer) and by art itself. The second relationship, between the bourgeois and his wife, is half verbal, half visual - his gesture, her watching of him watching - and is based on deceit. Then there is the third relationship - 'invisible', 'transparent' - between the cartoon and the readers, who, alone, see the whole picture; a simple dramatic irony, not unlike the scene in which we, but not Spica, understand the first conversation between the lovers.

⚜

The classic example of montage is precisely that of the voyeur. Film a man kneeling at a keyhole in Moscow; film a woman undressing in St Petersburg; show one after the other, and the audience will read it as a narrative.

The Belly of an Architect has its own keyhole scene. We see Kracklite at work on the exhibition, at the Victor Emmanuel monument, in a spectacular open space, half study, half museum; the prototype for Prospero's study. He asks Caspasian's father why he divorced; jealousy is the answer, a mistaken belief that his wife was unfaithful, but in fact the man he suspected was probably more interested in his daughter, Flavia. (Kracklite has wrongly suspected his wife of poisoning him, but she is having an affair with Caspasian.) As this conversation continues, we see the scaffolding which is an unmistakable reference to Piranesi, to his fantastic prison etchings in particular; the scaffolding is for the construction of huge Boullée models, but here it exists in its own right, a reconstruction of the irrational spaces and staircases leading to nowhere of the poet of ruins who is the symbol of Rome and the Roman, of everything which is conspiring against Kracklite. We see also the photo-copier, daubing Kracklite with flashing, deadly green, light, and the photocopies in close-up, again flashing white and green, the poisoned belly of Augustus with which Kracklite identifies, which we have seen him hold up against his own belly like a map of his illness. Kracklite leaves down the Victor Emmanuel stairs, and then climbs the staircase to his own apartment, awkwardly holding a briefcase, some papers; a photocopy of the belly happens to cover his own. (In the next scene but two, he says he dreams of stairs; in these dreams, he is always climbing stairs - or falling down them.) Halfway up the staircase, on a landing, is a young child, in a white towel (very like the white robe Kracklite wears in Flavia's studio), looking as if he has stepped out of a painting; Courbet's *Studio*, perhaps, or an altarpiece: he is an angel. He is holding an orange and a toy, a dinosaur. The boy follows Kracklite for a few steps as he ascends the second flight of stairs, then stops, and watches him; Kracklite looks back at him. At the top of the stairs (and he first turns left, not right, though his apartment is to his right) he hears, as do we, Louisa's voice, giggly, a man, laughing, and then the sound of a dog barking - actually Caspasian, indulging in horseplay. We see Kracklite facing us, his

back to his apartment door, a door shown framed by open double doors, a common motif in the film, but it is unusual to be denied a view through the frame within the frame; here it is Kracklite who is framed, excluded like our own view. He half turns - we see him from the stairs again, exchanging glances with the child - then goes to the door and listens - we now hear the dog noises - and looks through the keyhole - as we do. We see Caspasian, still barking, on all fours beside and then on top of Louisa, who is lying on a sofa; they are both naked. There is a close-up of Kracklite, in profile, at the door; another keyhole shot of the lovers, who are now standing up, embracing, making duck noises, framed by the open door behind them; a middle shot of Kracklite reaching behind him for the red chair beside the door, clumsily, without looking, for he is still looking through the keyhole; we see the lovers again, further back in the apartment in another room, moving down onto a bed which is framed by the open door they have now passed through; we see Kracklite again, with the child now entering the shot, having climbed the stairs, and turning to look at Kracklite, standing where Kracklite first paused, so we see the child from behind - and then briefly from the front, a corridor behind him - and then Kracklite at the keyhole again, though he is no longer looking through it, but wiping away a tear. He is at the door, his head and one hand against it, as if at a wailing wall. During this shot we hear Louisa making noises. We see the child again; from behind him, down the deep corridor perspective, we see his mother enter; she calls to him in Italian, he replies, he turns to Kracklite and asks him, in English, 'Why are you crying?' We see Kracklite and the child from behind again, in front of the door; Kracklite replies that there is a draught through the keyhole that is hitting his eye; he is watching again; the child turns and repeats this answer to his mother, and we again see the mother and child, with the mother beginning to approach the camera from the end of the corridor, one of many such exits and entrances in the film; she is a dark silhouette framed by a light wall and arch, as if walking out of an altarpiece. Through the keyhole, we see Caspasian strutting around before Louisa with the very phallic model of Boullée's lighthouse between his legs; it covers and brags about his penis. (A much larger model of the same 'building' features in the final sequence.) We see Kracklite at the keyhole, and then, closer to the door than before, we see his chair collapse beneath him; for a second he repeats the pose of Michael Andrews's painting *A Man Who Suddenly Fell Over*. Kracklite puts his finger to his lips to call for silence - a little like a comic drunk - as the child approaches him to help. We see them together, back in the established middle shot, Kracklite picking things up. There is a shot of the interior, for the first time not a keyhole shot; we see Caspasian approaching the camera to put the lighthouse back on its 'plinth', a small table in the room nearest to us; he 'wears' it until the last moment. Kracklite now has his back to the door, and is standing; the child (who has taken one of the scattered photocopies from the wreckage) gives him the orange (it is featured in the next scene). In profile, holding out the fruit, he looks more than ever like a figure in a religious painting. Kracklite reaches into his pocket and gives him, in return, the gyroscope which will be seen in the final shot of the film. The child, delighted, approaches his mother (and the camera) with it; there is a cut to his mother as he finally reaches her and turns back so they both are facing Kracklite, then a close-up of the gyroscope in the boy's hand, against the white towel, a shot of Kracklite leaving the scene, moving away from the door to descend the stairs (an exit which rhymes with the child's entry), and another shot of the mother and child. The child then leaves his mother and approaches the door - from behind which we can still hear the lovers - and the sound of a door closing. He sheds his towel, and wearing only his equally white pants - almost a nappy - he climbs onto the door and, hanging from it, looks through the keyhole. Another keyhole shot - we see only the lighthouse, brilliantly lit in the dark interior; the bedroom doors behind it are closed, the sounds of love-making muffled. We see him get down from the door, retrieve the photocopy he laid down with his towel, and, as Kracklite himself has done, place it over his belly as he approaches the camera, pauses, looks up. (In the postcard scene of *Les Carabiniers*, Michel Ange and Venus hold bra and Y-front advertisements from magazines across themselves in much the same way.)

Kracklite could have interrupted the lovers, made a scene; his passivity contrasts with Caspasian's own confident intervention between Kracklite and Flavia. He has witnessed (perhaps not incidentally) one of the few happy scenes of sexuality in Greenaway's oeuvre, in which sexuality is generally linked to death, often immediately, as in all three of the drownings by numbers. The death involved here is Kracklite's own, premonitions of which were cut into his own happy love-making with Louisa at the start of the film.

Greenaway, who sees his film-making as partly an opening up of debates, has himself offered a commentary on this sequence in *The Stairs Geneva*:

Every film-space itself is a framed peep-hole for us, the voyeurs of the audience, to be witness to other people's privacy, secrets, joys, miseries, embarrassments. It is voyeuristic because, in the very nature of cinema, the players on the screen are deemed to be ignorant of the fact that they are being watched by us. It is a perversely ironic state of affairs of course that this is not the whole truth, for cinema requires actors who know - and indeed it is the most essential part of their contract, to know - that they will be watched. They are paid to assume the innocence that their activities are not being watched. In *The Belly of an Architect* this is exemplified by a deliberate act of voyeurism on behalf of the architect and on behalf of a child, who both watch an act of adultery through a keyhole - that most ubiquitous of voyeuristic frames.

Greenaway is mostly concerned here to explain how *The Belly of an Architect* led to *The Stairs*, to his mega-cinema. He is also using theory closely related to the theatre, an aspect which I shall consider later in the present chapter; and, importantly, this leads to a definition of voyeurism which is not gender-specific. Nor, equally importantly, does the shooting of this scene clearly involve male viewers in a radically different way from female viewers. (There is not, for example, the straight-forward doubling up of voyeurism of the scene in *Basic Instinct* which unapologetically rhymes the male viewer watching the screen with Michael Douglas watching Sharon Stone undress behind a picture window.) Having sketched in a context within the history of painting, I would like now to first consider Greenaway's cinema, and in particular those aspects of it related to the areas loosely describable as voyeuristic in specifically sexual terms, in relation to other films.

There is, beside this paragraph, a still of the child looking through the keyhole, captioned 'Peeping Tom from *The Belly of an Architect*'. This naming of the child inevitably suggests a film of 1959, part of the roll call of cinema history in *The Stairs Munich*, which was as badly received as *The Baby of Mâcon*, for not dissimilar reasons: *Peeping Tom*. The central character is a killer, and his weapon is a movie camera, with a deadly attachment; he films his (female) victims as he kills them - making snuff movies in which the spectacle of death witnessed by the audience is precisely that of the murderer. The narrative (which includes another contrast/link between photography and blindness) creaks, and the central performance is unpersuasive, as is the combination of heavy-handed psychological motivation with a characterisation of psychologists as themselves mad (the father, present only in film within the film, and as an author) or barmy (the police psychologist). But the film has an undeniable emblematic power, mostly condensed into its opening sequence. We see a closed eye, in close-up, suddenly open, startled. We see a street scene, with a prostitute;

a man approaches her. We see, again in close-up, a movie camera, held under a coat. It is working. The narrative camera closes in on it. We see the prostitute, closer now - from where the man was in the second shot. This time we see her through a camera viewfinder, a grid similar to the draughtsman's. The camera, become the narrative camera, the camera as point of view, closes in on her; she is standing in front of a clothes shop window, a premonition of the film set scene of a later crime. We look down her body and up again; she looks up, says it will be two quid. We follow her down an alleyway and, pausing (an empty cardboard film carton is discarded, distracting us from the woman, temporarily breaking our identification with the camera/character), upstairs to her room; a matron is descending the staircase, and glances at us in disgust. In her room, we see her begin to undress, matter-of-factly, bored. The camera moves away (there is the knowledge, immediate or historical, in the audience, of what is showable, what is allowed, in a film made in 1959), we hear a sound, the camera returns to her. This time she is frightened, and there is a circle of reflected light playing on her face. The camera closes in on her. She screams. There is a cut to a projector. Then a man, his back to us, is shown beside the projector, now seen from behind. We see on the screen, in black and white, what we have just seen in colour, beginning with the prostitute at the shop window, though it is edited[9] and extended at the end to include the murder. The credits are rolling. The man rises up and then sinks back into his chair as, with the killing, the screen goes blank. We see once more the projector from the side, as the credits end, with 'Director, Michael Powell'. Fade.

This complex metaphor of photography, vision and narrative (and others like it; in *Rear Window*, James Stewart's camera is described as a 'portable keyhole') is easily relatable to the oculophobic strand of theory, traced in Martin Jay's invaluable *Downcast Eyes: The denigration of vision in twentieth century French thought*,[10] which has increasingly come to influence not just contemporary art history and criticism, but also contemporary art practice. Sight itself - or the heterosexual male gaze, identified with perspective - is categorised as (literally or metaphorically) fascist (it surveys), sexist. The piercing eye, in this reading, is at once disembodied, a symbol of timeless, objective, and of course mythical reason, and a kind of phallus, tirelessly penetrative. Both linear perspective and the trouser snake are one-eyed.

The links which this dominant theory, or metaphor, makes are there, quite clearly, to be made. They should, however, be located in an analysis which argues out of, rather than onto, that history of painting and perspective central to any analysis of Greenaway. This involves prising apart the notions of the voyeur and the member of an audience, while examining two central aspects of artistic spectacle, in Greenaway and dominant cinema alike, in which art allows the eye forbidden pleasures: representation of the naked and the dead. Ralph Rumney has written of the strategy of blatantly showing the voyeur what he fears to be caught observing;[11] Greenaway's equivalent of this strategy is to shed the grammar and structures, often teasing, always complacent, of genre narrative, so that those pleasures can be considered, not merely serviced.

Greenaway's remarks on Witkin might serve as a useful introduction to what is at stake:

I came across Witkin in the late seventies and was disturbed. The images - and they are heavily prefabricated images - not acts or events - were undoubtedly often pornographic however you twist the definition of the word to legitimise de Sade or Bataille or, indeed, Balthus. But these images also mock our outrage and show up our hypocritical disgust, which never stands up to much logic or sense anyway, when we condone so much real obscenity around us without so much as blinking an eye. Extravagant sexual behaviour, gratuitous posing, the exhibition of the freak, but not Diane Arbus exploitation, nor the double-standards of that meretricious movie *Freaks*, or that bourgeois, bogus, tidied-up titillation of *The Elephant Man*, or the contemporary standard interest on English television for the sexually savaged dead female from *Brighteyes* to *Twin Peaks* to *Prime Suspect*.[12]

'Get a life', Sharon Stone says to camera at the end of *Sliver*. She is talking to the voyeur, the creep, the baddie, but also to the audience. The film suggests that we all have voyeuristic impulses - Stone's character is given a telescope, so she spies too, as well as being spied on by surveillance cameras - but it also explicitly addresses the audience's sexual interest in its star. The narrative camera and the villain's camera are identified often enough to make the point clear.

The film is a contract, of a kind. Buy a ticket, and you will see Sharon Stone naked; the film is a version of *La Bain de la Femme du Monde*, but with a star. Stone is always Stone, and the scene where she is shown, where she shows herself, masturbating in the bath (apparently without hands) can only finally be analysed as a career move. She is (unlike the character she plays) no Susannah, but clearly exhibitionist in relation to her audience at this point. And, since Stone is in full control of the image, there is no danger of any illusions being shattered.

Films about voyeurism, which almost invariably make a self-referential link between photography and voyeurism, are common enough. They operate within the culture of cinema as the paintings of Diana and Actaeon or Susannah and the Elders operate within Western painting, between the dual possibilities (often, no doubt, mingled) of endorsement of and challenge to what is elsewhere implicit. One of the most recent, *Exotica*, invites (like many contemporary artworks) an exposition which draws on oculophobic theory, with its two controlling metaphors of surveillance, voyeurism and control: the mirror/window, used both by customs and in the night-club, and the figure of the DJ, whose position overseeing the action, though visible and troubled rather than invisible and impersonal, recalls that of the jailor in Bentham's Panopticon, the model prison which, although unbuilt, has provided unlimited ammunition for identification of sight with power (helped by the French pun: *voir/pouvoir*).

Voyeurism is linked often, too often, with power, as if the voyeur was always a killer, the camera always a murder weapon. *Exotica*, more interestingly, is a narrative of a taboo - the clients can look but had better not touch - so that the client in the club Exotica is, despite the presence of the girl at his table, no better placed than we ourselves, or than Michel Ange in the cinema Le Mexico, to link sight and touch. But sight - as painters have long realised - is also linked to helplessness. One can also be wounded by what one sees.

Kracklite is an accidental voyeur (and the child, despite Greenaway's account, is a failed one; he does not in fact witness the adultery). Indeed, since Kracklite's spying was not premeditated (his position is similar to that in the bathroom scene when he discovers the suitcase full of banknotes), and since he is very far from gaining sexual pleasure from what he sees, and since his wife's body is hardly unfamiliar to him, he hardly qualifies as a voyeur at all. (Nor is he like a member of an audience.) He cries. He is himself watched, absurd in his watching, in his fall as his chair collapses. He is mocked on both sides of the door: by the love-making itself, and Caspasian's clowning with the model (Kracklite is identified with Boullée throughout, and here 'unbuilt' and 'impotent' begin to coincide, coupled with appropriation; Caspasian is taking his place in his bed and in his exhibition); but also by the child's innocent parody of his obsessive comparison of his belly with Augustus.

The scene involves two deep perspectives: one, open, the corridor with its Madonna and child; the other that of the major establishing shot, blocked off by the door, reopened by the keyhole shots, then finally blocked off again by the closing of the bedroom door. The space is very different from Flavia's studio, but the keyhole and the camera are both framing devices for adultery. It is one of the rare uses of the point of view shot in Greenaway (one straightforward way of avoiding the identification between character and audience that Greenaway so distrusts is simply to avoid such shots - as, also, do Bresson, Eisenstein, Buñuel, Godard), but the point of view is doubled: we see what Kracklite sees (rigorously, when he is no longer looking, the view of the interior is no longer shot as if through the keyhole) but we also see him looking from the child and/or the mother's point of view. This, together with the reaction shots and the business with the chair, prevents any easy voyeuristic response to the scene. So does the childishness of the lovers. The scene, in stark contrast to *Sliver* (and like a Degas pastel), offers no concession to fantasies of voyeurism, fantasies in which the viewer is at once unseen, invisible, and *addressed*. (As viewer/voyeurs we are, perhaps, tacitly and ironically acknowledged in the lovers' final closing of the bedroom door, an exclusion relatable to all those slammed doors - dramatised exclusions, sometimes temporary, sometimes decisive - which briefly make us self-aware in so many films of our position as viewers.)

The point of view shots, in the context of the film as a whole, are, like Flavia's journalistic camera, details in a detached, directorial presentation of framing, examples of a conventional kind of composition ('the half-view, the ambiguous viewpoint, the composition that insist[s] on considering two-dimensional interests rather than three- ... the viewpoint that [does] not necessarily offer an attempt at a spatial understanding')[13] which is present rather as content than as form. (In fact, even the point of view shots offer a scrupulous account of the space of the building.) One basic, and crucial, distinction between 'witnessed' perspective and 'narrative' perspective is in the way the frame itself is conceived in relation to what it contains. In witnessed perspective, the frame involves cropping, of necessity; selection from everything else in the world. The edge becomes far more important, and becomes also a flattening device. In narrative perspective, what we see is performed, not selected; the space is self-contained, there is nothing outside it; it is theatrical, but without an off-stage. Centre-stage, rather than the edge, becomes important; the frame is a frame, and not a guillotine. (It is precisely this division which the great Baroque illusions redefine; the architecture in which we stand itself becomes part of the stage.) In the actual making of cinema, there is, however (because photography always involves cropping, and because film sets do not have the rigidly divided spaces of theatres, stage, backstage, auditorium), a mix - clearly, for Greenaway, a heady mix - of artifice and actuality. Introducing *The Belly of an Architect* at the Cambridge Film Festival, Greenaway remarked that his viewing of his films was always, at least initially, inflected by his strong memories of the actual shooting of the film, so that each individual shot also reminded him of everything that was just out of shot. It is now clear that this was to prove a more important point than it then seemed. 'The back or wrong side of a set can be as interesting as the so-called right side.'[14] There are enough films about film-making, and enough back-stage dramas, to suggest that many directors are fascinated by this fluid margin; what is peculiar to Greenaway is his attempt to pursue this element of cinema through other means, through metaphors of cinema rather than through film sets of film sets. *The Baby of Mâcon* also springs from this, of course. (There are early theatrical projects of Eisenstein which are comparable; his sets for *Puss in Boots* and *Heartbreak House* both staged an off-stage area as well as a normal set. *The Wise Man*, and Eisenstein's plans for the premiere of *Battleship Potemkin*, included various *coups de théâtre*, movements from the screen to the stage of the kind developed in *Rosa*.) Again, what is new is the thoroughgoing confusion and instability between what is on and off stage, and also between theatre and film. In terms of Greenaway's account of voyeurism and acting, we have actors (and extras) pretending they are actors in and audience of a play, but denying that in fact they are all in a film.

This account (which surely defines all narrative as voyeuristic, even if we 'witness' as readers only metaphorically) underplays the importance of convention, of our constant knowledge that we are seeing not 'people' but characters. It makes it difficult to distinguish between watching *Kramer vs Kramer* and watching a documentary, in which there are genuine problems to do with voyeurism

- the film-maker's, and the audience's - complicated by the extent to which the taking of the footage is actively affecting what is going on. (Documentary footage of, say, Dylan at a press conference in 1965 is footage of a performance; documentary footage taken with hidden cameras is voyeuristic. Most documentary material is between these two poles.) It also defines the convention that 'players on the screen are deemed to be ignorant of the fact that they are being watched by us' as part of 'the very nature of cinema', which is puzzling, even in terms of dominant cinema, let alone the austerity and richness of the scene itself. Stars are always in front of their parts - that is the difference between film stars and film actors. Comedy has always involved a direct address to the camera/audience, from Oliver Hardy (*passim*) to Woody Allen (*Annie Hall*), although a performance can acknowledge the audience without such a direct address. In my terms, the problem arises from the use of the word 'witness' in relation to an audience.

But let us return to voyeurism as a term used to describe the relation between an eye and a (naked) body, an area in which Greenaway's cinema is unprecedented.

Part of the shock of the razor across the eye in Buñuel and Dali's *Un Chien Andalou*, a still unrivalled example of montage as exploitation of the brain's helpless, uncontrollable capacity to make connections between successive images, is that although on analysis the image is carefully set up - Buñuel sharpening the razor, the cloud across the moon - it is not set up within any narrative context or conventional cinematic grammar. However much like an actual dream it may or may not be, it is not at all like a fiction. It is far too soon - just seconds into the film - and far too explicit.

Similarly, there is a 'grammar' of nudity in cinema, which Greenaway simply ignores.

'Outside of the strip-club, the art studio, and domestic intimacy, all of whose purposes are circumscribed to a different local usage, it is not possible to legitimately stare at the naked human body without censure.' Greenaway is writing here[15] about his exhibition *The Physical Self* in Rotterdam, in which a roster of thirty people, 'male and female, old and young', posed in glass cases, in the attitudes customary in the life class; he is writing about looking at real bodies. We could add to his list, perhaps, contemporary dance, and performance art. And a Greenaway opera.

'Don't concern yourself', he tells the reader of *Rosa* (who is, of course, looking at words on a page, and not the actor playing Rosa, still at this point as fictional as his character), 'it's human nature to look at the genitals of a naked body at the earliest possible opportunity'. (The 'you' in this generalisation is either male or female, as are the genitals in question.)

Greenaway's presentation of the body begins with this truth, acknowledged, in Western culture, generally in the tease. I remember, from an exhibition of Indian art years ago at the Hayward Gallery, a small painting of a reclining nude, clearly influenced by the Western genre; the woman looked towards the viewer, her arm rested on her body, but her hand did not conceal her sex, or operate in the tense, ambiguous repertoire of modesty, promise, self-pleasure, negotiation developed from Titian to Manet. It rested on her belly, the central premise of the Western female nude being too foreign to the Indian artist for assimilation. That premise was finally abandoned by Klimt, Schiele, Picasso. The use of photography in so much contemporary art, however, has led to a new examination of the relations between art and pornography - a split as artificial and (before it was exported) peculiar to the West as that between art and craft.

But the nude in Western painting is not restricted to the prototype pin-up. It is central to the narrative tradition, across pagan and Christian myths and allegories, whether linked to pleasure or shame, Arcadia or the expulsion from paradise, mortality and decay or immortality, the heroic or the mundane.

This is the language which Greenaway reinvents for cinema - but, since he is a modern artist, without the tease (or 'modesty') which survives elsewhere in film, in its grammar, at least, even if what is revealed has increased down the years. It is that grammar which makes the connection between the movie camera and the voyeur so easy to establish, whether we view a narrative set in a strip-club, like *Exotica* (which keeps cutting away from the leading actress's strip routine, a doubled tease), or view domestic nakedness or intimacy.

Here, least of all, can the actors admit they are being watched. (Although, in *Betty Blue*, as the heroine climaxes in the notorious opening scene, the hero speaks to us, directly, through voice-over; a device which apes the narrative voice of the novel but always compromises the present tense of cinema, leaving an unacknowledged rift between what is told and what is shown, between the first person narrator and the narrative camera, which retains the freedom of the omniscient novelist.) And here, most of all, it is a question of performance. Whatever the realism that surrounds it, the nude scene is the ultimate site of artifice. It is one of the places, along with the publicity still, the fashion shot, the magazine feature, the pin-up, where the human body is cosmeticised, restricted, remodelled; where illusions are created, not lost.

In Greenaway, in stark contrast, the naked body - for all its associative possibilities - earths the artifice of the narrative in corporeality. Many of the bodies he shows us are beautiful, many are not - he ignores the aesthetic/commercial ban on bodies insufficiently exceptional to be displayed which holds sway elsewhere - but whether beautiful or not, they are all bodies that belch, fart, eat, drink, vomit, piss - and impregnate, and conceive, and die. Human bodies are animal bodies. Our interest in the nude, he suggests, is more than sexual: it is also to do with our knowledge of our own mortality. Many of the bodies he shows to us are dead, or at least (there is a long passage in the text of *Rosa* about this) *acting* dead.

And nudity ceases to be an interlude in the narrative, an idyll, in brackets, or 'the nude scene' - for which the narrative is a pretext, allowing us to still distinguish, for her sake and our sake, a film star from a porn star, the cinema audience from the 'audience' in a porn cinema. (There is no collective noun for voyeurs, least of all 'audience'.)

Greenaway's emphasis on the naked body begins to restore to the nude the enormous repertoire of actions and poses and meanings, by no means restricted to the sexual or to ideal beauty, which it possessed in the traditions of Western image-making. Simply by offering cinema as a dialect of an apparently exhausted language (the language of Degas as well as Rubens) he exposes - almost incidentally, by wanting to do what he does as much as by not wanting to do what is done elsewhere - the peculiarly twentieth-century sense of shame involved in any nudity not arbitrarily defined as perfect.

Nothing is easier than to admit in words the truth of the universal struggle for life, or more difficult - at least I have found it so - than constantly to bear this conclusion in mind.

CHARLES DARWIN [16]

THE DRAMATURG: I get it. You want to find out about the world. We show what takes place there.

THE PHILOSPHER: You haven't got it entirely, I think. Your remark lacks a certain uneasiness.

BERTHOLD BRECHT [17]

Of course it's not real blood. You would not expect it to be. But it's powerful enough to remind us of slaughter.

Rosa [18]

At the peak of the theatrical deception, the film attempts to convince a cinema audience of two phenomena I have never been able to suspend disbelief about in the cinema - copulation and death; at least not copulation outside the pornography genre, and death outside the documentary... *The Baby of Mâcon* plays with these impossibilities and with an audience's suspension of disbelief about these impossibilities.

The Audience of Mâcon

There is a way in which the Hollywood tradition tends to keep its heart on its sleeve, and ... if you do that often enough the heart stays on the sleeve and not in its rightful place ... films seek to offer us condolence for grief, condolence for loss, and I don't think that's the human condition.

Anatomy of a Filmmaker

Empathy is not the sole source of emotions at art's disposal.

BERTHOLD BRECHT [19]

We have seen the screen in *Rosa*, the sheet which - unlike the pristine cinema screen which can retain no trace of the histories in light that touch it - is also a picture surface, a diary, stained by the fluids of two bodies and two lives. There is another screen in *The Baby of Mâcon*: the curtains around the ubiquitous prop bed which display what they conceal, becoming a screen for a shadow play, the death by rape of the daughter. It is in this scene that the artifice reaches its height, and the doubling of the audience enters the script: at the start of the rape the actors talk, as if to each other, about the audience - the audience of Mâcon - who cannot see them; at its finish, at the moment that the 'body' is rolled from the bed, the soldier/actor mutters 'what a fine actress'.

This may also be the second death in the film which is at once a stage death and a death on stage; the first is that of the bishop's son, the death for which this serial rape is the revenge. In the play, the daughter cannot be hanged for the child's death. 'In this city, in this sanctuary' a virgin cannot be hanged, as the 'saints', the female martyrs, swear by their attributes (which are body parts, or clumsy properties representing body parts). Cosimo offers a solution to the bishop, which since he is not a character in the play, but only in the film, establishes a paradox, a flickering duality, a *trompe l'oeil* play on the real and unreal. The play, for the first time, continues as if his intervention is a necessary part of its action, and not a nuisance, a naive disruption. The bishop accepts the solution - despite Cosimo's second thoughts - announces it (Cosimo had only whispered it into his ear) and sets it into action. The daughter is handed over to the militia, who queue up to receive absolution, and then to rape the daughter.

This scene, which determined the hostile reaction to the film, is the most chilling of Greenaway's counting games: an unlucky number is multiplied as a death sentence. This is quite literally sadistic; Sade invented complex mathematical patterns for his own fictions.

A virgin can only be deflowered once, and one rape would be enough to allow the daughter to be hanged, but she is raped two hundred and eight times. (In the one complex shot, we leave the action for a highly theatrical account, staged around an architectural *sacra conversazione* frame, of the fate of the daughter's family - the child's sisters, in another expulsion echo, are condemned to a life of prostitution, and the mother and father are shown dead in a sculptural tableau, respectively hanged and with a cut throat - and then return for the final rapes.) The figure of two hundred and eight is arrived at through a strange quiz game. The bishop asks, how many times did Caligula's sister serve the Roman senators? How many times did Diocletian abuse the daughters of Maxentius? How many times did the Christian virgins suffer the abuses of the Macabees? He is answered twice, reluctantly, by Cosimo's confessor and finally, like a schoolboy pleased with himself, by Cosimo himself: thirteen times; thirteen plus thirteen times; thirteen times thirteen times.

As the sentence is carried out, each rape is counted twice: by Cosimo putting a piece of paper with a number on it on a metal spike;[20] and by the knocking down of one of the two hundred and eight skittles set up on a giant chess board set into the floor. It is a new version of 'Dead Man's Catch'; a male revenge for it, even. (An unforgiving analysis of misogyny, this is the only feature film fully scripted by Greenaway without a strong - or, more precisely, powerful - woman character. One of its plays between the real and the unreal is centred on virginity, not just, as in this scene, the virginity of the daughter - endlessly physically examined in the play, in one scene, farcically, by Cosimo - and of the actress who plays her, but also the ways in which the male control of mother church is exercised over the real bodies of women through a cult of the Virgin. More universally, the daughter - or rather, at this point, the actress - suffers terribly for what is almost her final line. In an echo of Spica's mockery of his gang's 'shrivelled contributions' in the first scene of *The Cook* (compare also Cissie 1's question in *Drowning by Numbers*, 'Do all fat men have small penises?') she derides the young soldier/actor's penis. (It is implied that he too - unlike the bishop - may be a virgin.)

To the soldiers queuing to perform the rapes, it eventually becomes boring; the banality of evil.

This 'knowingly savage' film, as it is described in Greenaway's introduction to the script, appeared on its release to be related to the reports of systematic rape during the civil war in the former Yugoslavia. Any imaginable re-release would coincide with some horror in the world which it might 'match'. As I wrote my first draft, the Church in Rwanda was being accused of complicity in massacres. As I returned to it I read in my paper: 'In Bosnia, the rape of women became once again routine'. If *The Cook, The Thief, His Wife and Her Lover* analyses the deep grammar of gangsterism, criminal violence, *The Baby of Mâcon* does the same for institutional violence. Theatricality makes this easier: any 'realism' suggests a specific situation, and therefore a demand for, a possibility of, reform - a specific injustice, and yet also a fictional injustice, involving a strange confusion or corruption of both political and aesthetic involvement. Still editing *The Cook*, Greenaway spoke of the Jacobean theatre: 'that great sense of brutality, but also the metaphors - that great moment in *'Tis Pity* when the brother comes on stage and holds up a bloody heart on a dagger - an impossible piece of theatricality, but if you're clever and can make it work - a heart on a dagger - what an extraordinary, universal metaphor that is. If you can make it both real and metaphorical at the same time, you've achieved something.' Spectacle adds to this, achieving something of the diagrammatic universality of a *Massacre of the Innocents*: the rape, like the cooked corpse of Michael in front of Spica, like the heart on a dagger, is narrative condensed into a single image, time that unfolds and stands still. In *The Baby of Mâcon*, repetition heightens this effect; it is like Orwell's image of a jackboot endlessly descending on a face, or a perpetual punishment in Dante's hell.

In *The Baby of Mâcon* there is also a Brechtian alienation effect at work, although as we have seen Greenaway's critique of history owes more to Darwin than to Marx. The analysis we are invited to make as the audience of the action involves an abandoning of illusions rather than the pursuit of the illusion of revolutionary remedies for existing power structures. (The structure of power, Greenaway suggests, is constant.)

Brecht's *Messingkauf Dialogues* challenged theatre practice in the terms which, as we have seen,

Greenaway applies to cinema:

THE DRAMATURG: What about the fourth wall?

THE PHILOSOPHER: What's that?

THE DRAMATURG: Plays are usually acted as if the stage had four walls, not three; the fourth being where the audience is sitting. The impression given and maintained is that what happens on the stage is a genuine incident from real life, which of course doesn't have an audience. Acting with a fourth wall, in other words, means acting as if there wasn't an audience.

THE ACTOR: You get the idea? The audience sees quite intimate episodes without itself being seen. It's just like somebody looking through a keyhole and seeing a scene involving people who've no idea they're not alone. Actually, of course, we arrange it all so that everyone gets a good view. Only we conceal the fact that it's been arranged.

THE PHILOSOPHER: Ah yes, then the audience is tacitly assuming that it's not in a theatre at all, since nobody seems to take any notice of it. It has an illusion of sitting in front of a keyhole. That being so it ought not to applaud until it starts queuing for its hats and coats.

THE ACTOR: But its applause confirms the very fact that the actors have managed to perform as if it weren't there.

THE PHILOSOPHER: Do you think we need this elaborate secret understanding between the actors and yourself?

THE WORKER: I don't need it. But perhaps the actors do.

THE ACTOR: For realistic acting it's considered essential.

THE WORKER: I'm for realistic acting.

THE PHILOSOPHER: But it's also a reality that you are sitting in a theatre, and not with your eyes glued to a keyhole. How can it be realistic to try and gloss that over? We want to demolish the fourth wall: I herewith announce our joint operation. In future please don't be bashful; just show us that you've arranged everything in the way best calculated to help us understand.

As the dialogue itself suggests, there are problems with the use of the word 'illusion'. One would not applaud a 'scene' one had actually viewed through a keyhole. The difference, which can be compared to different kinds of painting, is to do with the viewer's or the audience's relation to what is represented. Either one enters imaginatively into a pictorial space or a dramatic action in a way which - through one's involvement with the fiction - leads one to 'forget' - to pay no attention to - the real space one is occupying, and (in theatre) also the real time of the performance; or one is involved with a representation which links its fiction, or discourse, to the body, space and time which it addresses; so that instead of 'leaving' the living room to 'enter' the 'landscape' 'through' the frame, one engages with the image in the space which it shares with the viewer; or one views a performance which does not seek to leave the material conditions of the theatre behind it - leaving the audience literally in the dark - but begins with them, and includes them in the way it represents, acts out, its content. (Put it in these terms, and there is an immediate and genuine problem for cinema, which, being photographic, is as much to do with absence as presence, and which has no option but to leave its audience in the dark. All the director can do is play with or refuse conventions, making the viewer aware - at a more abstract level - of what viewing cinema involves. Greenaway's dissatisfaction with cinema as a medium makes sense in this context, too.)

But what is important is understanding, and understanding, for Brecht, can only be reached by down-grading empathy and identification, both for the actors and the audience: 'the actor must give up his complete conversion into the stage character. He shows the character, he quotes his lines ... The audience is not entirely "carried away"; it need not conform psychologically, adopt a fatalistic attitude towards fate as portrayed. It can feel anger where the character feels joy, and so on. It is free, and sometimes even encouraged, to imagine a different course of events or to try and find one.'[21]

As the Actor in the *Dialogues* immediately realises, this potentially implies a return both to Shakespearean and pre-Shakespearean conventions (asides, direct addresses to the audience) and to entertainment (the low theatre of comedy and shows 'with the girls showing off their legs to the officers in the boxes'). In *The Baby of Mâcon*, this is precisely the kind of acting produced by the Father, in the scene in which the child's wet-nurse is selected (with the actresses indeed showing off their breasts to the audience), and criticised for its vulgarity by Cosimo's majordomo, who wants to play a part in the play himself. There are also Brechtian placards announcing each act.

Alienation, distantiation, the *Verfremdungseffekt*, might now be described as empowerment: it allows the audience a critical purchase on the action as well as a critical detachment from it. It might also be argued that the narrowing range of contemporary drama and cinema is truly alienating, by demanding that a widely diverse audience empathises with such a pathetically restricted range of (often fantastic) characters, an empathy that denies the variety of the audience's actual experience. So it is not just the action on the stage or screen that needs to be critically examined, but the whole context of its financing. In any case, empathy in the context of contemporary Hollywood product - in which the film is merely part of the entire range of merchandise - is closer to complicity; one buys into the whole entertainment deal as a part of one's lifestyle. One also buys into the spectacle, which is also a spectacle of violence, as if it were a roller-coaster ride. *Natural Born Killers* was a fascinating film, because there were clearly two views of violence involved in its making which were fundamentally irreconcilable: Tarantino's, which produces images of violence out of other images of violence, and Stone's, which relates images of violence to actual violence - ultimately, to Vietnam. But it made it clear that the visual culture it distorted, parodied, took to new lengths could not be criticised within its own language of MTV editing and channel surfing, only endorsed.

Empathy is linked to identification in cinema in particular, where we are not equidistant from the characters. In thrillers and horror films in particular, the camera drags us from one point of view to another: we are now the victim, now the killer, the rapist. So long as the film as a whole makes clear who is good and who is evil, it can offer us complicity in the crime, a momentary participation. Perhaps, for the male viewer, sympathy for the female victim, but empathy with the male who attacks her. Certainly, the culture links rape to 'normal' sexual desire rather than to power; the judges seem to, and when the tabloids print photographs of a rape victim it is, surely, to allow the male reader to decide whether she was pretty, whether *she was worth it*. This is why the not uncommon rapes of old women, or of men by heterosexual men, are so inexplicable in the culture; why women are questioned so closely in court about their dress, their behaviour, their sexual history.

The way in which the rape is filmed hinders an easy sympathy for the victim; there are no shots from her point of view. Yet this heightens, restores the horror of the act, since it escapes genre conventions; it makes us consider rather than ride the action. It separates (at one level) motive from action; the soldiers are obeying orders. On another level, the rape is a conspiracy of actors, a settling of scores. Either way, it both prevents the unacknowledgable identification of male viewer with rapist which dominant cinema allows (along with voyeurism), and denies that rapists are loners, madmen, not like other men. Rape here is shown as it is in war and in prisons, a display of power.

This makes it hard to take, as the representation of violence should be, and so rarely is. Pasolini's *Salo, or The 120 Days of Sodom*, which linked Sade's novel to Mussolini's Fascist Republic of 1944, had something of the same detachment in presentation. Godard, creating his own kind of Brechtian cinema, suggested in the firing squad scene of *Les Carabiniers* how the true nature of violence can only begin to be represented by a language which widens rather than closes the gap between art and life.

The rape scene ends with the Prince (played by Jonathan Lacey) being comforted by the women in his retinue. There are two babies in the film, and the Prince is the second of them: 'he often behaves curiously like a child - oblivious to bodily proprieties - he doesn't mind being literally spoon-fed in public, or using his close-stool in public. He stares at people a great deal, and, like a child, he is insatiably curious.'[22] He pulls together all the ambiguous threads of reality and unreality; he is credulous both in his piety - he is an eager bidder for the fluids of the miraculous child - and in his response to the action of the play. (He resembles, perhaps, the seven-year-old emblem of empathy described by Eisenstein in 'How I Became a Film Director' whose total involvement with the action on the stage of the Moscow Art Theatre was reflected in his facial expressions, which mimicked every feature of the action. The child's expressions acted as a 'Newton's apple' to the young Eisenstein, who determined to 'Kill this nightmare! Destroy theatre!' since it replaced reality with fiction.) The figure who cannot tell dramatic action from reality is a familiar one in the history of criticism, along with the dog who barks at a painting and the bird who flies down to peck at painted cherries; Reynolds is harsh on such anecdotes in the Thirteenth Discourse. 'Raffaelle is praised for naturalness and deception, which he certainly has not accomplished, and as certainly never intended; and our late great actor, Garrick, has been as ignorantly praised by his friend Fielding; who doubtless imagined he had hit upon an ingenious device, by introducing in one of his novels ... an ignorant man, mistaking Garrick's representation of a scene in *Hamlet*, for reality. A very little reflection will convince us, that there is not one circumstance in the whole scene that is of the nature of deception ... what adds to the falsity of this intended compliment, is that the best stage-representation appears even more unnatural to such a character, who is supposed never to have seen a play before, than it does to those who have had a habit of allowing for those necessary deviations from nature which the Art requires. In theatrick representation, great allowances must always be made for the place in which the exhibition is represented; for the surrounding company, the lighted candles, the scenes visibly shifted in your sight, and the language of blank verse, so different from common English; which merely as English must appear surprising in the mouths of Hamlet, and all the court and natives of Denmark. These allowances are made; but their being made puts an end to all manner of deception: and further, we know that the more low, illiterate, and vulgar any person is, the less he will be disposed to make these allowances, and of course to be deceived by any imitation.' It was not a happy idea to recreate this figure as a Maori in *The Piano*, but in the context of *The Baby of Mâcon*, in which all boundaries are blurred, it is revitalised. And it leads to a reworking of the old Shakespearean conceit, in a moment - after the death of the child - which suggests the emotion at the core of the film, and maybe Greenaway's whole oeuvre:

COSIMO: So small a life cut dead, so lately started, so soon departed, was God impatient? He was only a child.

The nuns - formerly so irreligious - now contribute true pathos.

NUN 1: Sir, it is only a play ... with music. (The orchestra play with irony.) Do not distress yourself.

COSIMO: It is only a play ... with music? Does God say the same at every death? It is only a play ... with music? When I die, will somebody say the same? He was only a prince. He died. It was only a play ... with music.

NUN 2: (very quietly) Sir, be grateful for the music. Most of us die in silence.

Religious ritual is also performance. Royalty is also performance. The prince is unselfconscious in a role in which selfconsciousness is a minimum requirement and this makes him riveting, embarrassing - at times he grabs attention like a child pleased with himself, although attention is already his right and duty. He is a spectacular vacuum, a series of rich costumes around a pale, effeminate face which cannot 'act', but only signal (mostly shallow) emotions, hesitancies, uncertainties.

His power is real, but he does not control it: the bishop tells him that his suggestion was in fact an order, but he still has no sense that he can revoke it; and so the moving of the daughter out of church jurisdiction to the militia in fact confirms church power. His piety amounts to abdication.

He is worried at the daughter's death, but - as with the child's death - really on his own account; he is worried at his part in it, but all around him seek to reassure him. He is forgiven.

HORSE SENSE

The Duke Prospero was blindfolded and sat upon a horse.
Ex Libris Prospero

LULLY: The newspapers said:
'There is a suggestion of unnatural practices.'

ALCAN: Let us perform some unnatural practices.

Lully and Alcan fuck Esmerelda inside the horse.
Rosa [23]

On stage (I am judging from two videos of record, production notes rather than cinematic re-creations of the performance) it was less horrific: choreographed, stylised, stagy as well as staged. The rape is, after all, a reconstruction, part of the investigation of the death of the composer. But reconstruction involves the possibility of a horror repeated, expanded. And, on the page, it is a tough image: the verb, like real bodies on the stage or before the lens, has a force that beats against the games-playing.

What has happened before this, in the text, is this: repeating a tabloid version of the action which we have already seen, Lully and Alcan have covered Esmerelda (Rosa's 'widow', in the press version, though they were not married) with ink, 'printer's ink'. They have bound her and gagged her 'with the same blindfolds that were the property of [Rosa's] horse when it walked the tread-mill'. They have made her walk the treadmill. Meanwhile, the horse itself has been gutted and stuffed on stage. Lully and Alcan have forced the taxidermist to stuff and sew Esmerelda inside the horse. 'Like Pasiphaë in the story of the wooden cow, the reproductive parts of animal and woman must align.' The dollars Rosa earned for writing theme music for Westerns have also been stuffed inside the horse.

After they have fucked Esmerelda inside the horse, Lully and Alcan set up Rosa's corpse on the back of the horse. He is now riding both his horse and his woman.

Rosa is 'crucified on a horse. He is a Christ for centaurs.' The horse is a kind of Trojan horse. These are not obscure references. Perhaps, when the dollars rained down, the dollars that are now stuffed inside the horse with Esmerelda, members of the audience familiar with Titian or Klimt -

if not with Greek mythology - will have thought of Danaë: 'At the centre of the stage, a fall of golden coins and green dollars starts to shower from on high into the naked lap of Esmerelda. She lies on the sofa like Danaë with Jupiter's hoard falling into the space between her open legs.'[24] It is another impregnation myth, in the original; the shower of gold leads to the birth of Perseus, who, as an adult, has to slay the Gorgon Medusa because he does not have a horse to offer Polydectes. Here it is ironised, as always, linked (in the text) to prostitution. But the story of Pasiphaë is more obscure. Are there any paintings that show it?

> Minos claimed the Cretan throne and, in proof of his right to reign, boasted that the gods would answer whatever prayer he offered. First dedicating an altar to Poseidon, and making all preparations for a sacrifice, he then prayed that a bull might emerge from the sea. At once, a dazzlingly white bull swam ashore, but Minos was so struck by its beauty that he sent it to join his own herds, and slaughtered another one instead.

> Minos married Pasiphaë, a daughter of Helius and the nymph Crete, but Poseidon, to avenge the affront offered him by Minos, made Pasiphaë fall in love with the white bull which had been withheld from sacrifice. She confided her unnatural passion to Daedalus, the famous Athenian craftsman, who now lived in exile at Cnossos. Daedalus promised to help her, and built a hollow wooden cow, which he set on wheels concealed in its hooves, and pushed into the meadow near Gortys, where Poseidon's bull was grazing. Then, having shown Pasiphaë how to open the folding doors in the cow's back, and slip inside with her legs thrust down into its hindquarters, he discreetly retired. Soon the white bull ambled up and mounted the cow so that Pasiphaë had all her desire, and later gave birth to the Minotaur, a monster with a bull's head and a human body.[25]

(Pasiphaë's brother, Phaeton, tried, and failed, to drive the sun chariot across the sky; there are three images of his crash landing in *Flying Out of This World*. Pasiphaë and the Minotaur had the Labyrinth built for them, to avoid scandal; Daedalus and his son Icarus joined them once Minos discovered Daedalus's part in the affair. Their flight, which, as Mellorder Fallabur and Armeror Fallstag were at pains to point out, was a triumph for the father at least - Daedalus managed to fly even while carrying the drowned body of his son - was an attempt to escape from Crete. *The Autobiographies of Semiramis and Pasiph*aë constitute the thirtieth of Prospero's Books listed in 'Ex Libris Prospero'; the nineteenth book is *The Ninety-Two Conceits of the Minotaur*.)

Rosa is subtitled 'a horse drama', not a bull or cow drama, but it is set in an abattoir. The progression from dead animal to beef has been unflinchingly chronicled on stage, with the blood from the carcasses captured in bowls, an echo of the angels who hover beneath Christ's wounds in so many crucifixion paintings. (The comparison between carcass and crucifixion is well established in the history of painting - Rembrandt, Goya, Bacon.)

The myth is reworked considerably. A real horse instead of a wooden cow, although it is finally given wheels; and a man's unnatural desires instead of a woman's. There is an echo of Milo in *A Zed and Two Noughts*, last seen heading for a zebra, but, as in that film, we think more readily perhaps of bestiality and hardcore pornography than of Greek myths. And also, perhaps, of blues songs, and the metaphors embedded in everyday language - sexual metaphors of mounting and riding and breaking in. The banal phrase 'you love [your horse, in this case] more than you love me' is taken literally, taken to absurd lengths, in *Rosa*. So are the horse/woman lyrics reaching through decades of blues songs to the Byrds' 'Chestnut Mare' (a riding/taming/flying song) or Dylan's 'New Pony'.

Such analysis, such a distancing piling-up of allusion, detracts from the savagery of the image - but only on the page, this page. On the stage, on film, these and similar images in Greenaway reactivate the physicality of ancient and Christian myths, a physicality simultaneous with allusion, meaning, association and knowledge - not least our knowledge both that this is not real and that in the all-too-human history and psyche such things, and worse, are commonplace. Empathy, too great an imaginative involvement with a realist narrative (the young Eisenstein thought), ultimately prevents us from dealing with, facing up to, what is really real. Self-reference, in this tradition, does not deny the world; it tries to establish, as best it can, what art's proper relationship with it might be.

The answer, for Greenaway, begins with the way that art already is in the real world: there is a real actor/singer on a fake horse, which has now replaced the real horse, on the real stage of a real opera house in a real city. Or there are real words on a real page which make us imagine these things. The actor is naked, which tests the limits of acting. How much of the body can act? Can private parts play the part of private parts, the way an actor's hands can play a sculptor's hands, or a pianist's, or a composer's? (The role has involved acting out sex, after all.) He is acting dead. The actress/singer is also naked, but she is not pretending to be alive, as the actor/singer is pretending to be dead. (Nor do actors pretend to speak. The words themselves are spoken.) There is real straw, and fake but not counterfeit money.

The answer begins in such details, but it does not end there. The image is an emblem of the whole opera, a final spatialisation of the 'story'; a composer, who writes film music for horses and riders and loves his horse more than he loves his woman, who tries to become more like a horse for him, is murdered. It is also two myths, one pagan, one Christian, collapsed into a single image, which itself merges two very different icons: the equestrian statue, already familiar in Greenaway from *The Draughtsman's Contract*, and the cowboy (perhaps, since he is dead, the cowboy hanged from his horse) - although Rosa was not a cowboy, but a composer who rode his horse unnaturally, and constricted it in a treadmill, so that it was moving yet static, like the film loop of landscape, and like a certain sort of music. The image is an astonishingly efficient - because visual (or, in the text, visualised) - compression and parsing of flesh and myth.

⚜

This is the second display of Rosa's body. Before this, it has sprawled as the murder victim, the corpse from a different genre entirely to the Western, a genre already considered in *The Draughtsman's Contract*: the whodunit. He has been, as it were, *the body in the library*.

Not, here, literally in a library, although Alcan takes his name from the composer who did die in a library: 'reaching up for the Talmud on a high shelf, he pulled the bookcase down on top of himself, and he suffocated. Cause of death - books.' And Michael was a body in a book depository.

There is, in classic detective fiction, an absolute opposition between matter and language: which is why the library is the most appropriate - because the most inappropriate, most disturbing - location for the body to be found. The body is flesh become mute, and yet, like the still life as clue, with a story to tell. The corpse and the clue must both be remade as text by the detective. (This is most beautifully illustrated in the P. D. James novel in which the description of the handless body floating in a boat, the visual, physical image with which the book begins, turns out to be word for word a passage from a book written by the murder victim himself. Which also reminds us of another way in which text dominates the body in detective fiction, Christie's in particular. Nursery rhymes or other word games structure the killings - even the alphabet will do, as in *The ABC Murders* - so that the bodies become illustrations of the murderer's text.) What makes every ending of a detective story disappointing is the way that the mystery of the physical has been finally erased: the visual has rendered up its meaning, and lost all its interest. We must begin again, with the finding of a new body, a new set of clues.

The detective story (and film) allows us also to participate in a voyeurism of death. It seems we want to look at the naked and the dead alike. Ideally, perhaps, both at once. Religious imagery - Sebastian, Christ on the cross - acknowledges our desire, removes from it all (surface) trace of voycurism, turns it into spectacle, demands that we look - and absolves us from all guilt. While murder involves (Lady Macbeth) blood that will not wash away, Christ's blood washes us.

Before the body in the library can become a text, it must move from three to two dimensions, from itself to a trace, a souvenir of itself: an outline.

Lully and Alcan draw a chalk mark on the blood-stained floor boards around Rosa's outspread body ... then, with a trick, they take up the chalk outline ... Alcan experimentally puts the line drawing in different positions in the room. Even on the sofa. Even on Esmerelda. Esmerelda tries to grab the silhouette. For a moment on the sofa she grabs it on top of her as though in a grim sexual embrace. [26]

Painting and sculpture began, according to Pliny, with a woman outlining the shadow of her man before he went away. Joseph Wright of Derby painted this scene; his picture is reproduced in *The Stairs Munich.* [27]

Irony And Tragedy

SIX NECESSARY ELEMENTS

Irony can be tragic; but can tragedy be ironic?

One way of considering Greenaway's cinema, and his feature films in particular, would be to call it tragedy ironised. Ironised, by Darwinism, crucially, by the absolute, rather than melancholic or rhetorical, unimportance of any 'hero'. And also visualised, spatialised, so that it is located in the body rather than in character, and in the image rather than the story, or what remains of the story.

Irony is central to a whole number of modernist strategies. For Manet and Degas (and Joyce, but irony in modernist literature is too big a subject to do more than mention here), it allowed a dialogue between the great art of the past and the unaesthetic surfaces and spectacles of modern life. It is (in ways not often noted) often central to 'documentary' as well as more recent 'fine art' photography: language, for example, when photographed, is almost invariably ironised by the frame which holds it. Above all, there is the Dadaist strand of modernism, and above all within that strand, Duchamp. One could tease out a thousand connections - with a playfulness appropriate to both artists - between Greenaway's cinema and the *Large Glass* in particular. Certainly secure parallels could be drawn between both artists' parodic love of systems, documentation and simulacra (Duchamp's notes for the *Large Glass* were meticulously, and completely unhelpfully, issued in facsimile); their incorporation of scientific ideas within art works; their interest in perspective (the ocular witnesses in the *Large Glass*, and also Duchamp's last great work, posthumously assembled, which can only be viewed by one person at a time); in sex and death and voyeurism; and in the relations of text and image. Despite Greenaway's commitment to the 'retinal' which Duchamp derided, both artists suggest the primacy of ideas; and both reduce to absurdity 'character', or the figure. *A Zed and Two Noughts* may be constructed like a Kitaj painting, in some ways, but it is also the closest Greenaway, or anything in cinema, has got to a great ironic machine like the *Large Glass*.

Catharsis means primarily evacuation of the bowels, and to this extent at least is close to Greenaway's heart, but in its metaphorical, Aristotelian sense of purging the emotions it is rigorously excluded from his films. If I take Aristotle's six necessary elements of tragedy as a starting point, an organising principle, for a final chapter which attempts an overview of Greenaway, it is not in an attempt to impose an Aristotelian reading onto his work.

The six necessary elements are: plot, character, diction, thought, spectacle and music.

PLOT

Cinema is far too rich and capable a medium to be merely left to the storytellers.
A Zed and Two Noughts [1]

Plot, for Aristotle, is the defining element of tragedy: the other five elements are what happens to plot. I have discussed the spatialisation of plot in Greenaway: *The Belly of an Architect*, with its simple, diagrammatic, narrative curves, and single dominant character; *Drowning by Numbers*, with its telling of the same simple story three times. The use of systems can be seen perhaps, in this context, as an ironised Fate.

But what the films wholly scripted by Greenaway all have in common is what allows a broad comparison with tragedy: violent death. There are many suicides, mostly of men (often fathers) without women: the twins in *A Zed and Two Noughts*, rejected by Alba; Madgett and Smut in *Drowning by Numbers*, rejected by all of the Cissies and by the Skipping Girl respectively; and Kracklite, cuckolded in *The Belly of an Architect*. In *The Pillow Book*, 'Jerome, in a bid to dramatise his love for Nagiko, stupidly fakes his own death by taking sleeping-pills. He overdoses, or is tricked by the jealous Hoki into taking the wrong pills. He succeeds in faking his own death only too well - and Nagiko finds him dead on her bed in her apartment.' [2] Other deaths are mostly murders: the draughtsman and Mr Herbert in *The Draughtsman's Contract*; the three husbands in *Drowning by Numbers*; Michael and Spica in *The Cook, The Thief, His Wife and Her Lover*; Rosa in *Rosa*; and the execution/murder of the daughter in *The Baby of Mâcon*. There are also acts of God - or the *deus ex machina*: the swan crash in *A Zed and Two Noughts*, and the death of the bishop's son, through the miraculous intervention of the Baby.

What prevents these deaths from being tragic is - within the overriding Darwinian framework, the refusal to posit a moral universe, or a notion of a final and universal justice as a frame for the action - what has already happened to character.

More precisely, theatrical forms underlie three of Greenaway's features. (Perhaps four, in so far as the quotation from *Romeo and Juliet* in *The Pillow Book* is clear. There is also a reworking of the story of Isabella and the Pot of Basil, familiar from Boccaccio, Keats, and, in the visual arts, the Pre-Raphaelites.) *The Cook, The Thief, His Wife and Her Lover* has the structure of a revenge tragedy, and theatrical structure is again used, but flooded, in *Prospero's Books* and *The Baby of Mâcon*. Flooded, in the former, by the fluid imagery and technology, and by the insertion of the material relating to the books; and flooded, in the latter, by a thoroughgoing confusion of theatre,

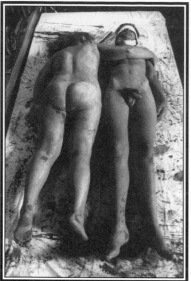

life and cinema which makes any simple account of what is happening at any point impossible.

Genre itself, of course, is generally a narrative system, and the avant-garde often flirts with genre conventions by disrupting the audience's expectations. *Blow Up*, for example, takes the device of the 'blind photographer' so often used in detective fiction and cinema as well as in actual police practice - the fact that a tourist snapshot of the Pope might unintentionally include an image of his would-be assassin - and uses it to make a film about photography rather than a murder mystery. *The Draughtsman's Contract* is in some respects a version of *Blow Up*; a detective story without a detective, in which the central character indeed is concerned, determined, to move away from the textual towards an impossibly pure notion of the visual; he draws clues as if they were simply a matter of light and shade and form.

Plot is disrupted in two contradictory ways: by the reduction of narrative to a system - the alphabet, or a countdown - still a narrative, but no longer a plot; and, perhaps at the same time, by a picaresque overflowing of stories within stories, often highly unlikely, of diversions growing like ivy over ruins. *Tristram Shandy* is a favourite book of Greenaway's.

CHARACTER

Visual works of art are not representations of character.
ARISTOTLE [3]

Is the most consistent character in Greenaway the character who is standing in for Greenaway himself, an authorial or directorial presence? Prospero, seen as an author, with his quill and his watery ink, putting words into people's mouths; Kracklite, the architect/director/maker of exhibitions; the draughtsman - these last two both developed from personal experiences, of drawing a house, of having stomach pains in Rome. Van Meegeren, perhaps, is a fellow forger of Vermeer. Even Smut, the great cataloguer of deaths, Greenaway suggests, is a possible author of the film he is in. It is commonly suggested by authors - most famously by John Fowles in *The French Lieutenant's Woman* - that 'the character takes over', but one cannot imagine a painter saying such a thing of a figure in a picture - 'the painting demanded', yes. Nor can we imagine a character taking over Greenaway as a writer/director.

The actors, in the most literal sense, do have to take the characters over, embody them. (There are, of course, plenty of non-realist theatrical traditions, often comic, unconcerned with the inner life of the 'characters' - or 'humours'; traditions in which character is displayed, not revealed, is a matter of surface.) Greenaway, although notoriously not an actor's director (any more than Hitchcock or Eisenstein), has managed to use the great resources of (mostly) British acting talent without ever producing - despite his interest in theatricality and music theatre - the kind of literary/actor's cinema-as-dramatisation so common in British film-making; though as a debut feature, with the director's reference points still unfamiliar to most critics and viewers, both the precise performances in and the setting of *The Draughtsman's Contract* may have attracted an audience accustomed to such heritage industrial drama. There have been at least two bravura performances in his films - Dennehy's and Gambon's - and he has spoken with enthusiasm and gratitude of both. But such performances sit alongside a figure such as Jonathan Lacey's Prince Cosimo, Michael Clark's Caliban, Sir John Gielgud's recital of *The Tempest*, and the fine ensemble playing in *Drowning by Numbers* which is pitched perfectly between children's and adults' games and narratives. Only in the minor characters, where well-known performers can and almost must be used as a shorthand, are there uncertainties. A familiar face from *Only Fools and Horses* at Spica's table threatens to render at least one character lovable on sight; Ian Dury (a contemporary of Greenaway's at Walthamstow art school) inescapably remains Ian Dury in the same film; and Jim Davidson takes

Left: Greenaway on set of Prospero's Books
Right: The Draughtsman's Contract

some getting used to in *A Zed and Two Noughts*.

One way of considering character in Greenaway is to use a different word: to talk of his *figures*, as one would talk of Mantegna's figures - of Christ, or of Virtue, some historical, some mythical, some allegorical, some painted as if they were flesh and blood, others as if they were statues. Painted figures have attributes to identify them; and serious critical discussion from writers such as Shaftesbury considered the limits of what figures in painting could be shown doing and still remain themselves. (Could a goddess of pleasure be shown displeased, for example, and still be legible?) Greenaway's commentaries on acting in *The Stairs Geneva* [4] and on Mantegna in his Sotheby's lecture concentrate on the question of whether such a 'strong visual identity' for characters is still a 'responsibility valid today in cinema'. If it is not, 'because of the knowledge that words will supply the meanings' (and Greenaway is insistent in the first interview on how important the soundtrack is to comprehension of television and cinema), the possibility remains of exploring such issues, in cinema itself, and in exhibitions.

There are clear parallels between such a discussion of character and Greenaway's discussion of still life and properties, and this is made clear in the proposed exhibition on acting, which would demonstrate '100 of the most celebrated, most utilised, most essential dramatic archetypes' in cinema, literature, theatre and painting. In the most recent relevant passage, '100 Archetypes' in *The Stairs Munich*, [5] crowds, heroes and archetypes have all become one. In Greenaway's own use, or conception, of archetypes, it is clear that individual figures, rather than simply repeating a particular stereotypical character, can pass through a whole series of archetypes in the course of a film, through their situation (the cuckold, say), or through visual quotation, most obviously and often of images of

Adam or Eve. This is thematised in *Rosa*, where the singers can switch from one character or stereotype to another. A passage from the scene discussed in the previous chapter describes how the rape of Esmerelda is met by

> A wild unfocused protest from the assembled Western band of characters. No Western they had ever played in had ever envisaged such an atrocity. Westerns are for servicing common morality and delivering good from evil. Crimes have to be committed but not as heinous as this. Poor Westerns! Poor Westerns that pretended morality was easily defined, easily encouraged, and easily put right by public indignation and courage alone.
>
> With a sudden savagery, Lully and Alcan usher all the protesting Western archetypes onto the cinema screens where they belong, and where they will be powerless to object to the grim reconstruction of events. They file back onto the Western film stock. Pushing and jostling, anxious about precedence, they harangue the calumny from the desert scrub of mesa and prickly cactus, boulders, rocks and small stones under the empty sky. The Texas Whore kills them all off by stopping the film-projector. The beam dies. The big screen is closed down, the show is finished, all the characters have gone home.[6]

One archetype is the nude, before it is related to any other archetype of Eve or Venus. We have considered the ways in which character is disrupted by the nakedness of the actor or actress. One

of the boundaries crossed, along with the move from the character to the actor, is that from cinema to the history of painting: Georgina/Mirren/Eve; Kracklite/Dennehy/Andrea Doria/Neptune. Often costume is used to extreme or absurd effect to establish a strong visual identity, moving away from dramatic character to art historical reference (Alba's Vermeer dress, the Skipping Girl; more loosely, the costumes in *The Cook*), creating extravagant, exuberant, effects (almost everything worn in *Prospero*), or suggesting the social impact or importance of how the character is seen (Cosimo, or the whole cast of *The Draughtsman's Contract*).

This frequent use of artifice in costume is part of the reason why, despite the Englishness of a film like *Drowning by Numbers*, Greenaway is able to suggest narratives of power relations (whether social or sexual) not narrowly related to the British class system - as they are in almost all British cinema, whether treated classic novels or the realist tradition from the sixties to the contemporary work of Leigh and Loach. (English actors tend to play roles within particular class stereotypes, another reason why the casting of minor roles can be disruptive of a non-realist cinema.) Perhaps the closest Greenaway came to dealing with these issues was in his assault on the heavily class-inflected documentary tone of voice in the films up to and including *The Falls*. Since then - and perhaps the strong European (particularly Dutch) and Japanese component not only in many of the subjects and locations but also in the financial deals behind the making of the films has been as important as Greenaway's European sources in both painting and cinema and his French cameraman - the work has been genuinely international (rather than provincial or mid-Atlantic) in its thought and ambition, and this is truly rare in that 'contradiction in terms', British cinema.

DICTION

Diction may be defined, in this context, as the question of the relations between word and image: dialogue; the voice-over; text on screen.

Dialogue comes late to Greenaway's cinema, because actors came late to it, not least for financial reasons, although it had also to do with an interest in land art, coupled with Godard's disjunctions between soundtrack and image in cinema and Greenaway's interest - still evident in *Fear of Drowning* and *The Audience of Mâcon* texts - in involved and absurd narratives with an intricate wordplay that no dialogue could present. *The Falls* has actors, but very little dialogue - and that is filtered through documentary devices; it relies on the documentary and narrative voice-overs familiar from *Water Wrackets, Windows, Dear Phone, A Walk Through H*. The documentary voice returns again, without irony, in the commentaries of the experts in *A TV Dante* (the experts include David Attenborough, whose voice is heard in *A Zed and Two Noughts*); and, more characteristically, in *Darwin* and the video version of *The Stairs*. Voice-over is used in *Prospero's Books*, already a kind of voice-over from start to finish, for the descriptions of the books themselves. Both Smut and Kracklite have voice-overs, for the rules of the games and the postcards to Boullée. In *The Draughtsman's Contract*, a voice-over gives the precise terms of the contracts for individual drawings. Storytelling remains a motif within the feature films; there are many stories or anecdotes in *The Draughtsman's Contract*, such as the tale of the trees named after children; and Milo is a storyteller.

Dialogue in Greenaway does many things. It always belongs to the film as much as it does to the characters, given the part that character plays in the artifice of the whole. It spells out the element of Greenaway's practice which is actually thematised in the particular film, sometimes laboriously, over-schematically (as in the discussion of symmetry in *A Zed and Two Noughts*, or some of the lines in *The Baby of Mâcon*) but often sharply (*The Draughtsman's Contract*), elegantly, humorously, even touchingly (*The Belly of an Architect, Drowning by Numbers*, the Prince on mortality in *The Baby*). The most challenging task it was given, in comparatively conventional cinematic terms, was in *The Cook*. The brutality of *The Draughtsman's Contract* was surely lessened, for the audience, by the distancing effect of the dialogue, cynical, witty, a commentary on the action which subtly framed and reduced the impact of its most physical moments - the enforced sex, the murder. In *The Cook*, Greenaway attempted to draw a portrait of evil - to use a pre-Darwinian term - without making it in any way attractive to the viewer, and Spica's dialogue was an important element of this. It is dialogue, for the most part, which makes gangsters attractive on screen; Greenaway wrote a script of immense crudity which ran parallel to the violence without anaesthetising it, making it

comic, or sweeping it up within the rhythms of verbal violence, as happens in any Mafia or ghetto or gangland film. In this respect, the play on literalism and metaphor is a rejection on the surface of the script of the kinds of slang euphemism for violent acts and violent death which are an essential part of the culture of the thriller.

Language, in painting, is fixed with an ambiguous life: it is word as image, with a meaning modified by its visual intonation - is it scrawled, or collaged, or in Letraset? - and by its relation to the image as a whole, a new meaning that does not proceed, but expands with viewing. Text on screen - most prominent so far in *Prospero's Books, M is for Man, Music, and Mozart,* and the staging of *Rosa* - has its own complexities, highlighting, delaying both the dialogue and the viewer's 'reading' of the image; a kind of subtitle, as *The Pillow Book* makes plain in its experimentation with actual subtitles. (Its use of Japanese calligraphy is a thematisation of the calligraphy that has long featured in Greenaway's cinema, and a welcome expansion of the familiar neo-Elizabethan hands.)

Language, in music, as libretto, is taken up by music, repeated, distorted; still voiced, but voiced as notes, as musical sound, with its own rhythms overruled. Greenaway is fond of using opera as a metaphor for what he is trying to do with cinema. One way of expanding this metaphor would be to say that his dialogue is a libretto for images.

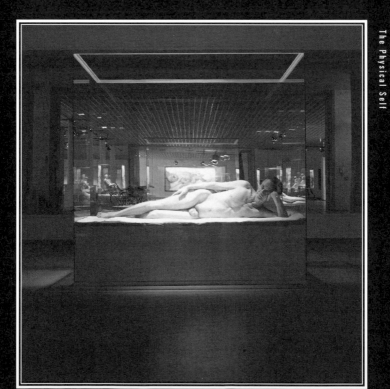

THOUGHT

The thought that is characteristically present in Greenaway's cinema is his own. Interviews with him generally include some echo or elaboration of a passage of dialogue from his films; the second interview in the present volume begins, for example, with my returning to a scrap of conversation, recorded after the first interview had finished, about intelligent painters making bad painters, a remark which had already been refined into a speech in *The Draughtsman's Contract*. He puts his thought into his films the way other directors - Truffaut, perhaps, or Fellini - put their lives into theirs. As the interview goes on to make clear, Greenaway also sees his cinema - his cinema of ideas, not plots - and, indeed, the rest of his work, as a way of starting debate.

Thought is generally thought of as verbal. At times, it is even thought of as unthinkable without language, is 'seen as' a particular use of language. The buried metaphors that constantly link thought to sight and space suggest otherwise, however, and counter-examples are easy to find: musicians think, artists think, chess players and sportsmen think, and although they often could put into words some sense of what they were thinking, they were not thinking verbally as they acted, or considered how to act. So in considering Greenaway, his visual thought should be considered first. In cinema, perhaps only Tarkovsky, another director fascinated by water, has developed so persistent a visual language or landscape across his films. Perhaps no other director has displayed so completely a painterly sensibility. Except in the increasingly frequent, and increasingly complex, tracking shots - more 'purely' cinematic, perhaps - it is almost impossible to freeze-frame Greenaway without discovering a perfectly composed, beautiful image. (In the first interview, he speaks of cinema as a way of making thousands and thousands of images.) I have so far, in considering Greenaway's vocabulary at length, refused any distinction between form and content, visual and verbal thought; and indeed, they are inextricably linked in any single shot. But if I were to separate them, the visual thought would include:

The nude: As archetype, within religion and myth; in its sexual context; as a *memento mori*, a corpse, discovered, laid out, or dissected; as a symbol of the pleasures and frailties of the flesh, of corporeality; as an accompanying figure in an allegorical/historical scene - as nymph, or cupid.

Symmetry: As a consistent principle of composition, often also involving doublings and contrasts.

Calligraphy, a constant fascination now being fully explored in relation to oriental languages,

and discussed at length in the second interview.

Costume: Exaggerated, capricious, theatrical, extravagant; often in black and white, often in rich reds, although Prospero also wears a particularly striking blue.

Tableaux, borrowings, quotations, structurings from painting.

Water, and light as water.

Falling paper (or feathers, or money, or confetti, or anything that pauses and glides in the air as it descends).

Still life; decay; the object as symbol and clue.

Landscape.

Interiors.

Meals, often out of doors.

Flashing lights, artificial lights.

Architecture: Buildings as 'characters'; doors and windows as framing devices.

Drapes, sheets, curtains, canopies.

Animals, particularly dogs, sheep, horses.

Statues.

Processions.

Photographs and photography.

Stairs.

Models, simulacra, maps, copies.

These are all constants, whether linked with the text, thematised, or not. They are also often the means by which more abstract notions are expressed, for example:

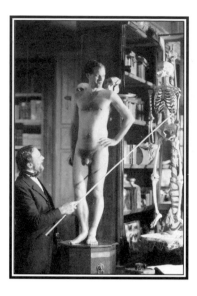

Darwin

Darwinian theory: Birth, copulation and death.

Artifice, self-reference (Greenaway, under pressure to defend his use of artifice, often underplays how he uses it to represent the world it isn't, but is a part of; particularly abstract power structures).

Encyclopaedic systems of thought, categorisation.

Irony.

Cinema itself, its unexplored possibilities.

These are all thought clusters and habits of thought discussed at length in 'Themes and Variations' or the interviews, or already made clear in extracts from Greenaway's writings. Let me try to suggest what is characteristic about the structure of Greenaway's thought.

It seems to operate consistently - and operate best - through oppositions and paradoxes, which are often ironic, but also initially driven by parallel urgencies, which, rather than cancelling each other out as they might in logic, flicker, alternate, like Wittgenstein's rabbit/duck drawing, or, more subtly because not a question of either/or, like the spinning coin of seeing and knowing, simultaneously heads and tails, involved in *trompe l'oeil*.

So the literal is paired with the metaphorical, the original with the fake, and with the map or simulacrum; an emphasis on artifice is paired with a dissatisfaction with cinema as insufficiently real, the corporeal with the emblematic; a distrust of narrative is paired with a love of language and a longing to tell stories, and text is paired with image; Darwinian science is paired with creation myths, and a Darwinian hard-headedness with a condemnation of the hypocrisy and cruelty of power far less complicit with the glamour of power than the average gangster film.

Around these poles, between them, thought accumulates threads and webs of connections, some fragile or broken or abandoned, others regular routes: the thought of the artist, and the thought of the viewer.

SPECTACLE

You shall see the very place, madam; said my uncle Toby.

Mrs Wadman blushed - looked towards the door - turned pale - blushed slightly again - recovered her natural colour - blushed worse than ever; which, for the sake of the unlearned reader, I translate thus:

> 'L--d! I cannot look at it -
> What would the world say if I looked at it?
> I should drop down, if I looked at it -
> I wish I could look at it -
> There can be no sin in looking at it.
> - I will look at it.
>
> LAURENCE STERNE, *Tristram Shandy* [7]

It would admittedly be difficult to find a single English word to express what Freud had in mind with *Schaulust* - a term that combines the German word for lust, or sexual desire, with that for looking, viewing, or contemplating - but a phrase on the order of 'the sexual pleasure in looking' would make his meaning clear; or, since 'lust' is a near-equivalent of the German 'Lust' and has the further advantage that it can be used both as a noun and as a verb, it might be preferable to 'sexual pleasure'. In either case, the reader would know immediately what is meant. Since we have all repeatedly experienced great pleasure in watching something, in taking it in with our eyes, and have occasionally been ashamed of doing so, or even been afraid to look, although we wished to see, it would be easy to have both a direct intellectual and an emotional understanding of Freud's concept.

BRUNO BETTELHEIM [8]

Cosmological, theological, geographical, didactic, and sensuous entertainment ... allegory, graphic symbol, map, mimetic gesture, idealised heroics, hedonistic display.
Flying Out of This World [9]

I

Spectacle: cinematic, painterly, operatic, theatrical; and now linked to exhibition. A spectacle arising from cinema's hybrid status, from Greenaway's route into cinema, and from his dissatisfaction with certain of its basic elements.

Spectacle is to do with the eye - what could be more obvious? But a crucial question, as we have seen, is how that eye is embodied. In a 'viewer' or 'spectator', it is simply embodied in someone who looks; the body is a support system for the eye (always in the singular, as we have noted, through some quirk of grammar or perspective-led habit of thought). It is easy to see how this conceit arose: through a particular kind of theatre architecture and use of lighting, through a particular kind of address made by a particular kind of perspective painting to its public. The suggestion that we should imaginatively 'leave', or ignore, the space we occupy in order to imaginatively explore, consider, 'enter' a pictorial space is one which, in an early triumph of Greenaway's examination of language through taking metaphors literally, is tested to destruction in *A Walk Through H.*

But this is not, as we have also seen, the whole of the Western tradition. (It is in fact misleading to suggest two completely separate traditions. Any suggestion of eye-contact between painted figure and viewer - and Alberti specifically asks for such contact - involves a linking of two worlds, a viewer who sees but is also seen. The fantasy of invisibility - either aggressive, the voyeuristic fantasy of seeing without being seen, or defensive, the fantasy of not being subject to the gaze - is no more a *necessary* part of perspective painting than is the notion of a real space witnessed from another real space.) The frame, in medieval and Baroque churches (the two periods linked by *The Baby of Mâcon*) is an architectural feature of an interior which acts as a whole to join with the theatre of ritual performed in the church itself; the frame does not distinguish or bridge two worlds, but punctuates the single world of the real but sacred space of the interior. The images are focused on our presence, on our corporeality, our spirituality, our bodies and our souls. We have, in fact, physically entered a three-dimensional picture space by passing through the doorway.

In such a tradition, which has of course its secular equivalents, the palace allegories surrounding a theatre of royalty and power, the lack of physical involvement can only be seen as a loss, as Greenaway sees it in cinema - and in cinema to an exaggerated degree: 'unlike a church or a house, a gallery or even a museum, a cinema means next to nothing to the historical-cultural value of the film it shows'.[10] We never entirely leave the space around a landscape, say; it will always transform the room into a room with a landscape (or 'a Hobbema') in it. But only physical discomfort or the behaviour of other members of the audience will connect the cinema with the film we watch while we watch it.

The making of the film has become, for the Greenaway of *The Stairs*, a Baroque extravagance or extravaganza, the film itself a dissatisfying by-product. (There is perhaps another parallel with land art, which in so far as it exists as documentation, more or less aestheticised, does no more than point to the real work, the artist's walk, to which the viewer has no meaningful access.) As a *Gesamtkunstwerk*, cinema comes a poor second to a service in a church such as Il Gesu, a drawing for which is included in *Flying Out of This World*,[11] the Mass includes costume, music, theatre, painting, as cinema can, but also real sculpture, real architecture - and the smell of incense. An exhibition like In the Dark (in Spellbound) can come far closer to such an experience.

Even within cinema, however, the parallels between Greenaway and Baroque are many. (Vermeer has been characterised as a Baroque artist, but I am thinking mainly of Rubens, of Italian Baroque.) Whatever its theological framework, Baroque as a style is based on an absolute and compelling refusal to separate mind and body, thought and flesh. It offers realism (defined as an acceptance of corporeality) against idealism, an ascetic or Platonic downgrading of the present and immediate world of the senses; it cannot imagine the divine without specific human detail, and even as it moves from earth to heaven it does so through a celebration of flesh, drapery, light - the fleeting externals of human vision - rather than the abstractions of anatomy, outline, the eternal verities that are masked by external appearance. This anti-idealism is nevertheless linked to allegory, to body-as-text, to property-as-attribute; to huge encyclopaedic schemes with fabulously or promiscuously mixed languages. There is a Baroque delight in illusionism which derives less from a petty desire to deceive than from a spiritual ambition to confuse the senses, to display what cannot rationally be imagined, to thematise the shared space of worshipper and image - so that Bernini sculpts an audience as well as an ecstasy, a self-reference which at once emphasises the viewer's own position in the space of the chapel and suggests, through the pouring out of the miraculous, that such physical realities can be, have been, transcended. Baroque is a confection of endless, and suspended, *coups de théâtre*; its overwhelming insistence on theatricality demands surrender to rather than analysis of its spectacle.

[As an (impossible) film project, *The Stairs*] was again to take place in Rome, but this time it was to be more naked in its self identification.

It was to concern a painter fascinated by the seventeenth century, who is persuaded to take on a commission for a film, a grandiose Italian costume drama, and specifically to make a ceiling painting, a Resurrection, based on 17th-century drawings of a destroyed epic work by Andrea Pozzo, a companion piece to Pozzo's *Apotheosis of St Ignatius* in the church of Sant'Ignazio in Rome.

This painting was to be a crowd-scene in the air, containing some eight named characters and eight hundred flying extras. It was an escapist religious picture, in subject and in metaphor, projected onto a high ceiling whose visibility was poor at the best of times, and whose sight-lines demanded a cricked neck.

The painting sought to make comment on the conundrum of pastiche and the deceit of *trompe l'oeil* - and on the special pretence of the painted surface, especially within the criterion of the Baroque, which can be used as a metaphor for the cinema itself - a phenomenon of total spectacle employing every means possible, but especially light, to fabricate illusion and make propaganda for an act of faith and for the suspension of disbelief - essential both for the church and the cinema.

How could we believe both locally that such a crowd of figures could fly into heaven through the roof of a Roman church, and how could we believe, more universally, in the concept of resurrection? And how could we accept that cinema tries to attempt this sort of miracle every time the projector light is switched on?

If this particular cinematic megalomania was insufficient, the film was also to reconstruct an apocryphal work of music, Monteverdi's *Marriage of Aeneas*, with a cast of twelve singers, eighty chorus and a thousand walk-on, run-on, fly-on parts. With horses. And elephants.

There was to be no cheating. The whole Pozzo painting and the entire Monteverdi opera had to be reconstructed. Formally they both represented the exact centres of their respective biblical and mythological cycles: the resurrection of Christ could be thought of as the pivot-point of the faith and history of Judaism and Christianity, and the marriage of Aeneas was to be considered as the pivot-point of Greek and Roman history and legend.

Despite this historical largesse, the drama was firmly rooted in the 20th century, and was to concern all those film actors and extras chosen to impersonate the many parts of the painting as models, and all those singers and figurants who were to enact the opera. Their existence was to be predicated on this reconstruction of a lost painting and a lost musical work, both representatives of huge mythological cycles. And as actors and extras they were also of course to be professionally involved in the business of re-creation, pastiche and all the deceits of representation. [12]

However, Greenaway, as an anti-theologian - his spectacle points to no faith - is usefully considered as a creator of Brechtian as well as Baroque theatricality: the light which is cinema exists as both wave and particle. It is not spirituality which is co-existent, doubled, with corporeality in Greenaway, but the presence of mind to imagine, to represent, as well as live out, physical existence. Illusion, in Baroque, is a metaphor, a content; an image of transcendence, of what is true despite appearances. Similar devices in Greenaway (and *Rosa* is full of *coups de théâtre*) are allegories of hollowness as well as the persistence of myth; we are free to make myths, but not to believe in them. Illusion is the most potent form of artifice, since, unlike 'realism', it draws our attention to the mechanics of representation: we look to see how it is done, and we fail, and so the tension between what we see and what we know is never released; disbelief is not suspended, but held in suspension; we become self-aware as viewers, as audience, in ways which can also include political and cultural self-awareness.

II

Baroque flesh is the site of pleasure and pain, both sexual, both spiritual, both existing as spectacle, and joined therefore to another pleasure, the pleasure of viewing - and not just the male pleasure in viewing female flesh, but human pleasure in viewing human flesh - across a wide spectrum of circumstances, as has been suggested.

Perhaps, briefly, we can consider the same ground in terms of what Freud calls *Schaulust* and his translators, to Bettelheim's dismay, call 'scopophilia'. [13] A dream analysis of Freud's in the *Introductory Lectures* suggests that in the dream the theatre is related to the primal scene; it is where

the desire to look at what is forbidden is legitimised and fulfilled. The connection, although not developed, is suggestive, especially if we remember that the primal scene, if actually witnessed, might well be connected by the child with violence - violence, unthinkably, towards the mother. (In Freud's discussions of the primal scene, he often refers to the wife being taken from behind, coincidentally a recurring image in *Rosa*.)

If we do see the theatre, the cinema, as places where we go to view representations of sex and violence - and that is simply undeniable - Greenaway is remarkable not in his subject matter, but in his treatment of it. Dismantle, or even merely question, the genre conventions that prepare us for the sight of violence in particular - deal with cannibalism in a restaurant and not some colonialist romp in Africa or a survival movie,[14] show the voyeur as cuckold, combine a rape scene with a paradox of what is real and what is only acting, show men widowed after a fatal accident seeking consolation not in religion, but in science, which offers no consolation - and the situation, however artificial, becomes difficult to bear because it must be thought about rather than consumed/resolved through narrative.

If we move the short distance from Freud to Bettelheim's translation/gloss - 'a term that combines the ... word for lust ... with that for looking, viewing or contemplating' - we might suggest that 'Baroque' or 'cinema' are also such terms. In any case, as Bettelheim insists of most of Freud's terms, we are talking about human constants, not 'perversions'. Much contemporary art does more than 'critique' the male heterosexual gaze; it empowers other gazes, and this is essential - to widen the visual, not restrict or censor it. 'Voyeurism', as a word applied to the Western visual tradition, marginalises and downgrades *Schaulust*; Greenaway is an artist who accepts and expands it. In Greenaway the spectacle is always sexual, but it also involves what we are reluctant or afraid to look at: the frailty of our nakedness, our mortality, the Darwinian drives underlying our sexuality which mock our vanity. Instead of sentimental involvement with the plot and characters, Greenaway demands a physical and intellectual engagement with a spectacle which is more than an image for a disembodied eye, which delivers pleasure in looking, without shirking the consequences.

MUSIC

A walk through G by a musician, or historian of music, would have been a very different one. It would in particular have concentrated on minimalism, systems music, and the music theatre of Robert Wilson and Philip Glass: 'after *Einstein on the Beach*, new perspectives opened up'.[15] The second interview offers some compensation for this lack.

Music is vitally important to Greenaway. In 1983 he made four documentaries, each fifty-five minutes long, on American composers: Robert Ashley, Philip Glass, Meredith Monk and John Cage. Cage, in particular, has been a major inspirational figure, the structure of *The Falls* being a (mistaken) homage to a work by Cage. He has worked twice with Louis Andriessen, on *Rosa* and *M is for Man, Music, and Mozart*. The catalogue to *The Stairs Geneva* has a CD with music by Patrick Mimran.

One is always contrasting Greenaway's cinema to the mainstream, and this is as true of his use of music as anything else. 'The best soundtrack music is simultaneously transparent - instantly readable as to mood or reference - and swift in shifting ... The point is less "mickey-mousing" - the trade jargon for music that sonically describes the action - than music that reads, subconsciously, in such a way as to pinpoint, flavour or otherwise render comic whatever might be happening, at that instant, on screen.' Mark Sinker is writing here (in *Celluloid Jukebox*)[16] about Carl Stalling, a cartoon composer - hence the emphasis on the comic - but the generalisation, widened, holds good for most film scores, from Prokofiev working with Eisenstein to Miles Davis jamming in front of the rushes for *L'Ascenseur au l'Échafaud*.

Rosa dramatises and satirises this conventional practice. Rosa sells out to Hollywood, writes music for Westerns, and the films he writes for - or rather the clips from them which are all that he ever sees - are projected onto the screens on stage. 'Rosa's footage-counter is fixed high up on the stage where its crimson neon digits glow. They count and re-count. They count forwards. And they count backwards as though music could be measured in negative time.'[17]

When Greenaway worked with Nyman, the music did not come after, or simply match, the action or images. It was introduced as a component in its own right, linked rather to the intellectual structures of the film (the eight stages of evolution, say, in *A Zed and Two Noughts*, or the decaying fish; the drawings in *The Draughtsman's Contract*) than to individual characters. (It is the inner life of the characters which film music conventionally suggests, and that is the least of Greenaway's ambitions for character.) Above all, it is not used subliminally. Artifice requires that we be consciously aware of music as an element in the film.

The music Greenaway uses is written, we have seen, in ways that run parallel to his own use of systems; and the music he likes, indeed, was an initial inspiration for his systems as much as Nyman's. It is a 'spatialised', repetitive music, as his narratives are spatialised, repetitive:

I want to consider this white consoling sheet [Rosa's shroud] further, in steady-state and static prose that doesn't advance but only runs with the smallest of variations on the spot. Music can easily comply with this request. It can preserve this hung-fire emotional state indefinitely, repeating a phenomenon without you wishing it to go away, or change, or move forward.[18]

Interviews

POSSIBLE EXCITEMENTS

⁂

Both of the two interviews included in this section have been substantially revised and expanded by Peter Greenaway for the present publication. the first interview (which as a result of the re-editing now has a kind of doubled present tense) was conducted as editing was in progress on *The Cook, The Thief, His Wife and Her Lover*, and began with a question about *A TV Dante*.

It sometimes seemed that the *TV Dante* series was a project where fools rushed in where angels feared to tread. An Italian classic treated with awed respect by Italians, subject of considerable painting, print and drawing illustration from Botticelli to Doré, rarely considered in film. Now to be treated as a television work in an English twentieth-century translation. Tom Phillips was a painter, I was a film-maker and we were working in a medium which was unfamiliar to both of us. And the question 'This is a text - why illustrate it?' A work conceived in words is best left there. However, the world of images is largely a world of illustrations of text. Look at two thousand years of European painting. Look at nearly one hundred years of cinema. Tom had a mission. He used words like 'illumination' rather than illustration. He had made a translation of the original *Inferno*. Against considerable odds, including the destruction by fire of his first effort, he had made an illustrated book of the same, following the great traditions of illustrated Dante from Delacroix to Rauschenberg. Channel Four put us together. I was interested in any project that might push the televisual language. I had long respected Tom's approach to image-making. When I was at art school, he, along with R. B. Kitaj, had helped legitimise for me what some called intellectual pop-art - the provocative freedoms of the use of very contemporary imagery without giving up long painting traditions.

For a pilot programme we attempted to make something of Canto V, the canto that deals with the realm of Hell devoted to the lustful, a sensationalist exhibitionist subject to start with. And we experimented. It took us a long time to complete. We were comparatively innocent about experimentation in the medium, invariably going the long way round, building up the imagery according to how we might compose it if we had been working with our own materials and methods. To the video engineers I am sure we were impractical academics playing with unfamiliar toys. I am puzzled when audiences laugh at film running backwards - if you work twelve hours a day on a Steenbeck, film running backwards is a commonplace, it seems normal. I suspect Tom and I marvelled at every commonplace video trick available, much to the bored irritation of the video editors. I suspect the first canto we completed reveals our innocence, an inventory of the available gimmicks which pop video makers and commercials editors play with in their sleep.

WAS THIS THE FIRST TIME YOU HAD USED VIDEO?

It wasn't the first time, but I'd never used it quite in this complex, multi-layered way before. I had a healthy respect for how expensive the commercial medium was in post-production - and I suspect Tom's *savoir-faire* about expense and how to negotiate with a producer was bolder than mine - he pushed hard for everything and we'd soon, in practice, used up half the budget to make one eighth of the programme. Previously I'd made four fifty-minute programmes for Channel Four - *Four American Composers*, Phil Glass, Robert Ashley, Meredith Monk and John Cage, made in the spirit, I like to think, of those composers' working methods - not so much necessarily to mimic their end products, but to reflect how they might have got there.

I think the most successful of the programmes were on Ashley and Cage, and I like to believe that they were the two that were the most television television. Cinema and television do have different requirements, different vocabularies, different audience attention requirements, and sometimes I feel that these vocabularies are racing apart in unsuccessful ways at a great rate of knots. And to the detriment of cinema - which indeed - in some rather sad rearguard action - is set on hanging on to its illusionistic picture-making traditions but by mimicking TV language - images now tend to be confined to the dead centre of the frame, there are a minimal number of wide shots, there is doubt at the fringes of the frame because of the chances of poor TV alignment, hesitation over extreme contrasts of colour and contrast because of the cathode-tube's comparative insensitivity. Instead of taking up what TV can offer as new language for example in post-production - the manipulation of the image after the camera has created it - instead we largely have a curious blend and mismatch of mimicry and conservatism and various cultural snobbisms.

However ... With *A TV Dante* we were nursed along by a surprisingly sympathetic and tolerant video-editor, Bill Saint, surprisingly because my experience in video-houses has not always been good - the equation of convenience, money, time and video-house lifestyle can be anathema for patient experimentation. The *Divine Comedy* is strong and

The Belly of an Architect

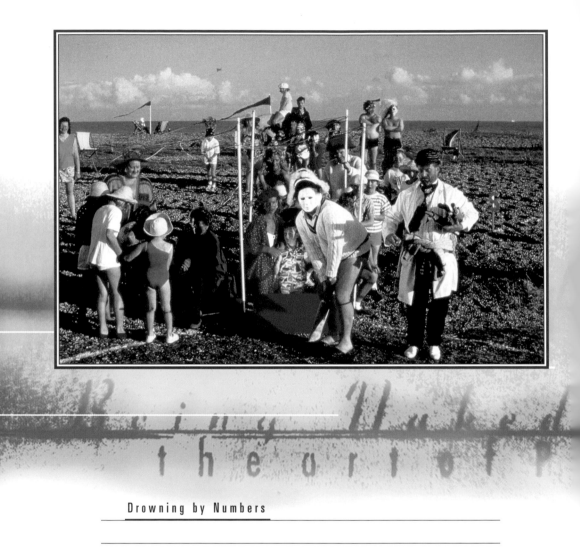

Being Naked
the art of

Drowning by Numbers

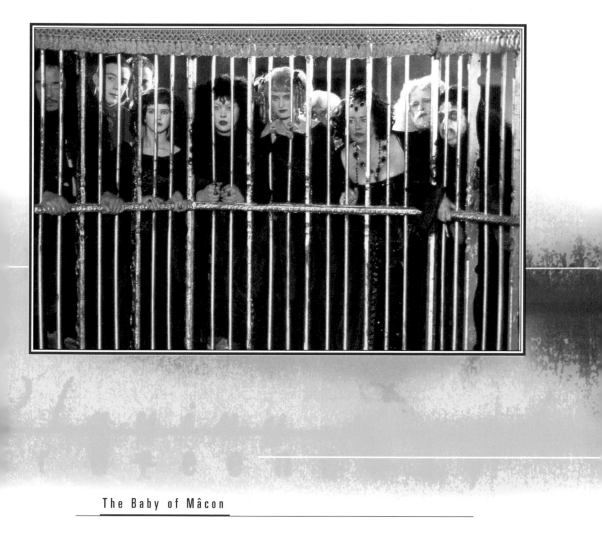

The Baby of Mâcon

Being Naked
the art of

The Cook, The Thief, His Wife and Her Lover

Prospero's Books

(Opposite Page)

The Pillow Book

The Pillow Book

Belly of an Architect

The Audience, John The Baptist Game

Mixed Media on Paper (Opposite Page)

39. Cire
41. the Moor
43. Diana
45. Mercury
47. the Mechanic
49. the Hangman
51. Minerva

Being Naked
the art of

Prospero's Books

Prospero's Books

(Opposite Page)

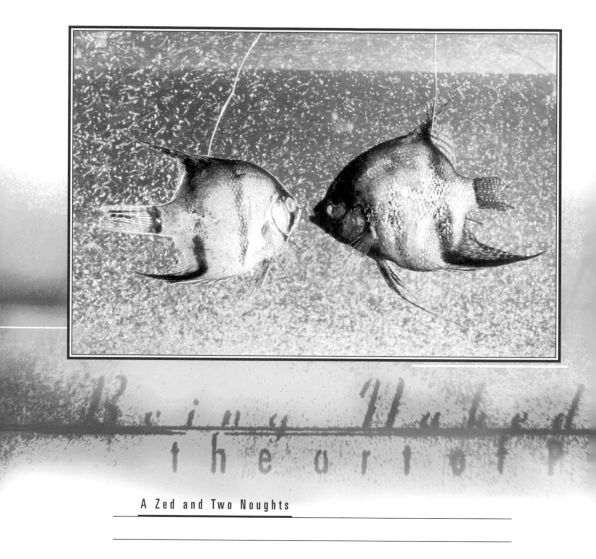

Being Naked
the art of

A Zed and Two Noughts

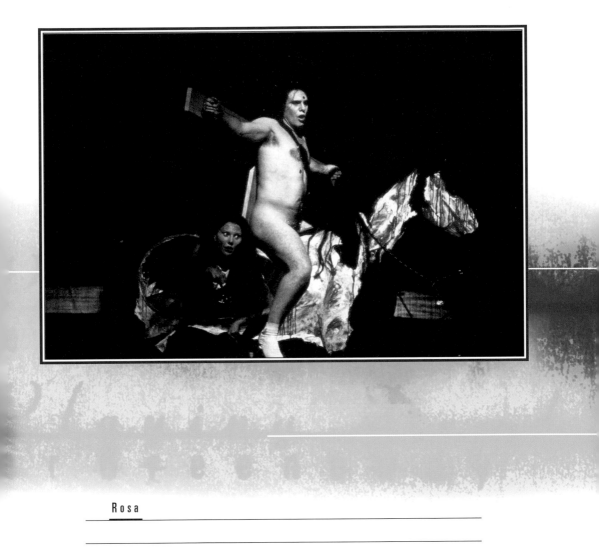

Rosa

Being Naked
the art of

The Draughtsman's Contract

Darwin

(Opposite Page)

The Football Field

Mixed Media on Paper

robust in structure - editable in sound-bite chunks relative to TV audience attention each canto lends itself to twelve-minute news summary timings, but it has vast complexity. Some have seen it as a compendium of all known information of the world, circa 1300. An encyclopaedic work - and we wanted to be lexicographers in sympathy with it.

How did the collaboration work?

One of the stipulations we both made was not to include the sort of characteristic images we were both known for in other media. In the event that was not so easy to fulfil. After all we were both in the business to make the images that we enjoyed, thought valuable, considered to be our own. But it was a ruling we tried to work with. To find some middle ground where individual interests could come together to produce some images that were not particularly either of us but rather a combination of both. Perhaps that could be a recipe for blandness. For me the series was exploratory and experimental. I think sometimes it works, sometimes it doesn't work at all. But there again, Dante's *Inferno* has so many ideas, so many metaphors, so many games to play, so many references to make, it would not be too difficult to include anything you wanted to include, which of course we did. The research methods, using large quantities of recently-old news items from Dutch archive sources, depended first on a delight in what the news items had to offer in themselves, and then a delight in the ingenuity of using them, making them fit, like pieces in a jigsaw puzzle. Large amounts of disparate material have been poured into the series of nine programmes; some of it is flicking through so fast that even an averagely attentive viewer would be hard pressed to tabulate what they saw. Repeated viewings are necessary. And why not?

There are considerable personal allusions, some private jokes, elaborate conundrums - but we thought legitimately so, for Dante did the same - maybe he played the game of personal reference more than we now know. He certainly paid off old scores with his enemies, real, unreal or imagined. We too found both personal and public references could be made with twentieth-century equivalents of Dantean personalities - popes, cardinals, policemen of one sort and another, politicians, statesmen, leaders, dictators, figures in the crowd doing the same job for us in the twentieth century as their equivalents had done for Dante in the fourteenth century. I felt it was valuable that we were trying to use a televisual language. When I first saw *The Draughtsman's Contract* on television I was dismayed. The film was made very much for the big screen. There were many wide landscape shots, many statically framed shots to examine and pore over in detail. Shot by shot, there were few close-ups, few American cut-at-the-knee figure compositions, little or no set over-the-shoulder conversation pieces. Narrative clues were frequently contained in the background. A considerable amount of this vocabulary did not mean so much on the small box in the corner of the living room. Many of those things which cinema does particularly well, that you can have some considerable control over to make a large-screen image, like colour grading, like organisation of minutiae inside a shot, like being able to make a sophisticated soundtrack, television does not take kindly to. It's a generalisation - but television basically takes well to close-ups and close-medium shots. Normally a television narrative uses the wide shot as a dialogue-less introductory device, reserving sync dialogue until the character-head is in close-up. The vocabulary of *A TV Dante* was anxious to avoid direct dramatisations, conversation pieces. It used straight-to-camera expositions - television's continuing and major characteristic - the statement, the interview, the acknowledgement of the camera - the 'I am talking to you' stance.

DID CHANNEL FOUR WANT THE FILMS THEY BACKED TO TAKE TELEVISION INTO CONSIDERATION?

I believe not. It seemed Channel Four, with the Film on Four project, was happy for film-makers to make films that would suit cinema screens and cinema audiences. Perhaps it was a market ploy - make the film successful in the cinema and then a showing on television would benefit. Better to make your own than buy those manufactured by others. But I am sure there was - at least with Jeremy Isaacs - a true spirit of encouragement. I am grateful to him, for I am certain that it was often his personal intervention on my behalf, over the scepticism of others, that we managed to make four films with Channel Four whilst he was there. And with David Aukin as Film Commissioning Editor, Channel Four's generosity continues. The films had very generous cinema-run potentials. In my case it was two and a half years sometimes before the film was seen on the box. Maybe the delay for me was for other reasons. Jeremy Isaacs, I am sure, wanted the product very much to be associated with cinema at large. In the end, of course, the situation of making film and making TV stretched the boundaries. There was much talk of the differences of cinema films and TV films. It became a question of urgent categorisation at international film festivals. The comparison is never really settled. *My Beautiful Laundrette* had the characteristics of a TV film, but it was probably Channel Four's greatest early cinema success. I believe the cinema projects and the TV projects for Channel Four that I have been involved in have tried to use different vocabularies pertaining to film or TV. *A TV Dante* is I hope very convincingly a different sort of work than, say, *The Draughtsman's Contract.*

But working with the video language, the opportunity to layer images, the ability to re-work and re-work, store for days and then come back and re-think, was, I thought, encouraging to make new uses of narrative that did not seem characteristic of conventional film and TV drama. At the time I was encouraged to think it might be more akin to the methods of painting or writing. There's a way in which Dante's *Inferno* is forever a chopped narrative, always developing new leads, wandering off in different directions, full of side-events, small stories in brackets. And the references needed some serious explanations to make significance. Perhaps now - in televisual terms - they might say it's ideal encyclopaedic CD-Rom material. We saw it as narratives in bursts interspaced with reflection and explanation. With the commentary and the footnotes interwoven into the central flow of things. Perhaps a classic travelogue - a journey through Hell with a good guide - which is a reference for me back to an earlier film - *A Walk Through H*, where indeed you could take your choice whether H stood for Heaven or Hell. At that time my introduction to the *Inferno* was virtually by name only. *A Walk Through H* and *Vertical Features Remake* were both similarly narrative and discursive - guides to a subject, a parcel of fragments, an encyclopaedic sequence. My early pursuits in cinema were very much to do with trying to create a cinema without narrative, which I've since realised is probably a contradiction in terms, because anything that moves through time - given human desire for cohesion and chronology - would seem to have some sort of narrative. 1,2,3,4,5,6,7,8,9,10 can be seen as a minimal narrative - it grows, develops. Perhaps, by association, it has greater narrative potential going backwards. I would argue now for delight and purpose in sequence. Sequence is inevitable in cinema, but narrative might not be. Does reading an encyclopaedia count as pursuing narrative? Working on *A TV Dante* brought me back to the possibilities of pursuing a cinema away from using those tight narrative concerns which perhaps have been a preoccupation of my last three films [*The Belly of an Architect, Drowning by Numbers, The Cook, The Thief, His Wife and Her Lover*]. That was good. It also encouraged me to believe that the post-production TV language could be used at large in cinema. And working with Tom was very valuable for me. He is extremely erudite, delights in academic reference, has a large range of literary interests that he can skilfully use in making visual imagery. I enjoyed using the aesthetic vocabulary of painters to discuss cinema and all it stands for. The process and the collaboration were stimulating.

WHEN YOU TALKED ABOUT THINGS HAPPENING IN THE BACKGROUND OF *The Draughtsman's Contract,* **WAS THAT A DEVICE BORROWED FROM PAINTING?**

I had long been curious about the idea of the figures-in-a-landscape genre - their significance and insignificance, the way they make a focus but do not shout for attention. The harmony of the characters with the landscape in a painting like Giorgione's *Tempest* - incidental, co-incidental - but how much duller the landscape would be without them. I wrote a film script with the imaginary dialogue of those two Giorgione figures - the soldier and the breast-feeding mother - some say gypsy parents, some say idealised Holy Family - where the background's every crash of thunder was the excuse to change the subject under discussion.

A more celebrated example, Brueghel's *Fall of Icarus*, where the incident that gives the painting its title has been minimalised, and the picture is about so much else - nonetheless, the whole being the completest illustration of the narrative origins of the Ovid myth that you could ever find - a true and faithful illustration of text. More relevant perhaps for me are the landscapes of Poussin - not the Mount Olympus crowd-figure paintings so much as the landscape architectural scenes with paths you can logically follow, piled up architecture and forest, and the important mythological event reduced to three figures beside a tree in the middle ground. The drama is strong but dwarfed by the disinterested round of Nature. It's a small conceit, but the ratio of the film frame of *The Draughtsman's Contract*, being 1 to 1.66, is the preferred ratio of those books of drawings by Claude Lorraine of artificially realised landscapes full of trees and sheep. Perhaps *The Draughtsman's Contract* itself is like flicking through a book of drawings of landscapes - a copy-book for reference, a training manual made for profit, a self-reflexive notion, because much of the film is about how to draw a landscape with conviction. And money. Those Claude drawings, I am sure, were the result of drawing what you know and not what you see - the dilemma that tripped the draughtsman.

DO YOU EXPECT YOUR AUDIENCE TO SEE THE FILMS MORE THAN ONCE?

I hope they do. I would like them to. But then perhaps what film director would not? There was an oil-rig worker in Glasgow who proudly told me he had seen *The Draughtsman's Contract* ninety-six times. Perhaps not necessarily through interested choice - given the isolation of his job. Is there significance in ninety-six? I know there are many people who have seen the film twice, three times, four times, five times, often stressing that their purposes were not to analyse in any academic sense necessarily, but to make and enjoy all the connections watching the film as a running continuous piece. An Italian architect saw it enough times to reconstruct the house and gardens as a coherent plan, and then come to England - to Groombridge, near Tunbridge Wells, where we filmed it - to check out his accuracy.

I can certainly remember seeing certain films that intrigued me many times - though there was no especial virtue in counting how many. Eisenstein's *Strike*, Resnais's *Marienbad*, Fellini's *Juliet of the Spirits*, Kurosawa, Antonioni, Godard, Frampton. But I suspect each film was pored over for different reasons. And sometimes of course not necessarily and exclusively filmic - we know that cinema is an excellent repository for nostalgia, personal association, shareable memory. Michael Nyman tells a story of a couple who met at a screening of *The Draughtsman's Contract*. Six months later he was invited to play *The Draughtsman's Contract* music at their wedding. Perhaps because of not dissimilar reasons, I have a relative who's seen *The Sound of Music* eighteen times - and he has kept the ticket stubs to prove it. He spends his holidays in Salzburg - nostalgia as a marathon event.

For me a second viewing of a film can be more important than the first. Understand and absorb the plot, get the narrative out of the way to concentrate exactly on how things happen rather than what has happened - see how things evolve, and examine the way the imagery has been put to use. I suppose for me this would go back to the deliberate, patient and painstaking activity of picture-making in painting, and I do know - for good or ill - that the most entertaining and exciting part of making films for me is not necessarily working with the actors, but it's working with the cameraman and the art department, and creating those hundreds of thousands of images, deliberating on their significances, stretching and pulling their meanings, planning and filming the location or studio-set to get the richest and most satisfactory image possible under the circumstances. Hence increased studio-shoots, increased artificiality. As Godard, with irony, suggested, cinema truth is measured at 24 frames a second - for every second of film you have 24 separate truths, each truth very minimally different from the next. In an hour-long film you've already achieved 86,000 images. A painter - maybe Tom Phillips - could find this a frustration - he may sit down for three weeks and produce one image. With Vermeer, after the passage of history and natural wastage, we have - some say - give or take a fake or dubious accreditation - only 26 images.

I've always believed it's up to me to make every film image as significant and satisfactory as I can. At the very least it's my obligation to pay as much care as Tom Phillips and Vermeer in an image's manufacture. As an aside it is curious how films are represented and identified by frozen stills - as though film was indeed a question of single static images since these are more easily communicated on paper - the vehicle of text-generated media - than their moving equivalent. Imagine a projectionless history of cinema in some future Dark Age - and we are obliged to make judgements on films by the evidence of their frozen stills alone?

I confess I had - and have - a great sense of impatience in the business of painting. Things do not move fast enough. Ideas are constantly on the flow, and there was no way that I could find a synchronous equivalent to the flow of possible excitements. Clouzot's *The Picasso Mystery* has a satisfactory procedure - a painting that constantly changed. All this of course is relevant to talent, ability and practice - and perhaps in my case all three were - and are - limited. Perhaps the cinematic manufacture of images is more suitable for what I have to offer. Though I never feel a natural-born film-maker. I have regrets and disenchantments about the film-making process as it can be compared to the business of painting. The painter is essentially working on his own, which is enviable. Despite the likes of Gilbert, Christo and Oldenberg and their respective partners, and despite the tradition of painting studio-factories of Rubens and Reynolds and the like, painting is traditionally a solitary pursuit. A man and a canvas and Radio Four's *Afternoon Play*. Tom reckoned he had heard every radio play there had ever been, plus repeats, and recognised every BBC sound-effect as it came around again for the umpteenth time. Film-makers have to be collaborators. I still enjoy writing a film in private more than any other part of the film process. Perhaps it's knowing it can be downhill all the way afterwards.

I enjoy the moment when the film arrives in the cutting-room, when the film comes back to me again. It's a relief after the ten weeks spent in company with hundreds of collaborators where you're not as much a picture-maker as you would wish - where there are more important qualities of communication required - like those of an invigilator, a public conscience, an instant psychoanalyst, a persuader, negotiator and cajoler - all necessary in order to get the company together to create the images you think you are looking for. However, I should not complain; the pains and anxieties of the producer are always greater and longer-lasting. But I'm getting better at the process. As each film comes along I'm beginning to enjoy its manufacture on the floor or on location a little more.

WHEN YOU INTRODUCED *The Belly of an Architect* AT THE CAMBRIDGE FILM FESTIVAL THERE WERE SOME QUESTIONS YOU FOUND DIFFICULT TO ANSWER, BECAUSE YOU STILL COULDN'T WATCH THE FILM WITHOUT REMEMBERING ALL THE SURROUNDINGS AND CIRCUMSTANCES OF EVERY SHOT - AND WHAT WAS JUST OUTSIDE IT. HOW LONG DOES IT TAKE BEFORE YOU CAN WATCH A FILM? HAVE YOU RECLAIMED *The Belly of an Architect* YET?

I haven't seen *The Belly of an Architect* for some time. The last time I concentrated on fully watching it was with Buckingham Palace press representatives. There was a curious notion that the film was eligible for a royal viewing. They were very polite and talked of visiting Rome some day themselves. I believe they took the film to be some sort of architectural travelogue. Perhaps they were right. I believe a viewing can be very different each time, and dependent on who you are with and your state of hunger, thirst, the smell of the cinema, the amount of available light, and of course what your experiences have been since the last time you saw it. Perhaps it's the same with viewing a painting. A trip to a gallery you know well can often set up certain expectations of recognising a known painting and suddenly being confronted with an unknown quality because of new company or a change in the light. I remember seeing the newly-cleaned huge Veronese in the Louvre, *Wedding at Cana*, by torch-light - battery-torch that is - and thinking that the experience should be for others too. Paintings after all, at least before the 1850s, were not designed to be seen in the neutral light and space of galleries. Sometimes I am surprised by coming across a film at a foreign screening - looking at *The Belly of an Architect* at an architects' conference in Philadelphia, or watching *A Zed and Two Noughts* in Sydney whilst I sat next to a Darwin scholar. Looking at the films several years after the making can sometimes be puzzling - the complexity is demanding. I have to work out the iconography again. In small ways the films can become strangers. I did watch *The Draughtsman's Contract* three or four months ago - in Barcelona - and was surprised. The sub-titles distanced the film a little, but parts of the film I had entirely forgotten. I remembered them in the script but not on the screen. Maybe that's not uncommon - with film-makers anyway. Perhaps with painters. There was a case where Miro didn't remember painting a picture and declared the item a fake, and his estate had to prove to him by documents and photographs that he had indeed painted it.

YOU MUST REMEMBER THINGS THAT WERE IN YOUR MIND WHEN YOU MADE A FILM BUT WHICH WERE NEVER FINALLY INCLUDED?

The imagination has to be more powerful than any image you can construct from it. And the imagination is always on the move; the image is invariably fixed. If the image is your own and you know where it comes from, it's probably alive and pulsing with the intentions you had for it - intentions which continue to inhabit and animate it ever afterwards. I know that it is almost inevitably true with painting that the image is always more dense with meaning for the author than it can ever be for a viewer. There are going to be private meanings, private perspectives, reasons for marks that are without meaning for a viewer. And the images I do strongly remember in the films are often accompanied by a remembrance of the minutes before it was made and the minutes after. Intentions for an image often remain strong beyond the manufacture. I had always thought for example that *The Draughtsman's Contract* was in a way a small personal remembrance and homage to Georges de La Tour, but it's not so easy now to find out why or how. Where are the images that relate to de La Tour? There are some figure-groupings which are perhaps blasphemously reinterpreted from a de La Tour *Nativity*. The Virgin, the Child, St Anne and Joseph seen by candle-light are now two pimps and a whore seen by candle-light. But that claustrophobic, quiet, mysterious, introspective atmosphere that you experience with de La Tour - so much less flamboyant than the other *ténébristes* - I don't see that atmosphere being so strong in the film at all now, so I was obviously imagining it. No matter, no matter. De La Tour's light was a considerable inspiration to me when we made the film. It was a communicable comparison and intention between myself and Sacha Vierny.

ARE ALL THE PAINTERS YOU USE AS STARTING POINTS FAVOURITES OF YOURS OR ARE THERE PAINTERS OR PAINTINGS WHICH JUST HAPPEN TO FIT INTO THE INTELLECTUAL FRAMEWORK?

It sounds manipulative, even idle, to suggest you should find a painting and then construct a narrative from it. This of course is not illegitimate. I mentioned the Giorgione scenario earlier. Composers have certainly used the process. A contemplation of a Gerald Dou painting by Leslie MacQuinney produced a disturbing narrative film. And contemplation and reconstruction of Caravaggio's paintings was instrumental for Derek Jarman. Since the majority of constructed images until the 1850s - in painting at least - were illustrations of text-conceived narrative, it is perhaps only fitting that paintings should be the catalyst to reverse the process back to narrative. In *The Belly of an Architect*, the painting references came quite late in the script-making process. In tune with all the mid-1980s discussion of architecture, I had wanted to make a film that commented on the responsibility of architects, and to make comparisons between the construction of a building and the construction of a film. Amongst other concerns of the public and the private, and the architect's claim to make art that was capable of a sort of immortality, I felt that the general public's shrill negative attitude to new architecture is so often simply the shock of the new. I believe such a strong reactionary element can be dangerous - witness the Prince Charles debates that have given confidence to architecture that I am sure history will despise. The crescents at Bath were regarded as overplain and jerrybuilt vulgarities when they were first erected; now they represent an epitome of desirability. So I wanted to make a film about architectural responsibility, and the architect as scapegoat. And I wanted to make it in Rome. I wanted to exorcise some personal ghosts about putting a domestic life up against a public life, and the resultant gains and losses. Perhaps the film was autobiographical in many ways I only understood much later. Its plot, for a start, is a reworking of a personal anecdote. I went to Rome to publicise *The Draughtsman's Contract* and swiftly fell ill with a painful stomach-ache - food poisoning, ulcers, cancer? I suspect it was nervous reaction, for on the plane back to London the pains mysteriously disappeared. A man with an ill-diagnosed stomach-ache is the plot of *The Belly of an Architect*. He believes in conspiracies, identifications with poisoned heroes, until finally indeed it turns out to be the worst it can be - cancer. An even more powerful autobiographical reference was my father - in fact both my parents who died of stomach cancer. My father was a large man with a large belly - like Stourley Kracklite - and a man seriously thwarted in an unrealisable ambition. All these ingredients were waiting for a catalyst. I had known the painting of *Andrea Doria as Neptune* by Bronzino for some time, but looking at it again I thought there was a way that I could use the image to bring everything together. Andrea Doria became the architect. Although the painting was finished around 1545, and was certainly an idealised portrait of a Venetian admiral as Neptune, and not associated at all with architecture, the heavy, vulnerable, solid, rather vain, and curiously innocent nude admirably fitted the notions I had for Kracklite. And indeed, I suppose, at a remove, for my father. And perhaps the vulnerability of posturing architects who thought they were heroes. Strip the clothes off Brian Dennehy and he looks like Andrea Doria. It's a curious image. Why did this man aged, say, 55, choose to have himself painted in the nude? Not just to identify with a classical Neptune? From Bronzino's other paintings, we can be sure of a powerful erotic imagination in the painter. What of the admiral? Was he advertising his corporeality? Perhaps it's a *memento mori*, saying, this is who I am, this is my flesh, I am an old man coming to the end of my career and life. Which is not inapplicable for the character of Kracklite. The Mannerist imagination can be vain, self-indulgent, putting the self under intense scrutiny, whether for scientific examination, or straight vanity. Pontormo wrote a journal which epitomises the sixteenth-century painter who examines his excrement, agonises over illness, constantly checks his digestion and the state of his humours. Accusations of intense introspection coupled with exhibitionism seems to be a public prejudice against the Mannerists. I enjoy those periods of cultural insecurity - like the period between the post-Michelangelo, post-Raphael, post-da Vinci, post-Renaissance and the Baroque, or between Louis XIV and the French Revolution, and perhaps now post-Picasso, post-Stravinsky, post-Corbusier. If Bronzino is a figure of the first Mannerist period, then Boullée can be seen as a figure of the second - when the Baroque changed to the Rococo and fought with Neoclassicism. Three interesting periods of Mannerism, a term of distaste coined by Victorian art historians keen to denigrate the fall from grace, as they saw it, of the Renaissance genius. For Mannerism, I'm sure you could better offer simply 'transitional', moving from one set of values to another, a period of searching and investigation, moving occasionally into dead-ends and U-bends, perhaps involving self-quotation and pastiche, but ultimately looking for a way through.

CAN THERE BE A PARALLEL IN CINEMA - IT'S SUCH A YOUNG ART FORM STILL?

One hundred years is a short time. I suspect the cinema has only produced one giant, a genius of great talent - Eisenstein. But then painting itself is not so prolific of genius per century as we might like to think. Perhaps the mid-fifteenth to mid-sixteenth century is an exception - and then in every sphere of human invention. Perhaps if cinema had had a greater synchronicity with the great investigations of the earlier part of the mid nineteenth century - the energy and curiosity might have produced comparable figures. Perhaps cinema was invented fifty years too late. I imagine the seriousness of purpose of a Darwin or Wagner or - if you take the early twentieth-century - of Joyce or Schoenberg, and it doesn't seem to work in cinema. But I do think you can place Eisenstein with Michelangelo and da Vinci without embarrassment. He had a seriousness of purpose, a knowledge of the cultural flow of two thousand years, did not see cinema in any sense as an isolated medium, could make all the connections which so many other film-makers either do not want to make or do not think relevant or even valuable. But I would always make my subjective appreciation on the use he made of film as language - and there is no doubt in my mind that though others discovered cinema, he invented it. There are not too many Eisenstein films - but to me they all seem extraordinary. He is a natural cinematic genius - the images constantly seem apt, relevant and irreproducible in other media. I have always been amazed at the first film, *Strike* - endlessly inventive, refusing to copy the direct narrative literary model of his American contemporaries. And made when he was very young. And the last two films - *Ivan the Terrible Parts I and II* - grand operatic cinema, intent on making self-confident images of great artificiality. Renoir, as a candidate, I think, does not indicate any such range, and I confess he - as a man and a film-maker - often, for me, has a jollity that irritates. Too much Father Christmas. His famous tolerance - 'Every man has his reasons' - seems a justification, not a programme. Chaplin's ingenuity is large, but I have trouble with his sentimental egotism, simple solutions, and self-righteousness. I feel that film to him was essential for the spread of his talent, but was allowed to contribute little as language.

TARKOVSKY?

I respected *Andrei Rublev*. I did not appreciate the over-stretched metaphors of *Stalker* or *Mirror*. I am suspicious of the Western enthusiasm for Tarkovsky's secular mysticism. I always felt he was happy to mystify and his reputation has much to do with the Solzhenitsyn factor, uncritical admiration for the dissident Russian, which towards the end of his life, amongst English admirers, became embarrassingly excessive - like an admiration for Tolstoy or Schweitzer. I suspect another decade and his reputation will be severely re-addressed. Bergman - certainly initially with *The Seventh Seal* - I am sure, encouraged me to think of cinema in ways I had never thought possible. Bold, confident metaphors, prepared to worry and feed on all the anxieties other film-makers, as I saw it, seemed to leave alone or not even countenance - loneliness, isolation, betrayals, desertions, faith. He always made me feel guilty. As each Bergman film came out in the sixties I dreaded going to see it, but knew I had to. But, as a language-making film-maker, on his own admission, he rated his theatre work more highly than his cinema, and, I think, a great deal of his cinema is very sophisticated filmed theatre - finally *Fanny and Alexander* proved it, if it needed proving.

BUÑUEL?

I always thought the British held Buñuel on a pinnacle as a form of glamorous liberal conscience - perhaps because the Hampstead Everyman always showed him - a prejudice. They saw him as foreign and Spanish and Catholic. And distant. Going to see and praise a Buñuel was to acknowledge their anti-Franco position, and consequently salve their consciences without too much effort. Whereas such audiences were not too aware of *L'Age d'Or* and *Un Chien Andalou*, whose images anyway were perhaps better disseminated as paintings, Buñuel's later films were regularly and lavishly praised by the enthusiastic liberal-minded audiences who eagerly read the Sunday paper reviews and were uncritically directed by them. Because he used Catherine Deneuve and Jeanne Moreau, in England the films continually seemed to receive a reputation as a form of liberal chic. His clever ironies seemed to me too easy, his Catholic-bashing institutional - it's what he was licensed to do. For anti-Catholicism, I preferred Fellini's more vulgar and Rabelaisian cynicism. The angry savagery of the early Buñuel films came out too rarely - I enjoyed the ending of *The Diary of a Chambermaid* that obstinately refused to permit retribution, and certainly thereby kept my anger alive.

For reasons I am sure I have tediously repeated, I have admired film-makers who seemed to me to really - and, I suppose, with great self-awareness - use true cinematic language, and not use the screen simply to make illustrations of existing text, or make a record - however beautifully and cleverly - of performances which would probably have been as effective on the stage. For these reasons, I have always thought Resnais was a true film-maker, in spite of the fact that he always closely collaborates with writers. I think the big trilogy of *Hiroshima Mon Amour*, *Last Year at Marienbad* and *Muriel* were brilliant films. There is a theory - but maybe it's only an idle game to be played - that the great film-makers are only allowed to make three really good films. In Resnais's case, as with Antonioni's *L'Avventura*, *La Notte* and *Eclipse*, he seems to have made them all together. With somebody like Houston or Kurosawa or Bergman or Altman, or Scorsese, they can be very widely spread apart.

WHAT ARE YOUR THREE? OR HAVEN'T YOU MADE THE FIRST ONE YET?

I hope it's going to be possible to make more films. I'm certainly aware of so many paper films that haven't reached the screen. *The Belly of an Architect* has Étienne-Louis Boullée as its secret hero, an architect whose reputation is based on paper buildings. Perhaps film-makers, like architects, are inevitably condemned to be always making dream projects - projects that never come to pass. I suppose you could call *The Belly of an Architect*, *The Belly of a Film-Maker*. Film-maker and architect share the same need for many collaborators of vastly different disciplines. They are both very costly, they both need large management skills. The film and the building are used and judged by a public that has many constituents. They both have a probable basis in a commission and a producer. They are manoeuvred and circumscribed by financiers, insurance guarantees, contracts with small print. They have to satisfy at the moment of completion and, one hopes, to find satisfaction with succeeding generations of users. They have in some sense to be both practical and aesthetic. They have to be judged in many currencies - money, technique, durability, kudos, aesthetics. And they both have a great many competitors in the market-place - competitors from the past and the present. As in *The Belly of an Architect*, there are not a few occasions when the central initiating figure - the film-maker or the architect - can be forcibly removed from his assignment.

HOW DOES THE FILM DEVELOP FROM THE INITIAL IDEA, WHEN PRESUMABLY IT'S FAIRLY CLEAR? IS IT LIKE HITCHCOCK, WHO HAD IT ALL PLANNED AND SIMPLY HAD TO GET IT DONE?

Frequently I have been asked, especially since I have had a training as a painter and a draughtsman, do I make detailed storyboards before starting a film? My feeling would be that such detailed working out of the movie could mean that essentially the film gets made before the camera turns. If the storyboards were good enough it could imply I could leave and someone else could make the film. There have been times when I've made vague sketches which have got me into trouble. Due to impatience, the sketches have been left unfinished, or decorated with indeterminate squiggles in the bottom left hand corner, marks which subsequently the art department would imagine to be a chest of drawers or a pair of copulating dogs or an asp in a basket. I would arrive on the set a week later and find, not exactly copulating dogs, but maybe an unwanted expensive and elaborate chest of drawers. I feel that rigidly defining an idea, a set or a situation can mean that you do not open yourself to happy accident. A favourite moment in the otherwise very closely controlled film *The Draughtsman's Contract* happens in a wide landscape shot, when the draughtsman returning to the house in a late scene says something like 'Now madam in this day of changing weather ...'. At that moment a large black cloud covered the sun. It would have been impossible either to accurately forecast that sudden change in weather or, considering the wide open landscape, have managed to make it happen by artificial light. Lighting by God.

The cameraman was not keen that I should use the take since the light level had dropped by three stops. Nor were the laboratories too happy about trying to adjust the grading to account for the change within the shot. We used it nevertheless and I believe it was successful.

The films are made on very low budgets - *The Draughtsman's Contract* cost less than

£750,000 in 1982. *The Cook, The Thief, His Wife and Her Lover* cost around £1.5 million. The shooting schedules have to be very practical and well-organised, and the script is often very full of a great many details and detailed instructions, but I am sure there must be room still to allow for the happy accident. I am fortunate in having a sympathetic producer who is happy that I should not draw storyboards. We have nonetheless developed a fairly constant working method to arrange sets and lighting and rehearsals in the mornings, and shoot in the afternoons.

As to where the ideas come from - invariably the ideas have been maturing for a long time - perhaps as vague images, perhaps as ideas pursued in some other form entirely - as a painting. The script ideas for *Drowning by Numbers* had been around for some six years before the subject was filmed, and there were scenarios for the film going back ever further - nostalgic references to the Suffolk coast and phobias about children hanging themselves could be taken back to childhood holidays spent at Southwold and Felixstowe. The final writing of the script came about by finding a structure for the film entirely outside of the narrative - the simple number count of 1 to 100. The initial idea for *The Draughtsman's Contract* arose from spending a summer in a friend's house near Hay-on-Wye, sitting in various chairs left out in the fields and gardens around the house to draw the various facades of the house at different times of the day. When the shadows had changed sufficiently to change the character of the drawing it was time to move to the next chair. The activity was leisurely and pleasurable and often interrupted by domestic errands, a meal, playing with my children, and perhaps being disturbed by the passage of sheep being driven from one field to another across the gardens. All this activity is essentially the plot line of *The Draughtsman's Contract*. A draughtsman, for money, sets about drawing a country house. Admittedly he is distracted by more dramatic events and certainly by more erotic entertainments than I was. But the temporal plan was not dissimilar.

Script ideas have come from a completely different source. In 1981, I wrote a script called *Jonson and Jones* which sounds as if it ought to be set in Chicago, perhaps in the 1920s, but it refers to the partnership and quarrels of Ben Jonson and Inigo Jones in the making of Jacobean court masques. Jones was essentially interested in spectacle and Jonson was interested in the spoken word. Together they put on some thirty to thirty-five masques for James I and Charles I, so despite their disagreements, personal and professional, their collaboration could be seen to be successful. The core of the movie was historically respectable. James had tried to marry his son Charles to the Spanish

Infanta. Charles and Buckingham returned from Spain in total failure. The King was downcast but his subjects were delighted. A marriage with Spain was unpopular.

A masque was arranged to rejoice at the safe return of Charles and to patch up public resentment. It was traditional that the court, including the King, would take part in the masque, they would dance and, within limits, recite and perform, but the strenuous or energetic or dangerous activities would be undertaken by doubles. So throughout the drama there were often two persons playing the same role: the courtly aristocrat would pose in costume, disdaining his double in the same costume, who would fall off the horse, jump from the gallery, fall noisily on his sword, etc.

So the film was about impersonation, fakery, doubling up, various twinnings, getting a substitute to do your dirty work all the way until feigning a death. The project was too expensive - budgeted at £5 million - the history drama making the costs high - but the interest of the Jacobean drama has stayed - and I have thought often of seeing if a modern Jacobean drama was possible, to shift Webster and Ford to the twentieth century - taboo subject matter, melodramatic shifts of mood, operatic drama, extremes of human behaviour, strong religious overtones, humiliations, the notions of shame which are largely foreign to contemporary audiences where good-evil balances are normally restored at the end of the film. Stomach-churning shame is rare in contemporary drama - how about Pinkie's girl in *Brighton Rock* and the priest in Golding's novel, *Rites of Passage* - and the Jacobeans' particular habit of turning the screws of evil to churn in the underbelly - and the feeling of anxiety at unsatisfactory redemption and unresolved revenge that persists after *'Tis Pity She's A Whore* and *The Duchess of Malfi* have ended. I have tried to make these notions of greed, sexual power and sexual humiliation and shame re-surface in a contemporary setting in *The Cook, The Thief, His Wife and Her Lover*. I have been fascinated by the almost unstageable melodramatic moments of great imagery in Jacobean drama - the bloodied heart held high on a dagger in *'Tis Pity*, seemingly an impossible gesture - being a symbol, a metaphor, and a grisly literal truth at one and the same time. For such a gesture consider cannibalism in a contemporary restaurant in a contemporary capital city - it seems as unstageable and as preposterous. But as symbol, metaphor and literal action perhaps it can be pulled off.

YOU YOURSELF SEEM TO BE BOTH JONSON AND JONES, INTERESTED BOTH IN SPECTACLE AND LANGUAGE. WAS THE ABILITY TO USE DIALOGUE - OR AT LEAST LANGUAGE, INITIALLY - IN FILMS A GREAT RELEASE FROM A FRUSTRATION AT WHAT PAINTING COULD NOT GIVE YOU?

I was accused of being too literary when making images at art school. One of the attractions of pursuing imagery in cinema was the possibility of full legitimacy in aligning it with text, words, dialogue. I found excitements in the possibilities of manipulating words and images together, and it of course permits you to do many other things besides. It's conceivably the closest we have reached to the Wagnerian multi-media synthesis, and I have tried to utilise as many aspects of its vocabulary as I can. The strategies are deliberately transparent, the language is used self-consciously. The colour-coding in *The Cook*, with the characters changing the colour of their costumes as they enter a room, is an example. The deliberate objectified camera-moves, staying back from involvement in the action, running the camera deliberately at a parallel to the action, watching the event like you might travel along a painted frieze. The use of complexity of conceit and wordplay in *The Draughtsman's Contract*, the by-play that some might construe as red herrings - though nothing I am sure is ever a complete red herring, everything is ultimately relatable. Many are irritated by this refusal to solely fulfil the canons of the linear narrative, tying ends neatly, finding solutions of completion, locking the whole together in an orthodox manner, sending the audience home satisfied that good has prevailed, a solution has been found, evil has been put back in its box, the waters have been calmed. The frameworks of these films are often tight and classical, which, I believe, gives room for much manoeuvre with-in. My purposes are to make a rich and enriching fabric of reference around the subject under cinematic consideration. This has been a long tradition in painting. It is true it often has to be worked at - but then what human cultural activity has proven worthwhile that has not demanded some reciprocal effort on the part of the viewer, reader or spectator?

I believe that cinema is at its most successful when it acknowledges its own artificiality. As in a fine painting synthesis, you can experience and appreciate the content and see how that content has been arrived at - when you can see the portrait and the brush-strokes that make it - so in cinema. For me - in cinema - there are few who can do this. Resnais, for me, has been the finest example - especially in *Last Year at Marienbad*. Lynch occasionally finds such a marriage. It seems to me that cinema is least successful when it pretends to be about the real, when it pretends to offer a slice of life, when it pretends to offer a frame around a window on the world. When it totally tries to persuade you that it is not cinema. The cinema as total illusory manipulation, to me, has always been suspect, perhaps deceitful. Select a frame, employ an actor, employ an editor, and you are into falsification. Why not admit that falsification? Arrive at some aspect, idea or comment about the world working with your audience with their belief intact, not cajoling them to retreat from believing that all they are seeing is shadows on a screen.

I suppose that one of the devices used in this respect must be the sense of irony. Passion devised by a film-writer, passed over to be played by an actor, then censored and nursed by an editor, then re-inflamed by a composer, is a curious object to be taken seriously. And the business of film-making is not so very special in the world. It is not easy to take the business and industry of film-making very seriously. Current suspicion of narrative and an equivocation about meanings - religious, political, moral - that once - even recently - seemed solid enough - has no doubt made ironists of us all.

The deliberate display of artifice aligned to powerful meaning, all made attractive and entertaining in the most positive way, seemed to me to be successfully reached by Kitaj. He legitimised dramatically for me in a Marlborough Gallery exhibition of paintings in 1963 how it would be possible to marry different styles of presentation, to be elitist if you wanted to, to be happy to shamelessly quote if you thought it relevant, to feel entirely at home with any collaging technique that seemed like multi-media. He also manages to treat politics and sex without restraint and without exhibitionism - not easy. This single painter and the earlier single experience of viewing Bergman's *Seventh Seal*, I suspect set me off first in full pursuit of trying to find my own vocabulary.

THERE ARE RECURRING IMAGES IN YOUR WORK WHICH SEEM TO BE CENTRAL TO YOU AND YOUR FILM-MAKING, CARRYING RIGHT ACROSS THE FEATURE FILMS, THE SHORTER FILMS, AND THE DOCUMENTARIES, WHICH ALSO FOREGROUND ARTIFICIALITY IN A WAY WE DON'T USUALLY ASSOCIATE WITH DOCUMENTARIES. DO YOU SEE A UNITY BETWEEN ALL THE WORKS?

I would like to think so. There is always, I think, a great sense of the presence of a conscious organising principle. Steadily applied and very visible structures which, if they do not dominate, then work very closely with a narrative. However, every film also suggests that the organising principle involved is only a device, a construct. I think all of the films have some sense of ironic stance. Many of them have a sense of black humour. And there are re-occuring images of flying, water and death.

It is true that after many years spent editing and then directing documentaries, and, for a very short spell, working for a TV news service, I became very dubious and suspicious about ideas of documentary truth. Time and time again - and I had some seven years to observe this, involved one way and another in what must have been more than a thousand documentary magazine items and full-length documentaries - I saw half-truths, prefabricated truths, half-lies, reworked truths, statistics swung in favour of truths, evasions which were tantamount to lies, actors employed to be members of the public supposedly offering unrehearsed vox-pop, extras using rehearsed lines written by the researchers, omissions which were deliberately economic with the truth, reconstituted factions which purported to be the real event - all being offered as documentary fact.

On the one hand, as an innocent enthusiast for Flaherty, Jennings, Cavalcanti and Grierson, an enthusiasm which I pursued with easy access to the BFI libraries, and on the other hand, and at the same time, as a practising editor working in a tradition these documentaries had started, it was not long before I became cynical about huge areas of film activity labelled documentary. Eventually Flaherty's documentary methods could be seen to be as bogus as the rest.

I suppose listening to Schlesinger talking about his film *Terminus* - a documentary about Waterloo Station shot in the early sixties which was offered to me at the time as a fine example of the documentary tradition - with all the re-staged events, and forced situations he used to make his film - I could see that some form of transparent honesty would be better offered if there was a total acceptance of artificiality, and a structure that deliberately showed no absolute veracity was being offered. This process of fabrication of the so-called truth - which I could also see was being used in all the fashionable Richard Leacock cinéma-vérité techniques being ushered in when I was learning to handle a camera - all crushed an early ambition I had to make documentaries, and certainly made me very dubious about the whole tradition of the 'naturalist' or 'realist' cinema. Subsequent readings of the films of the Italian neo-realists, and the way that their films were made, further convinced me that the documentary was as much a fabricated item as a feature-film fiction. There are times when *Umberto D* and *Bicycle Thieves* could look almost as phoney as those Harry Enfield Mercury phone commercials - themselves a spoof on the early BBC and COI [Central Office of Information] vox-pops that purported to be real. I suspect it will not be long before we think something similar of the 1960s New Cinema realism.

In the 'artificial documentaries' like *Act of God* and *26 Bathrooms* and *Death in the Seine*, there is certainly a use of established documentary characteristics, the authoritarian voice-over with the educated BBC non-regional voice. The careful presentation of evidence with sober long-shot, medium-shot, and close-up, the bogus notions of 'This must be true because look how carefully and thoroughly and consistently we have reported it.'

Act of God, a thirty-minute TV programme for Thames, was a catalogue of witnesses relating their experiences of being struck by lightning. I wanted to find the most random event and see if it could be systemised - a reduction to absurdity of the notion of statistical research - that by exhausting the probabilities we could arrive at important conclusions - which in the case of lightning strike were as valuable or invaluable as that if your surname initial was L, and you wore a hat, and your favourite colour was blue and you enjoyed spinach - watch out - you are bound to be struck by lightning.

According to the insurance companies, being struck by lightning is about as extreme an Act of God as you can hope to achieve, making them not responsible and not liable. But I had hoped for some Act of God-inspired reactions - some solid eighteenth- and nineteenth-century reactions - victims who had experienced some Road to Damascus conversion, people who, having been struck, would change their attitude to life - but no such luck - this Act of God is no longer an awesome sign of punishment or warning, but simply an unlucky meteorological freak - in England at least. Perhaps it's different in Mexico or Calcutta where I am told some graveyards are overflowing with victims of lightning strike. Whereas I tried hard to report faithfully on all the witnesses' statements to camera, the circumstances of filming them were patently artificial - in composition, stance, lighting and incidental happening, and certainly the editing was self-conscious and extra-frame - rigorously imposed as a system that did not take its pace, measure or empathy from the witnesses themselves and was obviously very contrived.

Act of God was made at the same time as *The Falls* - a bogus documentary, using the same techniques but - transparently - it was a fiction. However, such was the plausibility of some of the fictional events in *The Falls*, and so absurd did some of the factual events seem in *Act of God*, that a confusion of fact and fiction was ever present, setting up many notions about presentation of image, use of sound, reality, artifice, and the conventions we use to do all these things. In the end, just as perhaps there is no such thing as history, only historians, perhaps there is no such thing as news - only news reporters.

The habit of telling tales and reporting news and exchanging statistics continues in the feature films. Characters in *The Draughtsman's Contract* tell one another stories. The brothers in *A Zed and Two Noughts* fire statistics at one another. It is a way of multiplying the communication, expanding the viewpoint, aiding the main narrative by elliptical asides that, by counterpoint, fashion and qualify and enlarge, I hope, on the fabric of the content of the film. I enjoy too the freedom that this fragmentary approach permits. Some of the films are becoming aggressively narrative-bound in a conventional way. I look back to the narrative freedoms of *The Falls* with something of a wish to return there to take the ideas further. There are one or two projects planned for the future that might allow this to happen.

ABOUT THOSE KEY IMAGES, OR MOTIFS, LIKE WATER, AND FLASHING LIGHT ...

Water, certainly. I am not so certain about the flashing light. There are other images - vomiting, paper burning, sheep, a hand holding a pen, groups of people eating, certainly groups of people at tables in the act of taking a meal. As in painting you don't actually see the food and drink entering the mouth too often. You will not see a mouth chewing or biting in Veronese. And it's difficult to talk and speak at the same time successfully. People sitting in the open, eating, are not infrequent. Le déjeuner sur l'herbe, picnicking. These returning images were not conscious at first. Now they have been pointed out - I admit their use has more than once been a self-reference, a pastiche.

There are other devices, images, characteristics, you could almost call them visual tics - I could make a list - a concern for seeing people and objects through bars or cages or slatted shadows, people entering left and exiting right in frames that are held very statically. When the camera does track, it normally tracks left to right. Static frames with deliberate distances seen as holes within the frame with the light retreating in an alternating pattern of strict light and dark. And of course the static frame in general. For me the camera has begun to move a great deal more - though generally in a very fixed way - a steady move - as objective as possible - certainly not corresponding to an actor or extra's activities, certainly not permitting the action to make the camera activity its slave. You are right - there are many favourite motifs that are repeated, but then who doesn't use a favourite motif repeatedly? And the major obsessions repeat because there is no end to the permutations and variations on a given theme, especially if that theme is sex and death. The painter Renoir said to the film-maker Renoir that artists have maybe one or two main ideas and spend the whole of their lives repeating them. He hastily added that one or two ideas could be more than enough for a lifetime.

Another formal returning motif is symmetry. I have a delight in painters like the three Bellinis who used symmetry very dramatically, and the Renaissance *sacra conversazione* traditions of the saints and donors grouped around the Virgin or an altar - figures circulating languidly around a fulcrum that exactly bisects the frame. I would like to believe the use of symmetry is always relative to the subject matter in hand; *A Zed and Two Noughts* was obsessive about twinship, duality, the left hand balancing the right hand, the dominance of two in human anatomy - eyes, ears, nostrils, breasts, lungs, arms, hands, ovaries, testicles, legs, feet - and of symmetry generally in all animal and vegetable life - symmetry a condition of life. If a tree is not symmetrical in its general outline - and many are - then its leaf will be symmetrical, or a cross section of its trunk will indicate symmetry. The desire to be identical governs the twins in *A Zed and Two Noughts*, making a pair, left and right balancing out. There's a use of symmetry in *The Belly of an Architect* related not to the same concerns, but towards those of a classical architect which is characterised by symmetrical balance and harmony. Many images in this film are seen very much as a classical or neoclassical architect would see them - through facades and plans and elevations that have a geometrician's regard for arithmetical symmetry - entrance in the centre, each facade having a determined bisecting line. The cameraman's eye is the eye of a classical architect. The only time you see a very strong compositional diagonal in *The Belly of an Architect* is when the architect dies and the symmetrical classical grid of horizontals and verticals collapses. Suddenly you view events and structures from a corner, not from a straight edge that is parallel to the picture plane.

Because of a self-consciousness about framing, and the formal devices used to construct a picture, I have taken much interest in finding a marriage between the form and the content so both reflect the other's concerns.

A self-consciousness about the use of light has also been a characteristic. When Sacha Vierny and I started work on *A Zed and Two Noughts* we closely examined the paintings of Vermeer. Godard suggests Vermeer was one of the first cinematographers because he is primarily interested in the two most important elements of cinema - the world modelled entirely by light, and the event of the split second; the maid pouring the milk from the jug didn't happen a second before, didn't happen a second later. We also noted that the light for Vermeer invariably entered the painting from the left hand side, and at about a metre and a half off the ground - this simple equation became a device for lighting the film.

The interest in Vermeer spread in the film beyond his image-making to his life off-canvas, and to his reputation after death. In 1890 when Vermeer's reputation was revitalised there were reputed to be something like 40 Vermeers in existence. By 1935 the total of attributions was reported to be in excess of something like 300 and by the 1950s it had gone down again to about 50, and now, by general recognition there are only, I am told, 26 truly authenticated Vermeers. *The Lady in the Red Hat* in Washington is now under criticism as a dubious attribution. All of which reflects an interest in his painting that is relative to a desire for more of him, perhaps to deal in his paintings as a fashionable commodity, and in improvements in art scholarship. The Vermeer faker Van Meegeren found encouragement to paint more Vermeers through the interest of German wartime collectors, though it is difficult now to imagine why anyone was taken in - but such was the desire to own a Vermeer, the undiscriminating were not difficult to deceive. Van Meegeren as a faker of animals, along the lines of Wells's Dr Moreau, entered *A Zed and Two Noughts*, and so did Vermeer's mistress, Caterina Bolnes. The style of the film relating to the paintings, I hoped, was complemented by the paintings' origins, provenance, and the details - some apocryphal - that we know of Vermeer's not over-advertised life.

The cinematic dramatic lighting of Caravaggio and de La Tour were intended to be influences in *The Draughtsman's Contract*. The work of certain mid-Victorian painters was important to *Drowning by Numbers*. Not the work so much of the Pre-Raphaeltes, but painters also working alongside them and influenced by them from about 1849-1860 - Arthur Hughes, William Dyce, William Windus, Madox Brown. I hope the influences of the painted images are fully integrated into the film images - quite extraordinary images of English landscape - not unmindful that these strong observations of mood and minutiae of English landscape were also intended to work as moral lessons. With Holman Hunt particularly they were often severely improving sermons whose ramifications are now scarcely tenable, but the symbols and metaphors are not lost - some more obvious than others - the death's-head moth, the bitter apples, the burning autumn leaves, sunsets, graveyards, dead trees, and certainly both a very English and a very biblical use of sheep - lost among the brambles on a dangerous cliff-top, let loose in the corn, bright and white in the strong sunlight - and the scapegoat in the desert. The Pre-Raphaelites were convinced that in a pre-literate population, visual symbols were strong and understood - like the Dutch references of broken lute strings, women with caged birds, bitten pomegranates, peeled lemons - a vocabulary of proverbs, homilies, fables, edifying tales which we are led to believe the man on the street in Dordrecht or Utrecht or Delft would fully understand. That particular language so relative to Christian beliefs and Dutch bourgeois ambitions has now disappeared, although I am sure it has been replaced - not so disciplined or codified no doubt, but by different sorts of metaphorical language. An examination I suppose of the imagery that's contained in advertising, commercials and pop videos would probably find an equivalent range of metaphorical meanings.

I believe it is legitimate to utilise the two thousand years of image-making that we are all heir to - to examine the encyclopaedic collection that has been amassed. To consider it, homage and refer to it. It is there for examination, appraisal, speculation, and re-use as our Western imagistic tradition.

Cinema is still, at one hundred years, extremely young, and there is much evidence that traditional celluloid cinema is already on the wane. Whatever is said about locally increasing audiences, they are still far below the great popular cinema days of the forties and fifties. The centre of popular fascination and interest is now elsewhere. But if traditional cinema does change thanks to social habit and new technological advance - certainly initially into something more televisual ... I'm sure people will always be painting and drawing when cinema or its successors are long gone. That continuity is important and I'd like to be a part of it.

There's much to say about television being now more innovative and exciting and certainly less conservative than cinema. Because of the structures, people and primarily money that go into making feature films it can indeed be an extraordinarily conservative medium. Channel Four with projects like the *Four American Composers* and *A TV Dante* supplied me with the space, perhaps, to produce more exciting and innovative work than perhaps I could have managed in cinema.

YOU GO TO SOME PAINS TO INTRODUCE YOUR WORK TO YOUR AUDIENCE; BUT ARE YOU HAPPY FOR PEOPLE TO BRING THEIR OWN MEANINGS AND INTERPRETATIONS TO YOUR WORK?

I am sure that however and with whatever seriousness and single intent you manufacture a work, when you let it go you must know that it is going to be interpreted and indeed used by sensibilities not always directly in line with your own - often in fact directly opposed to your own. I have grown used to this now but I was not a little surprised to find that *The Draughtsman's Contract* had apparently so many contradictory interpretative possibilities, and provided so many cudgels to shake. It was reviewed as a piece of pro-establishment propaganda and as an anti-establishment diatribe; it was regarded as pro-Thatcherite and anti-Thatcherite; it was heavily censored as being anti-feminist, and applauded for being pro-feminist. I was labelled a misogynist and a misanthrope, but also a serious commentator on the Married Woman's Property Act and morganatic inheritance laws. It was described as cold and intellectual but also as sensuous and romantic. In a lighter vein, one critic saw the movie as being an exposition of a classic English league football game with players in opposing colours, changing strip at half-time, with ripped shirts, illegal offside favours and own goals. Opponents with less irony and a strict Marxist-feminist programme to pursue at that time saw it as the wrong sort of movie in which the BFI should invest their small funds - which in hindsight is curious seeing that *Orlando* has been described as *The Draughtsman's Contract* for the nineties and at one time or another tried to involve most of my collaborators including Kassander, Vierny and Nyman, and captured Ben van Os and Jan Roelfs to win them an Oscar nomination. And Alan Parker with Barry Norman and eight million viewers as witnesses vowed to educate his children abroad if the maker of *The Draughtsman's Contract* was permitted to make another film. Peter Sainsbury of the BFI said I should be so lucky that sufficient interpretations and reactions were considered necessary.

WOULD YOU GO AS FAR AS ELIOT'S POSITION WHEN HE SAID THAT HE WAS NO BETTER QUALIFIED TO SAY '*The Waste Land* IS ABOUT X' THAN ANYBODY ELSE?

Eliot's remark I am sure was deliberately disingenuous - perhaps to preserve what Braque suggested, that too many proofs spoil the truth. I am aware certainly that too much self-interpretation can sound like justification and not explanation. But I have no wish to mystify, or erect deliberate barriers of incomprehension. I believe the films are rational. I am not a surrealist. I have definite points of view as to what I believe I am manufacturing at the time, and I have little sympathy with the film-maker who hides behind false inarticulateness - with the sort of shrugging defence of 'I do what I do because that's what I do'.

It's sometimes harder to agree with a favourable report arrived at, as I see it, for the wrong reasons, than to deal with an unfavourable view argued with conviction. I am still - two years after the event - in almost weekly correspondence with a German critic and an Australian film-maker - both women - who continue to take very strong issue about *The Baby of Mâcon*.

I used to feel irritated about easy categories like a criticism suggesting that *The Draughtsman's Contract* was about painting and death, *A Zed and Two Noughts* was about animals and death, *The Belly of an Architect* was about architecture and death, *Drowning by Numbers* was about numbers and death, *The Cook, The Thief, His Wife and Her Lover* was about food and death. But I admit to a small pleasure about cross-over possibilities where *Waterworld* was critically rechristened *Drowning by Numbers* and an article [in the *Guardian*] about the attacks on the architect of the new British Library was headlined *The Belly of an Architect.*

IN *A Zed and Two Noughts* THERE WAS OBVIOUSLY AN INTEREST IN SYMMETRY AS CONTENT - THERE WAS THE SCENE WITH ALBA WHERE, AS ALWAYS, SHE WAS SHOWN IN BED IN A VERY SYMMETRICAL SHOT, AND THE TWINS WERE EITHER SIDE OF HER, AND THE ONLY FLAW IN THE SYMMETRY WAS IN THE VIEWER'S IMAGINATION, BECAUSE UNDERNEATH THE BEDCLOTHES SHE HAS A LEG MISSING - AND AS A VIEWER, YOU GET THAT - THEN AT A LATER POINT THE DIALOGUE ACTUALLY DISCUSSES SYMMETRY; AND I FELT THAT IF THE DIALOGUE HAD TO DO THAT, HAD TO UNDERLINE A POINT THAT HAD ALREADY BEEN MADE SO STRONGLY VISUALLY, THEN PERHAPS THERE WAS A LACK OF CONFIDENCE IN THE AUDIENCE. WHEREAS IN *The Belly of an Architect* THERE'S JUST ONE REFERENCE TO THE FACT THAT CASPASIAN IS WORKING ON PIRANESI, AND AS KRACKLITE GOES DOWNHILL THERE IS ONE MOMENT WHEN HE IS FRAMED AGAINST SCAFFOLDING THAT IS REMINISCENT OF A PIRANESI PRISON, AND THAT POINT WAS MADE PURELY VISUALLY.

I am sure you could be right about the symmetry - a lack of nerve that my fascination with the body's relentless regard for dualities stressed in dialogue by twins - the ultimate human symmetry - wasn't coming over strongly enough. I have only recently read new confirmations about twinship that suggest at least ten per cent - and maybe more - of all conceptions result in twin embryos, one of which, ninety-five times out of a hundred, perishes in the womb, and is mourned for evermore, having to be recreated and substituted by a stranger in a later adult pair bond. Maybe this is a Darwinian imperative - create an involuntary longing in the womb for a lost partner that has to be fulfilled to produce the circumstances for procreation. What are the statistics on true twins pair-bonding with strangers to produce children on their own? The information seemed to go further to suggest that these original embryonic twinships are true symmetrical left-right twinships with normally the right-handed twin making it into the world, proving, since this is normal, twinship neither one way nor the other. But if a left-handed twin is born, then he or she is surely the survivor of twins, proving the superstition of the sinister to the prejudiced that his twin was slain in the womb - a predetermination not proven by Cain and Abel, and Romulus and Remus until their adulthood.

Perhaps it wasn't a lack of confidence in the audience, but a lack of confidence in being certain that I had communicated my interests. I have always hoped the films were nicely encyclopaedic - amputees, zoo specialists, Darwin scholars, Van Meegeren fans might be as critical of the film as cultural referees would be of stating the unnecessary. I remember Annabel Wright, the COI producer who first hired me as a director many years ago, saying the pantheon of gods in *A Zed and Two Noughts* was too obvious to follow once you realised de Milo, the zoo prostitute, was the Venus who had no arms in a world where heroines had no legs. But a *Daily Mail* writer said how come Jim Davidson was everyone's pimp and messenger and wore a pair of wings on his cap? I am slow at picking up pop-cultural references that my children would take as ringed in red. Maybe your erudition travelled to places where some other eruditions don't reach.

DO YOU WORRY ABOUT THAT SORT OF POINT?

Am I worried that I need to signal such things? I'm sure the messenger is to blame if he makes the message unclear - especially if he considers himself to be a professional messenger. Perhaps he deserves to be shot for dereliction of duty.

I THOUGHT THE MOST EFFECTIVE REFERENCE IN *A Zed and Two Noughts* WAS TO MUYBRIDGE, WHO WAS BEAUTIFULLY QUOTED AND TURNED, BUT WHO WASN'T TALKED ABOUT, UNLIKE VAN MEEGEREN AND SO ON, WHICH AS AN ART HISTORIAN I OBVIOUSLY KNEW ABOUT, SO, IN A SENSE, I FELT VERY FLATTERED BY ...

Perhaps Muybridge is now a fully-fledged public cross-over figure. Advertisers use him more than enough - he must now equal Magritte and Dali as a visually quotable source that most will recognise. I've found French curators who mischievously confuse Muybridge with Marey, and one student who thought the photographs were taken by Francis Bacon to make his own personal source-library.

Muybridge is also quoted in *A TV Dante*, using the photos perhaps in a way Muybridge might have wished - as stock - stock for 'a man walking', stock for 'everyman', and, more elaborately - as from the strip *Man walking downstairs* - as Christ walking down into Hell - following the theological necessity that Christ was God remade as man, every man.

In *A Zed and Two Noughts*, the intention was to make a double-take quote - quoting Francis Bacon quoting Muybridge's *Animal Locomotion* studies - with the animal specimens - this time, not alive but locomoting with the movements of decay - presented on the meticulously squared-up backgrounds. It's meant to be a pre-cinema quote as well - Muybridge quoted as proto-cineaste, pre-cineaste, moving the still picture into the moving picture, relative to what the two natural historians Oliver and Oswald were doing in the film with their stop-motion photography.

I enjoy, as I suspect you do, the art historical reference - it's legitimate material, it's the way the image-making process works, it's the information which makes looking at any image that much richer. Of course there are different ways of making the reference, different degrees of digesting or absorbing it. It's probably always easier to be certain of making the point by a vocal or textual quote because our educational systems are geared that way. Terry Gilliam's painting quotes in film are rarities. As in a different way is the *Dr No* visual quote of the missing Goya Wellington, based on the act of the painting's theft not on its image. I am sure visual references have all too often to be nudged into value by textual or aural pointers. Cinema relies so heavily on its soundtrack, that one can often suppose that it's scarcely a visual medium at all. Think of the yards of dialogue track in an average movie - so often the film operates to see the lips move, not the visuals speak. Perhaps cinema's a case of soundtrack with images rather than images with soundtrack. Considering that the manufacture of a film follows the directions of a textual script, that should be no surprise. And it's particularly true of television; turn the television soundtrack off, and on average with the majority of soundtrack voice-over, voice-on, voice-off programming, within five minutes you are losing comprehension.

As regards this situation and the general area of your question, I doubt whether I was successful in communicating the self-reflexive visual programme in *The Belly of an Architect* by visuals alone. The film debates whether immortality is possible through art. It starts with visual imagery in the Vittoriano that supports the concept of man reproducing himself in terms of sculpture and statuary - perhaps the most sophisticated mimetic three-dimensional art representation - the visual space around Kracklite is full of sculptural representations. The sculpture then gives way to Kracklite's image being associated with painting - more abstracted, more created, three dimensions into two. Then the preponderance of painted images of man on the walls of the baths where Kracklite goes to recuperate gives way to photographic representations, which in turn are replaced with the banalities of the photocopied representation. Sculpture then painting then photographs then photocopies.

Working backwards, there are more photocopies in the world than there are photographs, more photographs than there are paintings, more paintings than there are sculptures. As the banalities of representation increase so do their number and proliferation, which is also reflected in the effort used to make them and indeed the financial value and cost of manufacturing them, and also a growing increase in the uses of a machine. In a sense the photocopy is the most exact copy of its original, a true cloning, but its purposes are scarcely art and its uses essentially practical. The greater the accuracy the lesser the value, aesthetically and economically. In essence, man reproduces his representation with increasing and cheaper exactness but with decreasing effect. Maybe in the immortality stakes of the art-object itself, the stone or bronze will outlast the oil-paint and the panel or canvas, which in turn will probably be more durable than the photographic negative and print which will last longer than the photocopied paper.

In the film, in all this visual elaboration there is no mention in text or dialogue of these ideas - all are presented visually as a background and adjunct to the film's other concerns - but I read and hear nowhere at all of any acknowledgement or appreciation of this - what price your optimism for a visual programme understood? Maybe aural or textual pointers are indeed necessary?

Those other concerns the film attempts to address through the job definition and character of the artist/architect in a film which could have been called *The Belly of a Film-Maker* are questions asked around the responsibilities of any architect or artist or film-maker. Or indeed architect/artist/film-maker. On the one hand public versus private responsibilities. On the other, questions of validity of art creation. No architect builds merely to provide a roof and guttering and a place to sleep. Why, in so many words, be an architect, or a painter, or a film-maker etc.? Was Kracklite an architect or merely a sham architect? Kracklite recycles art in the form of his homage to Boullée. That is a question not a million miles from myself as a film-maker homaging de La Tour or Vermeer or Hals or Resnais. The fact that Boullée himself was a paper architect puts him in the centre of contemporary conceptualism and makes him, as I found with a Swiss architect, as important as any architect who ever built a public building, not merely designed it. More so perhaps. For they built and found themselves imperfect. Boullée never built and found untested perfection. I asked the same architect whether he would agree that you can have a valid conceptual baker - a man who dreams up bread-plans but never bakes. He had to agree that you could. The making of paper-architecture and the making of paper films is, I am sure, a fair analogy - never have two professions shared so many frustrations of so many untried and untested and unmade dreams. If you are interested in immortality then perhaps it's best to be an architect - think of the evidence in bricks and marble and imperishable stone. What price the immortality ticket for a film-maker with brittle celluloid and fading emulsion? Is art anyway a ticket to immortality - if so, how? How can it be done? Make *Gone with the Wind*, *Jaws*, *ET* or *Jurassic Park*, certainly not *The Belly of an Architect*. This film, I suppose and hope, represents me asking some of these questions, musing, ruminating, speculating about these problems, about these significances. What do I intend? What am I supposed to be doing?

In the end of course the film comes down heavily - perhaps too heavily and too neatly to hear the cry of a baby - intimating that Darwinian proliferation is the only means to immortality - man-made art is denied the immortality status.

CAN I ASK YOU ABOUT THE ROLE OF CRITICISM WITH REGARD TO YOUR KIND OF FILM-MAKING, WHICH SETS UP A NUMBER OF REFERENCES AND A NUMBER OF SYSTEMS. ARE CONTINENTAL CRITICS MORE READY TO FIT IT INTO A WIDER CONTEXT OF IMAGE-MAKING?

I certainly look at the criticism in newspapers and film journals and consider what they are interested in - I make comparisons between the English and foreign comment on my films. The most heartening reviews I have ever read were in Dublin newspapers - not necessarily always favourable, but perceptive and encouraging. I used to believe that the French situation of film appreciation was of greater sophistication than the English in their terms of enquiry and relationships with the total cultural field - though, I am told, the new French critics are by no means as familiar with the possibilities of film language as their post-*nouvelle-vague* predecessors - the template for comment being now essentially the Hollywood tradition which sets standards and creates the sliding rule of comparisons. It is sad and tragic that a reduced availability of presenting alternative cinema seriously affects critical appreciation - but it's not surprising - criticism and comment relies on making comparisons with other examples, not by making comparisons with life - and if the material to compare is not available or viewable or obtainable - and, in the end, no longer made in the face of the very same ignorance - then what price change? We must patiently wait for the templates to exhaust themselves - which of course they will.

Reading and considering what film comment seems to want to see does indeed make me feel often like a hippopotamus in a giraffe race, or, when I'm feeling superior, like a giraffe in a hippopotamus race. Both these creatures inhabit the same terrain, are mammals, are vegetarian, and have certainly become highly - even exorbitantly - specialised - perhaps too specialised in a Darwinian sense - but communication between them seems as good as nil except to glare at one another at the watering hole.

I know for certain that it is more interesting for me to talk to a painting historian or an art critic like yourself because my terms and attitudes are rooted in what you know and have studied. My ambition has always been to try and bring that sort of language, those criteria, that vocabulary, those processes into cinema - and not ivory-tower cinema, but mainstream cinema.

We have been talking about reference and quotation. Although everyone does this constantly in conversation and text, journalism and literature - it's essential to our processing of memory without which there is no culture - there is often a resistance to the prospect of being permitted to do it with legitimacy in cinema. Art-networking has always been legitimate and honourable - Moore quotes and references Michelangelo, Picasso and Bacon reference Velasquez, Manet references Titian. The Renaissance referenced the classical world, Neoclassicism references classicism. It's good to be a member of the club. But the membership is open. No exclusions. There's no bouncer on the door and no club secretary. It's there for all to see, use, enjoy and meditate upon. Painters legitimately standing on another's shoulders to try and see the next horizon, and over it.

It is the English commentators who often search for the easy keys - they believe there must be a Rosebud. The traditional hierarchy of English education and its relevant snobbisms graciously permit or retract permission to speak. The traditions they have, on occasions, permitted themselves in my direction, are comparisons to Powell and Pressburger on the upside, Russell on the downside. Apart from *Peeping Tom* I am not a great fan of the first, whereas I have always enjoyed *The Devils*, and remember Ben Kingsley more for his playing of Russell's Rossetti than Attenborough's *Gandhi*. A critic once wrote I was the intellectual Ken Russell - when I asked her to comment further she replied - 'Oh, did I say that?'

Continental critics search for genre analogies. I have been pleased to be variously considered to be part of the traditions of Monty Python, the Hammer House of Horror, Carry On Filming. Amused accusations of dandyism were current after *The Cook, The Thief, His Wife and Her Lover*. The French newspaper *Libération* is always hostile. *Positif* has always been positive thanks to Michel Simon who is always encouraging and wise. The Germans have recently talked of Melancholy and the Grotesque. The Catalans and Slovaks, feeling Wales is a similarly underprivileged and comparable political ally, have strenuously pushed the fact that I was born in Gwent. A Polish university rowing eight have just christened their new boat *Drowning by Numbers* - I cannot tell you whether it's with affection or disdain. In general, as a first step, anglophile eccentricity is amicably accorded me, though there is respect for a cinema of ideas which the French can easily fit into their traditions, and a delight in the Baroque which the Italians feel very comfortable with.

RETURNING TO A PREVIOUS POINT, A FRENCH FILM LIKE *Death in a French Garden* CAN ASSUME VISUAL LITERACY, AND CAN USE BALTHUS EXTENSIVELY, FOR EXAMPLE ...

The references are used without special effort. Working with Sacha Vierny and often with a French or French-speaking - Belgian or Swiss - camera crew, I am aware that their film language and reference is rich. Although needlessly over-sensitive about canteen meals, the French crew will use a painter's name like a common adjective. A film-shot Mantegna is any lying figure seen feet-up. We can legitimately talk about sitting Mantegnas. And Sacha will discuss standing Mantegnas if pushed. A Renoir focus speaks for itself. Crossing the line unprofitably brings up Magritte, profitably, *Las Meninas*. To make a Crivelli is a little arcane - making a miracle but showing how it's made - like the Crivelli haloes attached to the head of a saint with an iron strap. The business of table-painting sets up problems. Relative to the images in *The Cook, The Thief, His Wife and Her Lover*, quoting table-paintings from Leonardo, Hals, Veronese, to Van Gogh's *Potato Eaters* meant frequent masking of seated diners by other seated diners. The French have been there many times before, and refer to the problem using a standard film-term related to the English word 'machicolations' - the alternating top-openings of a castle wall. Perhaps I should work with English-speaking film crews more often to make favourable comparisons. It's a rich semi-private etymology - full of xenophobia and male chauvinism - Paganinis, dollies, blondes, redheads, brunettes.

YOU'VE BEEN WORKING ON ANOTHER DROWNING FILM, ABOUT DROWNINGS IN PARIS, *Death in the Seine*.

I'd come across Richard Cobb's book, *Death in Paris*. He'd discovered a mortuary archive in the Bibliothèque Nationale, supplied by two morgue assistants, Boule and Daude, who in the years just after the French Revolution had very carefully, if naively, written up accounts of corpses they'd been responsible for between 1790 and 1801, years that would include the Terror, the Directoire and the Consulate. I think they recorded something like six hundred bodies brought to them to identify, of which 410 were taken out of the River Seine. It was a list of death, a catalogue of corpses - incomplete, unfinished - like all catalogues - providing findings and statistics which, as always, asked more questions than they provided answers. What I wanted to do was to attempt some sort of resurrection of these people dredged dripping from the Seine - the people of the Paris crowd just after the Revolution. Because the TV programme was short at forty minutes, we chose some twenty-three subject-cases to provide a cross-section, representing likely murder, suicide, industrial accident, drunkenness, disposal of a body after robbery, teenage pregnancy.

The mortuary assistants had recorded in a haphazard fashion details of sex, hair colour, physical wounds, details of clothing and contents of the pockets, and, where witnesses and relatives had come forward with information or to identify or collect the corpses, some indication of the corpse's profession or trade or circumstances. These mortuary notes are largely about what these two morgue assistants see and not what they know - perhaps a similar concept to that which governs *The Draughtsman's Contract*.

These lists of bold uncomplicated facts are often poignant, always unsentimental. The naked woman in her seventies, who is dredged ashore clasping two leeks in her left hand. A boy whose pockets contain a bent nail and a button and length of string - then as now familiar. Sometimes the initials of the clothing's laundry marks did not fit the initials of the corpse. Sometimes the wounds on the corpse could have been caused by the body bumping against the piers of a Seine bridge or maybe were the marks of foul play. I wanted to make a catalogue-movie presenting the mortuary-note facts via representations with present day subjects pretending to be corpses - dredged from water, sometimes revived, searched for clues, open to interpretation. It is possible to match the very hot summers and the very cold winters of those eleven-odd years – that persuaded Parisians, especially children, to go swimming and skating - with the tragic consequences of their enthusiasms.

The image of the drowned female in this list was tragically frequent. Cobb makes surmises - April is the favourite month for young female suicides - nine months after summer. Whereas hanging was the favoured method of suicide for males without access to gunpowder, drowning was favoured by females. Unrequited love, unwanted pregnancy.

I was also working at the same time on the scenario for an opera set in a swimming pool, to be called *Massacre at the Baths*, where death was by drowning - prominent among the characters were Ophelia and Virginia Woolf, and as a side-show, Marat dying in his bath, and as the heroic lovers, Hero and Leander.

ONE OF MY FAVOURITE PICTURES IS TURNER'S *Hero and Leander* IN THE NATIONAL GALLERY ...

The gap is wide between the original and reproductions of it. Size and texture is a surprise on a revisit. You think you are familiar with the image, often reproduced, then seeing a Turner again is disturbing, though I am sometimes surprised about what he thought he could get away with in the figure drawing. I like those Turners in the Clore Gallery that have been left unframed. They look like white textured holes in the wall - or like Monets. Without a frame, seeing how he took the paint around the edge of the canvas - as they are hung, they are certainly objects, not through-a-window illusions - anticipating painters that are much more recent to us than Monet.

THE LAST TIME I SAW MONET'S *Water Lilies* IN PARIS, IT WAS THE MOST EXTREME SORT OF PAINTING I'D COME ACROSS, FAR MORE EXTREME THAN MANY AVANT-GARDE WORKS OF THE TIME - TO TAKE REALISM TO THAT LIMIT AND THAT SCALE, WITH THE CENTRE OF IT SOMETHING COMPLETELY TRANSIENT AND UNDEFINED - YOU COULDN'T GET THAT IN PHOTOGRAPHY, YOU COULDN'T GET THAT PLAY ON FOCUS, YOU'D HAVE TO CHOOSE BETWEEN SURFACE AND REFLECTION AND HE REFUSES TO. DO YOU GET FRUSTRATED EVER OVER PAINTERLY EFFECTS THAT YOU WANT THAT THE CAMERA CAN'T GIVE YOU?

There was one particular example. In making *Drowning by Numbers*, a country bourgeois drama of sorts - with great use of bright sunlight in interiors full of flowers, furniture and stuffs, I wanted to use the painting characteristics of Vuillard. I enjoy the way that his people become etherealised up against wallpaper and upholstered furniture, so that the wallpaper and the clothing and the carpets and the characters become one in the same light. His people often become united with the armchairs and settees they are sitting in. Flesh and cloth melt together. But we couldn't get it. Sacha made some tests. We did some experiments and it didn't work. It was no good throwing the focus a little, or putting the equivalent of Vaseline on the lens and making it feel soft - it just looked like a bad Hovis advert. There was no way that we could tone and synthesise everything. The best bet was to rely heavily on the art department to over-emphasise pattern and texture with restricted colour. We considered painting people's faces so that they were the same colour as the wallpaper. It was OK when Juliet Stevenson was still and in the appropriate light but as soon as she moved the artifice would fall apart. I know that the exercise was as much to do with capturing the cosy, comatose intimacy of Vuillard - people - family, children, relatives, friends - often seated, often asleep or dozing in summer light - as to do with abstracted cinema-painting language. The sitting-room of the film's first drowning in the bath-tub with Joan Plowright and Bernard Hill has something of the ambition - but not at all to say we were anywhere near successful at honouring some of those Vuillard comfortable sitting-rooms looking through open doors into sunlit gardens. We abandoned the attempt but we'll try again sometime - but the chances of the same content asking for the same style is not perhaps likely to come again.

Honouring a painter or a painting enthusiasm, and I delight in it in a way others might delight in honouring a favourite author, there are constant and amusing pitfalls. A constant frustration is the question of space and perspective. If you look carefully at della Francesca, who has an obsessive and complicated concern for perspective, he's probably using some dozen different perspective systems in one image. Unless you deliberately built the set with false perspectives, you cannot compete. But false perspectives only work from a given fixed point, so the chances of taking the della Francesca as a starting point to develop and move into other cinematic concerns, is not so profitable.

With Renier van Brummelen, Sacha's lighting partner on the film-sets, we are lighting many exhibitions with the equivalent of false perspectives in using light projections which have been - in some cases - very heavily keystoned - placing silhouettes, masks and gobos in the light-beams to light impossible angles with amazing accuracy - which gives encouragement to imagine all sorts of possibilities. Much of this knowledge came from working in the Amsterdam Opera House on *Rosa* - where the fixed stage proscenium and the rigid auditorium seating meant it was impossible - unlike on a film-set - to put your lights exactly where you wanted to. To examine these quite small lighting masks in your hand, is to see very large distortions - as excessive as the distorted skull in the National Gallery Holbein's *Ambassadors* - but by computer-calculating the necessary distances and angles, the distortions are righted over great distances to produce surprisingly large image-projections - light almost literally can be made to travel round corners or squeezed through nearly-shut windows and nearly-closed doors, through letter-boxes and keyholes.

Concerns for borrowing painting's use of aerial perspective in the cinema are often frustrated as well. You've got to be very strict about where you put your lights in order to get that sense of recession - to flatten as in a Japanese watercolour where foreground and background are of the same substance, or infinitely extend as in a Bellini landscape where the distances can be physically walked but where every object is still very sharp and in focus. The cornfield studio sequences in *Prospero's Books* with Mark Rylance were fine if the camera stayed still, but as soon as it travelled the illusion became transparent. Sacha suggested the use of the old painting trick of making the sky darker than the land - always beautiful and dramatic - used by Hobbema and Rubens and later by Constable - such that by making the audience feel God himself was using a theatrical trick on real landscape, an audience can be lured into a belief that the cinema's theatrical trick is only recreating a known reality.

Discussing these objectives with Sacha is fascinating and entertaining. Not a painter or particularly knowledgeable about painting, he is intrigued about how to achieve means to an end. After talking about the industrial tenebrism of Joseph Wright of Derby for the yet unmade *35 Men on Horseback*, or artificial rainbows for *A Zed and Two Noughts*, or special lighting phenomena like St Elmo's fire and shooting stars and the Aurora Borealis for *Prospero's Books*, or architecture lit by fireworks in *The Belly of an Architect* and again in *The Pillow Book*, he will consider the problem for an hour or so and always come back with an ingenious solution of how to do it.

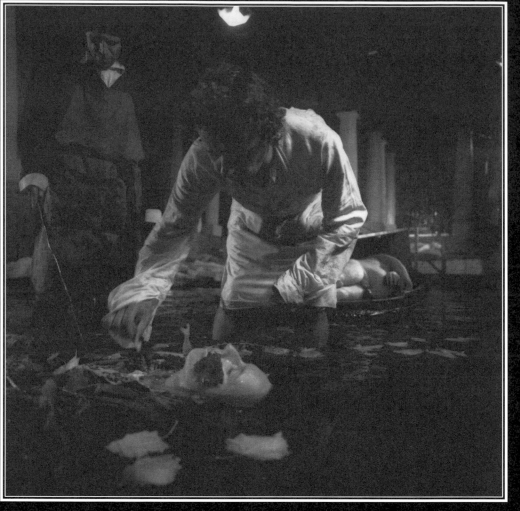

Death in the Seine

CONTINUAL EXCITEMENT

The second interview was conducted as editing continued on *The Pillow Book*.

THERE IS A REMARK RIGHT AT THE END OF THE TAPE OF OUR FIRST INTERVIEW, A REMARK WHICH IS ALSO AN ECHO OF A PASSAGE OF DIALOGUE IN *The Draughtsman's Contract*, WHERE YOU SAY THAT INTELLIGENT PAINTERS MAKE BAD PAINTERS. THE QUESTION IS ALMOST TOO OBVIOUS TO ASK AN ARTIST WHO IS ALWAYS BEING CALLED TOO CLEVER OR ESOTERIC, BUT I'D LIKE TO BEGIN THERE.

The reference in *The Draughtsman's Contract* was brought about, I suspect, by opinions I had - and have - about painters whose reputation is obviously related towards some forefronting of their intellectual qualities - painters like della Francesca, Mantegna, Vermeer, Poussin, Klee, Kandinsky, Mondrian, Kitaj, and perhaps also painters like Vasari and Reynolds - who can all easily be accused of excessive academicism and delight in the exhibition of learning - image-makers, who perhaps have not been generally as highly credited as, say, those who have a more forthright attraction. Although the views of Mrs Talmann - who may have been a cultural snob in *The Draughtsman* - do not necessarily have to be the views of the author. Perhaps these perceived intellectually-intelligent painters sacrifice too much for an intellectual programme. An intellectual process - as demonstrated in the draughtsman's own perception and in his blindnesses - can be too much of a knowing one. And the dictum in the film is draw what you see, not what you know. Perhaps a certain blindness, a certain obsessive blinkeredness is necessary for a great vision. Saints, martyrs, fundamentalists are perhaps better at supplying the goods. Painters like Mantegna had ambitious intellectual programmes probably requiring considerable amounts of background knowledge to interpret the images, as with his allegorical paintings made in association with Isabella d'Este, now in the Louvre. Perhaps the intellectual painter relies too much on text-supported image, and not enough on the image itself. And these sorts of problems and anxieties are relevant in cinema, and maybe in my cinema - especially relevant to my anathema to a universal dominant cinema that is predominantly illustrated text. I am never sure with della Francesca whether he can be considered intellectually astute because of his commentators, or in spite of them, or indeed, bringing it back home, whether Reynolds could be an example - a discourser, certainly a self-conscious thinking man, a man conscious of putting forward a theoretical position, though certainly not a consistently good painter. But a painter like Rembrandt is the painter who scores high in the professional and public imagination, whose painterly intelligence seems to be of a different order - less self-conscious, less intellectually exhibitionist (though exhibitionist in other ways), more intuitive, more consistent and more focused - not allowing exactness of an intellectual examination of his material at all to break his concentration, or spoil his single-mindedness.

Rembrandt would not need to establish an iconography test to make him obviously one of the greatest painters of all time, whereas Poussin would have been pleased to be intellectually respected - certainly Reynolds would have been pleased, though with Reynolds it would have been more to do with public and society status. In the end I suppose it is intellectual against intuitive intelligence. The ideal painter is the one who achieves and balances both, which was not the case that could be made for the draughtsman. We could play a game of cross-reference. Poussin is to Resnais as Rembrandt is to Renoir the film-maker. Renoir the painter is to ... as de La Tour is to Bresson. Chardin, Köllwitz, Le Nain are to Loach, as Caravaggio is to Pasolini? I'll leave you to fill in the gaps and make up some more examples, because I can see other factors entering into the equations.

In *The Cook, The Thief, His Wife and Her Lover* there are two completely opposing acting approaches represented by Michael Gambon and Alan Howard. Alan Howard with a large knowledge of classical literature, certainly Shakespearean literature. We talked very entertainingly about the ramifications of the plot and the metaphors of *The Cook*. I learned a great deal about what I had written through him. Michael Gambon in rehearsal, after expressing amusement and delight in the part of the Thief, argued no special position, said little. But it is Gambon who comes over with the big performance, intuitive, inventive, adding in performance on screen what Alan Howard laid out in preparation in rehearsal. Alan Howard is excellent, but it is Gambon who attracts the eye and the attention. The casting as a result seems correct, though it might very well undermine my own case. I had always thought Michael Gambon should play the Lover - I had called the Lover Michael thinking always of Gambon whilst writing the script - a casting I am sure that I had believed to be right after seeing Gambon in *The Singing Detective*.

IN THE CATALOGUE FOR *The Stairs Geneva* YOU DESCRIBE YOUR AMBIVALENCE TOWARDS CINEMA; HOW IS YOUR SENSE OF IT NOW, AS YOU EDIT *The Pillow Book*?

Well, I feel very much the same. Many of my disenchantments were laid out in that catalogue - cinema's restrictive frame, its lack of an ability for simultaneity, its passive audiences, its non-existent iconic presence, its poor narrative qualities, its slavery to text. Against such criticism - and it's a deliberate provocation - I don't think we've probably seen any cinema yet; we've seen one hundred years of cinema prologue, a medium of recorded theatre and illustrated literature, and I think that when we look back perhaps in another thirty years' time to the cinema we regard as sophisticated now, we will see that by comparison to what will then be achieved, late-twentieth-century cinema will look like some kind of mid-nineteenth-century lantern lecture.

Eisenstein, and I think without irony, suggested that Disney really was the true film-maker, because his world, Disney's world, was entirely prefabricated, and had nothing to do with mimetic photographic realities. You can see what Eisenstein meant. I am no great fan of Disney, but when the full possibilities of an entirely prefabricated cinema are possible with all the new technologies, Eisenstein's Disney dream might be possible in a very sophisticated and adult form. It has been said that the technology of the new Gutenberg revolution that is surfacing is going to completely change our notions of the manufactured image, and I think for the first time we will see something which we can really say is autonomous cinema, cinema cinema, and which doesn't have all the mimetic associations that are a characteristic of what's come before. We will truly have the ability to make infinitely manipulated images - the freedoms of a painter. After a hundred years it is perhaps about right to see that change. Many aesthetic/technological revolutions have taken that time to develop, to mature and to fall away into conservatism and then some form of fossilisation or senility, and I think cinema now needs some form of revitalisation, it needs to be reinvented, and I'm optimistic, I am sure it soon will be.

SINCE WE LAST SPOKE A LOT OF HOLLYWOOD CINEMA HAS MOVED AWAY FROM DRAMATIC REALISM, FROM *Kramer vs Kramer*, AND TOWARDS IRONY, SELF-REFERENCE AND ARTIFICE AND, ABOVE ALL, SPECTACULAR AND PATENTLY UNREALISTIC AND MANIP-ULATED SPECIAL EFFECTS; IT SEEMS TO BE A LOT MORE KNOWING.

How knowing is it? If you take *Jurassic Park* and *The Mask*, for example, both have a predictable conventional drama at the plot and narrative level, and both are only using the devices of new post-production manipulation - which can be free of illusionist necessities - in an essentially three-dimensional, illusionistic space. The original Tex Avery cartoons that *The Mask* homages are still more sophisticated in idea and execution in their original form. A classic case of the Disney vocabulary fusing with the new technology to gain nothing, whilst pretending to participate in the technological revolution. It's not really offering anything new - only taking old models and re-dressing them with new tools. When Hollywood picks these things up, it picks them up with that sort of notion - squashing them down and packaging them to fit old forms. Again, although we all might be amazed and delighted at the special effects in *Terminator 2*, as indeed I was, it's only servicing the same narrative and formulaic cinema of Griffith.

HOLLYWOOD MAY NOW BE PUTTING GENRE IN QUOTES, BUT IT'S STILL DOING GENRE?

However much we might respect Scorsese, he's still making the same cinema as Griffith, the vocabulary's not changed or challenged ... and that seems tragic. We've had a hundred years of this so-called medium, this great magical medium, but consider and compare the language changes which have taken place in literature and painting in the same hundred years.

There have been huge jumps and lurches and investigations of new language schemes in literature and painting, against which cinema has remained conservative. We can of course offer reasons why - it's supposedly a highly collaborative medium, and collaborations don't make for great individual statements, however much you want to deny *auteur* theory; and it's also because apparently cinema has to be expensive, which forces its language to exist behind conservative fencing. There cannot be extremes of imagination and radical possibilities if you need to make forty million at the box-office to cover your publicity costs. The demands of the market place - apparently - will allow for nothing that is not familiar. John Cage said introduce 20 per cent of novelty into an art-product and you lose 80 per cent of your audience. However, my carping is almost irrelevant. If I moan about the Hollywood cinema of the world from Beijing to Mexico City, from Tokyo to Sydney, I couldn't survive without it - I could certainly not keep a cinema open; I need the commercial successes of other films to pay the usherettes and cinema managers and cinema distributors and cinema heating to permit me just a little screen space.

SOME THINGS HAPPEN ALL THE TIME IN YOUR WORK, BUT THEN ONE FILM WILL MAKE A THEME, A SUBJECT OF THEM, SO A CONSTANT MOTIF BECOMES A STRUCTURING DEVICE. THIS SEEMS TO BE HAPPENING WITH TEXT AND IMAGE IN *The Pillow Book* - THOUGH OBVIOUSLY THIS WAS CENTRAL TO *Prospero's Books* AS WELL - AND THEY ARE BEING BROUGHT TOGETHER VERY SPECIFICALLY WITH THE BODY. I DON'T KNOW IF THIS IS

A BAD OR AN IDEAL TIME TO BE TALKING ABOUT *The Pillow Book*, **WHILE YOU ARE STILL EDITING IT?**

The Pillow Book is certainly occupying most of my current enthusiasm and imagination. Sometimes I feel very depressed about the film, and sometimes I feel a very panicky elation, because I feel the vocabulary we're exploring is fascinating and I just want to be allowed to go on exploring it. But thinking about John Cage's warning, I've got to be aware of what's going to happen to this movie when it's out. I have to keep a balance; I want to go on making movies, and if my movies become too difficult, the finance is not going to be available. The question of the relationship between text and image has indeed caused disquiet in many films. I have tried to see if a really satisfactory relationship can exist between what some call the primacy of the text versus the primacy of the image. As I see it, one of the dissatisfactions of cinema is still its inability to find a definitive synthesis between these two things. Much of my cinema has tried to deny the text, has tried to deny the narrative, but it's contradictory - I also have a deepfelt desire to tell stories, though I want to tell those stories visually.

However, if I want to believe that making images is a primary and autonomous art, I have got to accept that we've had three thousand years where, in essence, the majority of all image-making - at least until the 1850s - has been largely illustrative, it's been second-hand, where all major painting has been illustrating biblical and classical texts, literary works, and texts of nationalistic history. And even if you consider landscape and portrait manufacture, you're still more often than not playing with fables, moral maxims, proverbs, allegories - all familiar first and primarily in text. Text, text, text. And now the majority by far of feature films are first texts then films - has all this serviced painting well, and does it service cinema well?

The disquiet is mirrored upside-down in *The Pillow Book* because it's self-consciously a film about text. But this time mainly Oriental text - maybe it's a wish fulfilment more than an actuality - but in the process of examining the Oriental written character where, it seems, text and image are synonymous in a gestural mark that can always be unique each time it is made by hand. That doesn't happen in the West. We lost our calligraphic traditions a long time ago. Whether we had them in the same way of course is to be discussed. Text is allowed to be the perpetrator of image, but in the West must not be confused or sublimated into image for here we have successfully separated out literature and painting - literature's over here, and painting's over there, they are to be seen and experienced as separate entities and not to be united - in some ways that is disastrous for cinema. This division of text and image has split us into two approaches, so that we're extremely sophisticated and highly educated in a textual way but not in a visual way - so there's a case to be made that we are textually literate at the expense of being visually illiterate. Perhaps this split began with the spread of literacy. If the charge of visual illiteracy is upheld, it must be viewed as a paradox for this is an age when there are more manufactured images than there have ever been in civilisation's history. So accepting that in the West most manufactured images are textual in origin, and that also a large gap has apparently been driven through the notion of combining text and image, I thought that if I could look at the notion of the Oriental calligraph as a completely synthesised notion of text and image that here would be a good template for cinema.

It is particularly fascinating to watch a calligrapher work. With the making of an Oriental character, it can be said that every single time you make it, it can in some senses be different. In the hands of even a five-year-old child, as we've experienced it in the film, and certainly in the hands of sophisticated calligraphers, the sheer gestural excitement of writing a character also includes the pleasure of seeing it drawn. To write and draw simultaneously still seems to be significant in the Oriental calligraphic tradition. I had some idea to make such a concept the basis of the film.

EISENSTEIN MAKES A COMPARISON BETWEEN THE CALLIGRAPH AND MONTAGE ...

I remember poring over those examples in Marie Seton, and wondering if the analogy was being pushed too far, because the montage application never fused two or more ideas together in the same way as the calligraphy. The sum of the parts in a montage sequence was never, it seemed to me, as synthesised to a whole as exists in even a simple Chinese or Japanese character. Watching Brody Neuenschwander, the calligrapher of *M is for Mozart* and *Prospero's Books*, also persuaded me to think that Western calligraphy, when it attempts to be more than purely functional, is also guilty of simply being decorative in a way that could not be said of Oriental characters. Montage seems to operate by displacement and is curiously very cerebral, whereas the gestural mark of an Oriental character seems very intuitive as I understand it. But I must be careful - first the traditions seem to be making Japanese calligraphy too special and rarefied - too much an arts and crafts tradition, and too much a Japanese 'national treasure' against the almost culturally political desire of many Japanese I met to want to use typewriters, word-processors and Western alphabets to the detriment of their calligraphic traditions, and, second, the teaching of Oriental calligraphy can be so severe and conservative. We met Japanese and Chinese calligraphers in Kyoto and Hong Kong whose tradition stopped and started at only using black ink on white paper - and that ink only being applied strictly on a flat horizontal surface. No colour, no mixing of colour, no mixing of technique and certainly no vulgarities like writing on the human body. Yet the combination of flesh and text itself - the essence of *The Pillow Book* - seems to be not a million miles from an example of montage.

Brody Neuenschwander has taught me a great deal. The excitements of just simply watching him perform, more than anything else, is enticing for the camera. There was a seductive quality about him and his Japanese calligraphers simply making the necessary marks, such that the film's stock could have been used up just watching the ink go on the paper and the flesh. The film's first cut contained much close-up material and I regret being obliged to remove it. The word 'calligraphy' does not seem to do the process justice - it implies penmanship rather than the process of transferring the thought from the head to the hand to the page. Though after a time, this special relationship of eye, hand and pen and paper can seem overworked. I remember, when working on the *Flying Out of This World* exhibition at the Louvre, curators making draughtsmanship-writing comparisons that implied, along with Barthes, that the physical act of writing by hand was essential and the computer was inimical to the business of literature because the essential physical contact of shaping the letters along the length of the body from brain to pen-tip was lost. One curator, insisting on this point of never using a word-processor because the writing bond would be broken, exasperated his publishers beyond endurance, and his contract. Calligraphy was obviously a product of a less time-conscious age, though now publishers by comparison seem often lazy, insisting on compatible software, where a hand-written word is a new form of special illiteracy.

You would however think by now that somehow the processes of literary imagination working through word-processors might have actually changed the character of writing - certainly as regards certain forms of literature. Umberto Eco tried to suggest something of the same in *Foucault's Pendulum*. Dorothy Parker said very few writers write, they spend 90 per cent of their time rewriting. From a modern perspective, this can be so much a chore that the whole business collapses through an equation that says it is just not worth the effort. Imagine Tolstoy's wife repeatedly writing out *War and Peace*. Imagine Dickens's workload. I am happy that it has all gone, because now you can perfect *ad infinitum* - maybe *ad nauseam* - to the detriment of spontaneity. Perhaps in fact the capacity to perfect is a condition of the word-processor influencing literature. I enjoy the process. Now exhaustion and boredom at copying and re-copying out the words is not an entity, perhaps the notion that a writer never finishes, he only stops, is not going to be so valid any more. Now he can truly finish.

One curiosity. A Belgian publisher, perhaps in opposition to the possibilities of the squeaky-cleanness of a truly finished word-processed manuscript, is interested in publishing film manuscript scripts in facsimile, with all the erasures and repeats, wandering scribbles and quick visual aids left in unedited. I had used such rejected first-draft, hand-annotated typed pages as the basis for paintings - something to read as text and image, something to eat, something to drink. Many years ago the film *Dear Phone* had something to say about the process of scribble to print. But perhaps this sort of publishing speaks too much of surrogate activity. A film-script is only a prelude to a film. And a dubious one at that - since Godard says once the producer has found the money, throw the script away. Perhaps it's like publishing Joyce's laundry-lists, Alan Weberman going through Dylan's dustbin, and the gibe that anything Picasso touched had a price-value, including the evidence of the hand of the painter wiping his own backside. I remember reading that a Belgian (again) collector of film manuscripts considered Bergman's *Wild Strawberries* was far superior as a script than a film.

As regards *The Pillow Book* and writing and calligraphy - the film was based on a notion that Sei Shonagon intimates that the most important things in life are physicality and literature. She does say how dreary and depressing and pointless life would be without writing. So the metaphors and images in the film are constantly about the stimulations of flesh and text. Not flesh and painting, and I certainly wouldn't say flesh and cinema.

The narrative concerns an emancipated woman with a love of literature who likes her lovers to write on her body. The text on the body is not permanent. There are no notions of branding and tattooing. The calligraphy is applied by a delicate ink brush, with the writing washed away by the rain, by bathing, by swimming in the sea. The page is constantly changeable, relating to the notions of writing on water, and on perishable paper, that makes an association with the ephemerality of the body, the ephemerality of the flesh - connections between the mortality of paper and flesh and writing.

The Belly of an Architect IS ALSO ABOUT EPHEMERALITY, BUT THERE EVEN ARCHITECTURE IS EPHEMERAL BESIDE BIOLOGY, SO THAT THOUGH FLESH MAY BE EPHEMERAL - AS

INDEED KRACKLITE'S IS - THE DNA IS ETERNAL.

If you are interested in the dubious attractions of immortality by leaving some mark, some stain on the wall, perhaps you should make architecture - or better still, be a potter - the earliest imperishable wholly man-made artefacts seem to be pottery fragments. What price the manufacture of a pottery fragment is in individual terms to a 25,000-year-old skeleton is, to say the least, highly dubious. Perhaps much the same could be said of the Sistine Chapel after 25,000 years. What price cinema in all this - the most ephemeral of the arts? With the biological links, certainly I would subscribe to all the notions that the Darwin inheritance has taught - *Homo sapiens* is cosmically insignificant, as individual he is infinitely disposable, the significant thing is the continuation of the species, which is alive and well in DNA, so all those concerns for the vanities of immortality in a debate between art and biology are writ large in many other films as well as *The Belly of an Architect.*

WHAT MARX WAS FOR EISENSTEIN'S CINEMA, DARWIN IS FOR YOURS. BUT YOU SUGGEST SIMULTANEOUSLY THAT DARWIN WAS RIGHT, AND THAT NATURAL SELECTION IS ONE MORE EXPLANATORY MYTH.

There's indeed a scene in *A Zed and Two Noughts* where Darwin and Genesis are discussed with the inference that just as Genesis has been pushed into the realm of a beautiful symbolic and nicely satisfying myth, maybe one day - perhaps measured only in another century - Darwin will be in the same position - creator of a beautiful myth. The evolutionary theories certainly appear to answer many questions for the moment in terms of history and geography but ultimately they may be no more satisfying than Genesis. Indeed, I suppose both critics and supporters of Darwin would argue, and Darwin would argue the same dilemma himself - that the natural-selection explanations can only be taken back so far, but then the big questions still remain, which creationists answer as acts of God and scientists as acts of nuclear explosion. The three big questions of that Tahitian Gauguin painting - where did we come from? where are we? where are we going? - are still unanswerable.

But if we acknowledge - as I suppose we all do now - the totality of a system which is related not only to the ecosystems of the earth but of the universe, then Darwin is the ideal late-twentieth-century prophet. In *Darwin*, we pushed through those connotations - Noah with God's rainbow, Moses with the tablets. His theories, with the effect they have on all the sciences, ties everything together in a rather beautiful and satisfactory way, and goes back as far as any other religion is prepared to go back before they all get slammed up against the final wall of unanswerable questions.

The irrelevances of morality in a world of natural selection, the accommodation of morality according to history or geography, the moral code as a device of convenience, the highly adjustable concepts of good and evil to suit individuals and communities - all stem for me from the post-Darwin explosion. But we should look how the medicine of Galen or Newtonian physics seemed irrefutable to their believers and agree that the Darwinian line of thought cannot be definitive. And I can see - rewording Marx's thoughts on Christianity - that maybe Darwin is my opium.

DARWIN IS IMPORTANT TO *Rosa*, ESPECIALLY PERHAPS THE BOOK. ONE OF THE CHALLENGES TO THE READER OF THE BOOK IS TO IMAGINE IT AS AN OPERA BEING STAGED, AND ONE WONDERS HOW IT COULD ACTUALLY BE STAGED. THERE MUST HAVE BEEN SOME INTERESTING TRANSITIONS.

The book was an attempt to consider all the many possibilities of knowing what the opera was about and finding for myself some way of staging it. One of the devices in the book is to look at what's happening on the stage through the different perspective of certain people in the audience. It's a literary device that is difficult to operate in a real opera-house audience. We tried to find a way of doing it by considering planting actors in the audience, but then that would not satisfy the interior monologuing. How would you make the private thoughts available? Would these planted audience-members stand up and speak, do they stand up and sing, do they leave their seats, how do they present their information? It all became too clumsy. It might have been something we could have put into the film of *Rosa* if we ever could make it. The box-office also reminded me that twenty-five audience-paying seats would become unavailable.

There were other surprises, like the lifting floor. I had written in the book for a device that metaphorically should signify that the earth moved. The book talked of the stage turning on its axis - that proved difficult - in the end the floor lifted up nearly vertically. To an unprepared audience, that was entirely unexpected and dramatic. You don't expect the floor to move - though working in Kyoto on *The Pillow Book* floors can unexpectedly move as on the morning of the Kobe earthquake. The hotel room indeed shook. In England we expect that three of the four elements are volatile, but we expect the fourth to be reliable. A floor that can move without warning with dire results must affect all your thinking.

I WAS INTERESTED IN YOUR IDEA THAT A FILM SHOULD OR COULD BE LIKE A GREAT HISTORICAL MACHINE PAINTING, WITH A HINTERLAND OF STUDIES AND SKETCHES AND RELATED WORKS. MORE AND MORE YOUR PROJECTS ARE LIKE THIS.

The traditions of making preparations for a painting are valuable, I would have thought, in cinema terms. I am grateful that my art-school training was old-fashioned enough to have thought them relevant. Now I see drawing is no longer even on the curriculum in some art schools like Newport. The reference to history painting often involved immediate criticism. Kitaj was attacked for his presumption in trying to revitalise history painting. David Sylvester said Kitaj did not have the necessary apparatus for being a history painter - it's difficult to see who has better claim. Shifting further forward, the process of visual preparation in note-form, in reworkings, alternative viewings and alternative solutions is nicely applicable to the manufacture of a CD-Rom, though I am dubious that at present there are only two strategies, the game and the index - both of which are, I think, still more valuable sought and found elsewhere. It's difficult to beat the methods, convenience, and browsing potential of a dictionary or textual encyclopaedia. And ideally most enjoyable games are played in company, not alone. I would also think scale is important - I would want the large-screen possibilities in relation to the CD-Rom. How about making CD-Roms on IMAX or OMNIMAX?

I would imagine that the CD-Rom has still some way to go before it becomes a major part of our total learning and entertainment servant. And most of the CD-Roms I've seen have become tedious after ten minutes. Again, it's like the Scorsese tradition continued from Griffith, the forms are there, but it's the brick wallpaper in a caravan syndrome again; this refusal to let go of the old forms, but at the same time not having the strengths of the form that is being mimicked. One curiosity is that the CD-Rom might break the monopoly of the alphabet as the major form of taxonomy.

I'm making a book with a video-house in Strasbourg to be called *100 Allegories to Represent the World*. The images are computer-collaged and the programmers insist on making conventional notes, conventional storyboards. The potential of addressing the ideas straight into the machinery is resisted. Here is an opportunity to put flights of fancy straight into the machine, but we have to go the slow route. The images are to be the slaves of thinking relative to the technique of the cell animated cartoon, the advertising cut-and-paste layout. The safety of the familiar. But of course I can see the dangers of exploring where we have not been before.

We are editing *The Pillow Book* on computer technology - advertised widely for its potential to speed up linear editing. But the possibilities of interfering with the filmed image, of manipulating, for example, its aspect-ratio, is too exciting to be missed.

The fixed frame has been a characteristic of painting, of photography, with cinema and with television. At least in theory, the painter chooses his aspect-ratio according to his content - if you're a landscape painter, it has been traditional to select an image which is broader than it is high - and if you wanted to fulfil your obligations to the sitter in a portrait, it's the other way round. Pushing the idea to extremes, to satisfactorily paint a giraffe, a painter might well choose a vertical narrow frame, to paint a snake a long horizontal one. A Boston art historian computer-recorded the dimensions of five thousand European paintings from the sixteenth, seventeenth and eighteenth centuries to try and find out the average aspect-ratio that was preferred - it came out, rather disappointingly, around 1:1.66, the basic ratio of cinema projection.

The Pillow Book was shot on Super 35mm and with computer editing could lend itself to recropping according to many different criteria - to sympathise with degrees of emotion or different significances to the narrative, different tenses, different character perspectives and so on. To some this might suggest visual indigestion, but I think it is worth taking the risk to experiment. Another risk taken is the huge amount of text on screen. There are many languages in the film: Chinese, Japanese, Vietnamese, English, French, Latin and even indeed a word or two written in Yiddish. We hope to play many language correspondences - with the vagaries of manipulating sub-titles either to conform or to contradict the spoken dialogue of the film. To contrast and compare texts on screen in different languages. To allow space for the individually written calligraphic text to communicate yet more meanings.

However the manipulations go, the overall intention was to demonstrate the literary origins of the film by constant reference to the words that made it, and made the film's heroine, but with little or no attempt to conventionally dramatise the events of the original. If, as the film suggests, the body is a book, the book a body, then we absorb text like a sponge, we are made of text - just like the film. The film's textual origins are explicitly stated repeatedly by quotation - much like the heroine's obsession with the original *Pillow Book of Sei Shonagon* - the film is a collection of acknowledged quotations. In the end these extend beyond the text, and include the various photographic styles of the film and the collage of music.

WHEN YOU SEE A SUB-TITLED ENGLISH FILM ABROAD, IT'S VERY DIFFICULT NOT TO READ THE SUB-TITLES IN THE FOREIGN LANGUAGE. EVEN THOUGH YOU UNDERSTAND THE DIALOGUE, YOU'RE ALWAYS LOOKING DOWN AT THE BOTTOM OF THE SCREEN.

Maybe it's a checking-out process - to see if they have got it right. I am sure that the retinal attraction to white celluloid shining through the emulsion must also be relevant - often the sub-titles can conventionally be the brightest thing on the screen, but I am sure that our reading habits are also to be credited - the captioned photograph in a newspaper, the impulse in a gallery to read the title of a painting before examining it, our overall literary education that persuades us to trust text more than images. But there is a large prejudice against sub-titles. Whatever the quality of a film, making a choice between viewing a sub-titled and a non-sub-titled film is, for many, immediate in favour of no sub-titles. TV audience viewing figures of sub-titled films indicate small acceptance. All of which is sad, and dangerous - for the market becomes limited to your own language, film distributors insist on dubbing, unfamiliarity with the sounds of foreign languages creates increasing spirals of ignorance and maybe xenophobia. A young audience at home may soon find the sound of a foreign language rare and freakish. This is also compounded by the colonisation of computer-text. If you do not live in a country of major production, you might well be obliged to learn English, French, German or Japanese to operate your PC. With *The Pillow Book* we are living dangerously. Already the foreign distributors are growling.

IT USED TO BE THE OTHER WAY ROUND, THOUGH MAYBE ONLY FOR A MINORITY AUDIENCE. AS A STUDENT IN THE SEVENTIES WATCHING TEN FILMS A WEEK I ALMOST THOUGHT A FILM, CERTAINLY A NEW FILM, WASN'T WORTH WATCHING IF IT WASN'T SUBTITLED.

Perhaps a case of admitted reverse prejudice. Used also not infrequently by commercials directors seeking a particular kudos. Even in cases where it's not strictly necessary, the sub-titles are supplied to get a certain cachet, the associated cultural superiority from a foreign-language film.

YOU USED SUB-TITLES IN *Rosa*, AS WELL.

Primarily because the opera *Rosa* was a set of instructions for an opera, stating in texts projected onto screens of varying size and visibility, this is how you do it, here are the instructions from the kit box - starting at very first principles - here is the stage, and I give you the actors, and remember this is false, and this is only representation, it's translated text ... just to push that sense of opera's impossible artificiality with its many complicated sophisticated conventions which do not exist anywhere else. Those conventions trap you and straitlace you, but also offer large degrees of freedom. You don't have to play the mimicry games of continuity, chronology, faithfulness to life, the games of psychodrama and the slavery to narrative. You can play the sequence in the knowledge that opera conventions are like no other.

THERE'S A GREAT PLAY ON CINEMA WITHIN THE OPERA, ESPECIALLY AS STAGED; THERE ARE SOME VERY COMPLICATED MANOUEVRES WITH MULTIPLE SCREENS; WERE THOSE EFFECTS YOU DEMANDED IN ADVANCE, OR DID THEY DEVELOP OUT OF THE ACTUAL MACHINERY OF THAT PARTICULAR OPERA HOUSE?

It worked both ways. My knowledge of opera as a production exercise was non-existent. I would present them with a problem, and they would come back with a series of solutions. Often I would pick up the solution that they would have rejected. It was important that the whole activity shouldn't be crashed with cinema language; the opera language had to be truly in evidence. The balance between the two languages was fascinating to play with. I was also very lucky to be able to use the resources of the Amsterdam Opera House. There are, I am told, very few opera houses which offer more technical possibilities. We are working now on an opera called *100 Objects to Represent the World*, the same title as the Vienna exhibition, not perhaps the same objects, but which uses a similar sort of shopping list as its structure, to make an ironic 'prop-opera'. It's scheduled for Vienna, Munich and Paris in the spring of 1997. The Munich theatre is a traditional rococo theatre and the possibilities for simultaneous back and front projection and multiple screens are severely limited. I had a hope of investigating all sorts of eighteenth-century notions of illusionism, painted clouds and *deus ex machina* and thunder machines and so on, to try and self-consciously use the technology of another age.

WAS THERE A BIG DIFFERENCE BETWEEN THE WAY YOU WERE WORKING WITH THE OPERA AND THE WAY YOU'VE WORKED BEFORE WITH THE SOUNDTRACKS OF THE FILMS?

Operas are known by their composers; we maybe know the librettists, but the impetus of the work is assumed to have come from the composer. *Rosa* will be catalogued as indeed a Louis Andriessen opera, but the relationship of idea to music, concept to performance, was not dissimilar to the relationship I would have had in making a film. The initial idea indeed came from me, opened up as much as I could to a total collaboration with the composer, as I had done for many years with Michael Nyman, only this time for a seen live audience rather than for an unseen one.

WHAT WERE YOU WANTING WHEN YOU FIRST STARTED USING MUSIC IN YOUR CINEMA?

I think it's true that there probably never was such a thing as silent cinema. Even Lumière was accompanied by a piano. Cinema can be impoverished by not having a musical association, for all the reasons that are self-evident. But again music seems not to be used in a primary way in most cinema, but as a decorative adjunct, being persuaded to adopt a secondary or tertiary relationship to the image, to emphasise what is already there in the image, to accentuate mood, supply relief, service the image. In the early days with Michael, there was a great deal of agreement about this. We tried to find an equivalence of image and music to move towards a useful collaboration - not just a music-servicing relationship - so that music was essentially structural. I think *The Draughtsman's Contract* proves the potentiality of that, the music and the images are often equally complementary. For purely practical reasons for the most part - time, finance, recording expediency - it never quite worked in the same way afterwards. But the ambition to find a satisfactory partnership between image and sound continued, with different composers, recorded music, live music, on and off the cinema screen - in opera, music-theatre and installations and exhibitions.

But I also have a plan to try and make a 'muted' if not truly mute film - with an absence of sound akin to the experience perhaps of a deaf-mute - though it should not be described as a silent movie. At the other extreme, the last noisy fifteen minutes of *The Cook* seemed to move seriously towards the condition of opera. And a true description of *Rosa* would be film/opera, opera/film. I believe there are a great many possibilities of exchange between the two conventions, though I have serious doubts that opera is filmable in any truly satisfying way; the wide one-view stage cannot be fragmented into cropping and cutting into medium shots and close-ups, subjected to moving cameras and the taping of sound, and still retain the opera excitements of the wide one-view live stage with its ability to use simultaneity, its costume and make-up traditions, its inevitable suspension of belief in the match of singing potential to acting potential to image.

Dubbing an actress with a singer's voice is no good, substituting real Verona, Venice or Naples for the scenery seems to miss the point ... and so on.

And perhaps just as cinema appears to be waiting for a reinvention of itself, there is a feeling that within music invention too we've reached a plateau - we are told that minimalism has played itself out, the Boulez tradition has become known and fixed. I am not so excited - and need to be convinced - about the various graftings of jazz and pop and modern classical traditions. We're looking for something new. The music of the New York composers in the late fifties, early sixties, continuing into the seventies, had a big influence on me. Reich, Glass, Riley, Adams, Branca. Whatever his current reputation, I still frequently listen to Glass. Michael Nyman introduced me - a little reluctantly I remember at the time - to the music of *Einstein on the Beach*, and the excitement was immediate. I had made my own discovery of Cage in 1959, first through a lecture-text, then through his paintings, and only later through his music. Cage's structures and non-structures and random structures were influential in *A Walk Through H* and *The Falls*.

LET'S TALK ABOUT *The Baby of Mâcon*, AND INDEED THE RESPONSE TO IT. IT WAS HEAVILY CRITICISED, NOT PRIMARILY ON AESTHETIC GROUNDS, BUT FOR THINGS WHICH I WOULD HAVE THOUGHT SHOULDN'T HAVE SURPRISED PEOPLE, OR NEEDED EXPLAINING.

I would have thought so. In a world of Tarantino and *Terminator 2*, the vocabulary is there for the taking of. But the purposes are different. *The Baby of Mâcon* is not violence and sensation and humiliation and exploitation of innocence for a quick cathartic giggle; this is cause and effect propositioning, and is intended to show and debate painful issues with a deep sense of seriousness. Perhaps the purposes were too moral. It's curious how audiences want to watch, but need the removal of the responsibility of watching; and from the explosive and disturbed reactions to *The Baby* I witnessed in many places around the world, the implication was that audiences felt both attached to and attacked by the film. People could accept what happened in *The Cook, The Thief, His Wife and Her Lover* but not in *The Baby of Mâcon*, not only because of its taboo subject-matter, but because *The Cook* also had a sense of distancing irony, and that sort of irony is not present in *The Baby of Mâcon*, it's eradicated, scraped away. Although audiences knowingly laugh about the strictures of the politically incorrect - and where convenient, suggest they are too sophisticated to subscribe to them - I saw time and time again that the film's political incorrectness, in a moral climate that has changed and hardened in the four years since *The Cook*, made audiences uncomfortable and embarrassed about their participation as viewers.

It was curious and sad to see the English critics falling over themselves to increase the damnation, each critic outdoing the last to heap up the infamy, inventing in the public's mind a film that did not exist. And their efforts were successful - the film was taken out of the London cinemas very quickly. The film indeed used blasphemy - though Catholic audiences were muted, amused or excited in Warsaw, Madrid, Rio and Dublin where I sat through the film with festival audiences. Audience reaction was violent in Hamburg and Toronto.

The film involves the financial and status exploitation of a child, it debates the destruction of innocence and the possibility that innocence is a myth. It has been seen in some eyes to be deeply misogynist. It is certainly anti-Catholic. Surprisingly French philosophers in Strasbourg took high moral ground about a film that slaughtered animals on screen. And I suppose, maybe its greatest crime, it makes a deep criticism of voyeuristic audiences. The last scene, audiences watching audiences watching audiences watching audiences, is intended to make a bond of identification with the audience in the cinema. Like the language of visual and moral sensation of the Baroque era the film evokes, the film works on the watcher to make him a participant, so maybe that was deeply unsettling. Gilbert Adair said he left the cinema in disgust as soon as the baby appeared in the film. His reactions were right to be disturbed but his diagnosis was wrong. The advent of the baby was the key not only to the actors within the drama but to the audience in the cinema. Babies cannot act, placing everything else in the film into immediate artificiality. The suspension of disbelief is violently disturbed. I had remembered a small incident in Kubrick's *2001*. In the prologue, actors simulate early man discovering technology. Obviously, no complete or even partial suspension of disbelief can be successful here - we as cinema audience accept the artifice as best we can - and the actors do a good job - but then - whether deliberate or not - and I suspect not - Kubrick introduces a real chimpanzee infant. It was a great mistake. What sympathy we had for trying to believe you can film actors playing neolithics, immediately and utterly collapsed. The real ape - and apes cannot act - brought the edifice to the ground. It proved the lie. It made the actors look ridiculous, and the intentions embarrassing. If that effect was uncalculated, the introduction of the baby in *The Baby of Mâcon* was very calculated. It proved the lie. It humbled the actors - both as characters and as actors prating in a costume drama - actors playing actors in a drama so patently a costume drama that they change their costumes three times in full view of actors playing an audience. The disturbance of the suspension of disbelief occurs again and again throughout the film, most provocatively in the rape scene, when identification of character, actress, play-acting and crime are thrown into painful confusion.

277

WITH THE RAPE SCENE IN PARTICULAR, PERHAPS WHAT IS MOST UPSETTING PEOPLE IS - AND IT IS ALMOST UNSAYABLE, SO CRITICISM IS EXPRESSED THROUGH DEFLECTION - CLEARLY, WE'RE NOT ALLOWED TO IDENTIFY, EMPATHISE IN THE NORMAL WAY WITH THE VICTIM, BUT FOR THE MALE AUDIENCE THERE IS ALWAYS A DOUBLE IDENTIFICATION, AND WHAT I SUSPECT YOU'RE REALLY NOT BEING FORGIVEN FOR IS THAT THE AUDIENCE IS EQUALLY NOT ALLOWED TO IDENTIFY WITH THE RAPIST, WHO BECOMES A MULTIPLIED FIGURE, A TEXT EVEN, A CROWD AND AN ORDER AND A BLESSING.

The representation of the act of rape with its connotations of violence, humiliation, dominance, torture, shame, intimacy and violation is always the most powerful, sensitive and disturbing of representations. I can think of no other more powerful. Murder pales beside it, for death for the victim cancels physical and mental pain. Cinema deals repeatedly with the representation of rape. Experience shows it's probably its most powerful dramatic weapon. To openly negotiate disturbances of the suspension of disbelief around this most powerful of dramatic representations is always going to be disturbing indeed.

I was given a TV right to reply to criticism of the film, in a programme [*The Late Show*, BBC 2] where Derek Malcolm implied he perceived the possibility of erotic pleasure from that scene. [Malcolm's exact words were 'Do we need something that's actually quite erotic?']

The Baby AND *The Cook* BOTH MADE CLEAR THAT THERE ARE SOME THINGS ARTIFICE ALLOWS YOU TO SAY ABOUT POWER AND POLITICS, IN A VERY GENERAL SENSE, THAT REALISM DOESN'T.

True.

AND IF WE GO BACK TO THE EARLIER FILMS, THOSE THINGS ARE THERE ALL THE TIME.

I hope so.

I WAS STRUCK WITH THE FIGURE OF THE PRINCE IN *The Baby*, A FIGURE OF THE POWER OF WEAKNESS, A POWER VACUUM.

It's power as a figurehead, power as an empty space, because of the necessity to respect it through convention and history and the status quo - the classic weak hereditary monarch. Cosimo Medici is patently unequal to the task. I was fascinated by him. He is a real historical character - by all accounts a religious hysteric, first by rote then by inclination, later to be cursed with a violently unsuccessful dynastic marriage, and with a passive character who hated disturbance of any kind. He did indeed turn into a highly puritanical prince who helped to bring about the final collapse of the Medici family, though it was his offspring who finally broke the continuity that had stretched back to the earlier successful and celebrated Cosimo Medici. We present him on his fifteenth birthday, being treated to a visit to the theatre to see an edifying play on the nature of miracles. Six months before, he had fallen from a horse, and since he was the heir that the Medici fortunes relied on, the family came together and tried to protect him in order to protect themselves, so he wasn't allowed to go hunting, he certainly wasn't allowed to go horse-riding, he had a considerable entourage to look after him, to satisfy his every whim and every necessity. His greatest character-forming influence was his mother; thanks to her and her reliquary obsessions and excessive exhibitionist piety, he was later responsible for all sorts of strange moral directives in Florence, declarations - hardly enforceable - that prostitutes had to wear yellow, nine o'clock curfews, anybody caught without a copy of the Bible on a Sunday liable to prosecution.

I suppose at that young age he still can be just about forgiven for his excesses, because he's still an innocent. He could not be excused ten years later. His borrowed sense of faith is continually manipulated by all those around him, so that he is manoeuvred into being the person who perpetrates the greatest tragedy; it's he who whispers into the ear of the very willing priest the ultimate solution to the problem that virgins cannot be judicially murdered unless they are deflowered. Emblematically, it's the collusion of state and church, each desperately hearing what the other wants to tell them. It is no new criticism that the Roman Catholic Church is conceived of as being not essentially a spiritual power, but as a temporal one. But the target is not entirely the Catholic oppression; I wanted to make comment on any power that is determined, come whatever the cost, to hang on to its power, and that any establishment will use every device it can, it will invoke ancient and apocryphal precedents, it will use all the myths that are perpetrated by itself about itself, it will perjure itself and betray itself repeatedly - like communism and capitalism - it will torture, abuse, humiliate, deny everything that it believes in, in order to hang onto power.

THE CONNECTIONS I WAS MAKING WERE WITH BRECHT, AND ALSO WITH PASOLINI'S LAST FILM.

I was also impressed many years ago by the Peter Brook performance of the Peter Weiss *Marat/Sade*, whose writing is certainly in a Brechtian tradition. I confess I have never seen *Salo*. I saw the Peter Brook production at the Aldwych and the use of grilles and a privileged audience on stage are shamelessly borrowed - through the fog of imperfect memory. The world of theatre-stage and church interior are intertwined - the film images constantly resonating sacred images. The original Nativity of the Child is distorted into a negative melodrama with Ralph Fiennes as a surrogate Joseph. And the classical *Pietà* does not see a thirty-three-year-old Christ, but a four-year-old Christ suffocated in the arms and on the lap of the Julia Ormond Virgin. Christ has been killed off in his innocence. And the whole drama stumbling about on the false power of the Virgin Birth propaganda myth - a political and theological expediency introduced late into the Catholic creed, creating impossible suspensions of disbelief that mock Christ's mortality and disservices human rationality.

IS SADE A FIGURE WHO PARTICULARLY INTERESTS YOU?

An uncomfortable perpetrator of anxiety, of pain, treachery, disloyalty. The literary representation of such pains and anxieties is one thing, their enactments in real life entirely unacceptable. But that could be disingenuous. An arch exploiter - totally unacceptable if you found a contemporary equivalent - and we are finding them surfacing all too easily in the English and American courts. Of course he had to be locked up, but on the other hand, as many - and especially French - intellectuals will be very explicitly supportive about his sense of exhausting moral behaviour, of pushing things to the edge, of opening up the moral taboos, he is important.

OF COURSE HE ALSO LIKED COUNTING GAMES.

If you look at the way *100 Days of Sodom* is organised, it's a complicated mathematical structure full of symmetries which would be very interesting to plot. Though planned carefully, its resolution was not completed. Circumstances, perhaps even boredom, never permitted the final stages to be anything other than a synopsis.

THERE ARE MAYBE PARALLELS BETWEEN SADE'S VIEW OF NATURE AS ESSENTIALLY AN AMORAL FORCE AND DARWINIAN THEORIES.

His writings predated the freedom that had to be discussed to ever permit a climate for someone like Darwin to operate in. But it is curious how morality still needs to be argued on what seems to be very familiar territory. *The Baby of Mâcon* was debated by the philosophical department of Strasbourg University with a conservatism that surprised me. The responsibilities of the artist as a high moral priest were repeatedly stressed. The belief that because we have language and memory that has separated us from the instinctual behaviour of animals, we have thereby also a learned or innate moral conscience that has to be acknowledged. A curious, as I understood it, refusal to admit that morality is a moveable, mutable, negotiable concept, and therefore a construct relative to the quantity and quality of the people who subscribe to it. The Darwin proposition still does not seem to have freed us from all that. Even Darwin, read carefully, with all his moral qualms, would never have accepted these moral niceties. Darwin often has been given a popular reputation as a mechanical evolutionist, but his responsibilities to his own theories are fascinating to read.

ARE YOU INTERESTED IN CURRENT DARWINIAN DEBATES?

I try to follow them. After the months of research preparing for *Darwin* several years ago, I still read as much as I can. I have much respect for Stephen Gould who sometimes reads to me like a pupil of Borges. I always enjoy the extravagant engineering of evolution that is repeatedly unearthed in the scientific papers - of obscure snails on Tahiti wiped out by accidental biological warfare in one summer after fifteen million years of patient evolution to inhabit one cabbage patch, of absurd mutations in fish and bird that become essential, and extraordinary specialisations that mean certain and obvious extinction. And I marvel that so much was going on in the mid-1850s to deliver versions of *The Origin of Species*, that sometimes Darwin appears as just an accidental figurehead, in the way Lumière is an accidental figurehead in the discovery of cinema - anybody could have been credited. They're still hammering away at the Darwinian edifice, but, for me it remains sound.

HOW DO YOU REGARD INTERVIEWS LIKE THIS ONE? ARE THEY A NECESSARY EVIL OF PROMOTION?

No, for the most part, I enjoy them. The debate is invariably more interesting than the product, and I know the process of making a film is always much more satisfactory than coming to any solutions about it. And if I proselytise my cinema as a cinema of ideas, then it's the engagement of the ideas that is most fascinating. The ideas are wrapped up in, I hope, an entertaining form, so that people can enter into them from many angles. If we really consider cinema to be an important sophisticated medium then let's discuss anything and everything in it - and that most importantly must include its language.

THERE ARE ALSO PHILOSOPHICAL IDEAS - PARTICULARLY IN DUCHAMP - WHICH ONLY HAVE THE FORCE, AND INDEED MEANING, THAT THEY DO BECAUSE THEY ARE PRESENTED AS OR WITHIN ARTWORKS - THEY COULDN'T BE ADEQUATELY STATED IN A LECTURE.

I suppose the large cross-over and popular theoretical areas of minimalism, conceptualism and post-modernism, which all, for the most part, started with painting, have helped fashion the opinions and culture of the last forty years. Just one work - Duchamp's *Large Glass* - must loom large in the responsibilities of all that's now labelled conceptualism. Popular high and low culture, directly, indirectly and by unacknowledged osmosis, would owe more to Duchamp than, say, to Bertrand Russell. It is curious that Cage and Duchamp as ideas-men may ultimately be seen to have more usable influence than, say, Picasso, or Cézanne or Matisse, who are regarded by many as pure painters, as being more interesting than Duchamp. I would personally be more interested in those artists who use painting as a means to an end, than in those painters who use painting as an end in itself. Have we got to that position with cinema? Is cinema allowed to organise itself and perpetuate itself in that way? There are very few people who would invest those sorts of notions in cinema - Godard would certainly be one of them; Eisenstein, of course long dead and buried, and his reputation fixed now, but he would certainly be another. But cinema still has not been given sufficient credence and responsibility for us to use its findings with full seriousness. In England I sometimes feel that someone like Stoppard is permitted legitimate space to debate ideas from notion to theory, from absurdity to exhaustion, because it's theatre and that's OK, but you're not supposed to be allowed to do the same thing in cinema. If you do, you're marginalised, or regarded as outrageous, or given a special joker's political license like Jarman, or patronised like Ken Russell, or respected, but not looked at, like Roeg.

ONE CLEAR CONTEXT FOR YOUR WORK - A CONTEXT IN WHICH THESE ISSUES ARE NOT MARGINAL - IS THE CONTEMPORARY ART WORLD, IN WHICH YOU OPERATE AS AN ARTIST.

I am sure that worrying about a job-description cannot be that important, but critics and journalists talk about artists and film directors, as though the latter cannot be the former. My greatest interest I suppose is still reserved for painting. It has always been at the cutting edge of investigation in making visual images, and still is, despite its so-called minority position. What is happening now in painting I am sure will continue to affect contemporary thought. Maybe it will take fifteen, twenty more years - look how long the *Large Glass* took to reach an initial understanding even with a suspicious art establishment. The particular private radical investigative procedure of the painter, I believe, represents the apogee of the manufacture of images. But it's taken two thousand years to reach that position of privilege. I've chosen to work in moving images, I've chosen to work in cinema, but I want to bring with me all the aesthetic preoccupations of, as I see it, an ideal radical investigative painter, to try to make them work in cinema. So that I can talk to painters and painting theorists in a more satisfactory way than I can to those equivalent people who associate themselves with cinema, whose preoccupations so often have little interest for me.

FINALLY, HOW IS *The Stairs* PROJECT DEVELOPING?

The next exhibition is in Munich on the subject of Projection. One hundred screens to be projected across the city on public architecture. It's a combined effort to unite city electricity, private electrical companies, the curator's Marstall theatre, the opera-house facilities. A public/social exercise as well as an aesthetic exercise. The example of Christo is evoked. His ability to persuade all those Californian conservative farmers to build the *Running Fence* to the sea was remarkable. He fought and fights resistance with great persistence. There are comparisons to being a cinema director. On a film set many social graces have to be aired and practised to get things going. On the whole though, on a film set you do not have to meet the mayor and the mayoress, and talk to the community and the lighting people and get the city on your side. Every time there's a certain weariness, because you know the thing has to start out fresh each time. But when it filters down and you get local theatrical companies being involved, and the local orchestra, and the student communities and so on, then it really begins - without wishing to sound like a community worker - you can see the spark of electricity flickering around. Everybody tends to interpret the project according to their own lights, which is fair enough as long as the combined effort is there to make the thing work.

Geneva was exciting, the whole city really took over on the day we opened, tens of thousands of locals and visitors became involved in a day-long opening that lasted until midnight. I suppose it's cinema as exhibition, exhibition as cinema, a debating platform again to discuss ideas, to examine language. The exhibition in Geneva was all about seeing and knowing, which connects back to *The Draughtsman's Contract*. So it's wheels within wheels, the germs and ashes of all the projects exist in all the others, whatever the medium, there's a continual excitement about the business of creating visual images.

NOTES

A Walk Through G: Some Organising Principles

1 *Guardian*, 7 September 1995.

2 *Circles of Confusion* (New York 1983), p 59.

3 'Foreword', *Notes of a Film Director* (1946; reprint, New York 1970).

4 All unattributed quotations from Greenaway are taken from the interviews to be found at the end of the book. The first of the interviews was published in *Transcript*, I.1 (1994) and has been revised by Greenaway for the present book. Some quotations are taken from the initial version.

5 This is neither a defence of Greenaway, nor a history of critical response to his work, but two paragraphs from an interview with John Walsh (*Independent Magazine*, 11 September 1993) are perhaps worth quoting:

> These [exhibitions curated by Greenaway at the Louvre, and in Vienna] are heady operations for a chap from Essex whose formal training stopped at Walthamstow art college. The passion of the autodidact can be discerned behind his ceaseless image-making, his ambitious lexicographies, his compulsion to put absolutely everything into his films and exhibitions - all the arts, all science, all four elements, astrology, medicine, magic, religion, class, evolution, animals, insects, music from Bach to Eno, painting from Dürer to Kitaj, sculpture from ... To follow Greenaway down his labyrinthine galleries and rapt taxonomies is to embrace madness. You wonder: does the ceaseless flood of Greenawayana amount to more than a massive showing-off of learning, a Xanadu of sterile connections?

Well; that is how language works. Walsh himself throws in a *Citizen Kane* reference, traceable back to Coleridge's poem, and beyond that to the book he had been reading which inspired it, and beyond that ... And, compared to Tarantino's or film school graduates' referencing of B movies, Greenaway's references should be straightforward for an educated audience - Bach, Eno, Vermeer, Muybridge, Dürer, Kitaj, Borges, Resnais, Duchamp, Jacobean drama (*Jurassic Park*, after all, stole an idea from *The Duchess of Malfi* without adverse comment). But consider the tone: 'heady stuff for a chap from Essex'. What does this mean? That for a gentleman from Shropshire it wouldn't be heady stuff? Is the journalistic association between Essex and Thatcherism enough to dismiss any native of Essex out of hand? Note also 'whose formal training stopped at Walthamstow art college' - that is to say, whose formal training stopped with his higher education. Like most people's, who get so far. 'Walthamstow' (Essex again) and 'art college' are used here as if merely to name them is make a case against them. This, like the implied sneer in the (incorrect) use of 'autodidact', which both dismisses any art history taught at an art college and further suggests that to learn from one's own reading and looking is in some way second-best, is the kind of snobbery and marginalisation which artists have suffered in Britain since Reynolds was supposed to have got help from 'real' writers whilst composing his *Discourses*.

6   Caux, D., Field, M., De Meredieu, F., Pilard, P., Nyman, M., *Peter Greenaway* (Paris 1987), p 110.

7   *The Stairs Munich* (London 1995), p 13.

8   See also *The Stairs Munich*, p 44.

9   There is here a conscious echo of the old Latin tag (from Horace) that so influenced centuries of European painting, *ut pictura poesis*: as with painting, so with poetry. Lessing and Shaftesbury attempted to shake it off by a division between temporal and spatial arts, a division still of great interest to Greenaway.

10   *The Early Films of Peter Greenaway* (London, undated [filmography included to 1991]), pp 2-3.

11   (Paris 1988), p 23.

12   *The Order of Things* (London 1970), p xv.

13   (*Les Bruits des Nuages*)(Paris 1992), p 105.

14   (Vienna 1992).

15   (London 1994), p 15.

16   See paragraphs 4-8, pp 9-23.

17   *Balcon*,1992, p 43.

18   (Paris 1993), pp 17, 28.

19   p 27.

20   Described by Stephen Heath, *Questions of Cinema* (London 1981), p 57.

21   *The Stairs Geneva*, p 3.

22   In fact 1895-1995 meant 101 screens; but the rhetoric of 1-100 remained intact.

23   Screenplay. In Robert Wilson's 1995 installation, *HG*, it remains equally uncertain just what 'HG' stands for. In *A Walk Through H*, Heaven and Hell are certainly possibilities.

Themes and Variations

1   *Guardian*, 7 September 1995.

2   p 41.

3   p 50.

4   *The Stairs Geneva*, p 9.

5   *Blitz*, October 1989, pp 24-30.

6   p 58. Braque's father, incidentally, was a painter with exactly these skills, and this influenced the cubist plays on *trompe l'oeil*.

7   *Questions of Cinema*, pp 165-75.

8   The horse recalls not just *Rosa, A Horse Drama* - to give it its full title - but also the final scene

of *The Draughtsman's Contract*, in which the mysterious naked figure, bodypainted to resemble a sculpture - or, perhaps more precisely, the remarkably 'alive' statues in Watteau's parks and gardens - sits on an equestrian statue (and 'sits', also, for the draughtsman's final, unfinished, unlucky thirteenth drawing).

9   The dialogue in *The Belly of an Architect* about the emperor's skin disease which was eased by water is easily enough read - once one becomes accustomed to Greenaway's world of repeated archetypes, in which historical and mythical characters are freely mingled - as a reference to, a parallel with, Marat.

10 The same toy ship has already been submitted to a 'tempest' which is a stream of urine. Visually, this scene recalls the opening of *The Belly of an Architect*, with Kracklite and his wife making love in their sleeper in front of the landscape they are rushing past; another bed in front of a curtained 'screen'.

11 'A Lecture', *Circles of Confusion*, p 19.

12 p 91. In the script, this scene is followed by what I take to be a direct parody of the race around Trinity Quad in *Chariots of Fire*.

13 *Questions of Cinema*, p 27.

14 *Questions of Cinema*, p 44.

15 'Initially it was technically difficult to make an alignment between what the optical device framed and what the camera framed, because the human lens is infinitely adjustable and rarely fixed at one viewing distance.' *The Stairs Munich*, p 46.

16 There is an image by Degas of a woman with binoculars who stares right at, or through, the viewer.

17 The 43rd section of *Watching Water* suggests that Kracklite himself makes the connection between himself and the portrait; in fact, he is concerned rather to compare himself with the Emperor Augustus, who was poisoned by his wife; it is Flavia who compares him to Doria.

18 Architectural models in particular, in *The Belly of an Architect* and *Prospero's Books. A Zed and Two Noughts* is full of animal posters and toy animals as well as real ones; and Beta, Alba's daughter, has her own zoo, with its own child-like system of classification - she puts spiders and flies together on the grounds of colour.

19 In *The Cook, The Thief, His Wife and Her Lover* menus are both texts and still life compositions.

20 *New Statesman*, 30 June 1995.

21 Quotations are from Greenaway's catalogue essay of 1993; unnumbered pages.

22 (Harmondsworth 1974), p 240. Polak's *The Painter and his Model*, which, like Greenaway introduces nudity into the scene, was part of the series *Photographs from Life in Old Dutch Costume*.

23 One of the acknowledged influences on Greenaway's opera/theatre is Philip Glass, one of the *Four American Composers* of Greenaway's documentary series. Glass's opera *The Photographer* is about Muybridge.

24 In 1872 Muybridge took a photograph of Leland Stanford's trotter Occident in motion, and established that at one point all four hooves were off the ground. In 1877 Stanford financed a series of studies - this time with a calibrated backdrop and 12 cameras with shutters tripped by the motion they recorded, the beginning of the format which has so fascinated twentieth-century artists - designed to be of use in the training of horses and athletes. In 1883 Stanford withdrew his patronage, and in the following year Muybridge began work at the University of Pennsylvania, producing the 100,000 images from which *Animal Locomotion* was selected. It would be useful to have a history of Muybridge's importance, if any, to the histories of racing, athletics and medicine to set beside the familiar accounts of his importance to art history.

25 Sotheby's. In fact Darwin, in the *Origin of Species*, places great emphasis on the lack of consensus regarding what is a species, what is a sub-species, what is a variety, on the arbitrary - or at least intuitive and fluid - nature of classification of flora and fauna.

26 Phillips, p 14 of the Channel 4 publication accompanying the first broadcasting of *A TV Dante* (1990).

27 Perhaps Sadie, like the painting *Blackbird Singing in the Dead of Night* (cf. *The Falls*), is named for the Beatles song; a line in *Drowning by Numbers* echoes a line from 'Rocky Racoon', a song from the same record, *The White Album*.

28 Who had taken the picture because he is attracted to Cissie.

29 The motif of a photograph being described to a blind person - although in this narrative it was a blind man who had actually taken the photographs - was the basis of a later film by Jocelyn Moorhouse, *Proof*. Greenaway has mentioned in conversation a link back to Hollis Frampton, whose writings on photography and cinema frequently include Borgesian fable/metaphors directly relatable to Greenaway's own narratives. The two most radical explorations of blindness in cinema are perhaps Buñuel's - the blinding razor in *Un Chien Andalou*, but also the attack on the blind beggar in *Los Olvidados* - and Jarman's, in *Blue*. I have already suggested that blindness has long been a motif within the history of painting.

30 Which recalls a Man Ray print of 'objects which do not reflect the light', also completely black; paint on photographic paper.

31 This last phrase is an echo of a line of Madgett's in *Drowning by Numbers*.

32 *Guardian*, 29 July 1995.

33 Compare the final sentence of *Fear of Drowning*: '*Drowning by Numbers* is a poetic, amoral tale told morally to support the belief that the good are seldom rewarded, the bad go largely unpunished and the innocent are always abused.'

34 Sotheby's.

35 See Caux et al. p 88-9.

36 *Rosa*, p 5.

37 Sotheby's.

38 p 37.

39 Sotheby's.

40 Caux et al., p 119.

41 There is one exception: the neo-Fascist site associated with Caspasian, in the scenes which anticipate his arrival at Flavia's studio.

42 'The home of a unique species of black maritime rook that mated with seagulls'; 'Against the disc of the full moon even white birds are black'.

43 This scene initiates a conversation in the interviews below about the relationship between what is stated visually and what is stated in the script.

44 Sotheby's.

45 *Works and Texts* (London (Royal Academy) 1992), p 246.

46 *Fear of Drowning*, pp 35-41.

47 *Anatomy of a Filmmaker*, BBC Omnibus, 1991. This detachment is, to some extent, a consequence of the gallery as an environment which brings together images originally intended for churches, cathedrals, dining rooms, bedrooms, palaces, town halls - for all manner of public and private spaces and seats of power, and brings them together under the strange category of the aesthetic - a category increasingly replaced or erased within the contemporary museum by the category of fame. Rome, especially, is a city with many great paintings still in their original location; sitting before an altarpiece next to a worshipper is to rediscover - or discover for the first time - the historical complexity of one's internalised aesthetic gaze.

48 *Anatomy of a Filmmaker*.

49 Compare Tom Phillips's category, in his notes on 'The Postcard Vision' reprinted in his RA catalogue, of the 'blind photographer', who records more than he knows.

50 pp 42-3.

51 Indeed. Veronese had to justify himself to the Inquisition, over a Last Supper, in 1573.

52 Sotheby's.

53 See *Transcript*, I.3 (1996).

54 *Circles of Confusion*, pp 193-9.

55 *The Stairs Munich*, p 39.

56 Ibid., p 49.

57 Ibid., p 51.

58 A marriage already celebrated by Elvis Costello. Greenaway's phrase 'urine stains like pale yellow flowers' also recalls Helen Chadwick's *Piss Flowers*, bronze sculptures derived from a man and a woman urinating into snow.

59 p 29.

60 Peter and Linda Murray, *A Dictionary of Art and Artists* (Harmondsworth 1975), p 406.

61 My source is a photocopy of an undated clipping.

62 *Anatomy of a Filmmaker*. This qualifies our interpretation of the 'verdant landscape' at the start of the film.

63 Compare Greenaway's discussion of photocopying in *The Belly of an Architect* in the interview below.

64 *Illuminations*, Glasgow 1979, pp 219-53.

65 pp 25-6.

66 See pp 27, 55.

67 *The Stairs Geneva*, p 73. Properties were also a key element of *In the Dark*, 'an ironic exhibit-installation' for *Spellbound* (Hayward Gallery, 21 February-6 May 1996). The objects were real, but real *properties* – objects about to represent themselves in an imaginable fiction. (Imaginable, mostly, through memories of earlier fictions.) 'This exhibit has a great advantage over cinema insofar that much of its substance is "real". We can give you the actors in the flesh (yet ironically they are in essence still acting), the props in the flesh - though they are taken out of a context in the real world to be presented in an artificial one.' (From the proposal.)

68 Cf. *The Stairs Munich*, p 38.

69 Bresson's *L'Argent*, centred on a forged 500-franc note, was released four years earlier.

70 *The Stairs Geneva*, pp 48-9.

71 p 139.

72 In *Henry IV Part 2* the Archbishop of York compares the people to a dog that 'wouldst eat thy dead vomit up, and howl'st to find it'.

73 By Mitchel, who uses a wooden spoon for the job. Albert, we later learn, also used a wooden spoon in his sexual abuse of Georgina.

74 pp 112-13.

75 Compare the catalogue paragraph on the fortieth object to represent the world, a human tattoo, although a more delicate calligraphy is involved in *The Pillow Book*. Barthes in particular, of course, has eroticised critical language.

76 'Illustration' is still a common, and disparaging, word in art schools. One immediate

explanation is that art schools have illustration departments, and painting students have consciously chosen not to be illustrators, in a very mundane, professional use of the term.

77 *Watching Water*, para 47.

78 Compare, perhaps, the clues recovered from the mouths of the victims in *The Silence of the Lambs*. The use of the French Revolution - foregrounded in *Death in the Seine* - in *The Cook* is one instance of my losing count; the connections I can make - the irony of a gentle man who reads about violence, and who meets a violent end - seem insufficient for the weight which the revolution is given in the film, basically a revenge tragedy, more concerned with sexual than with revolutionary politics. Astrid Seriese, the Singer in *M is for Man, Music, and Mozart*, wears a thin red ribbon around her neck, another French Revolutionary reference perhaps - it was a fashion amongst aristocratic women who had lost relations to the guillotine, and Ian Hamilton Finlay based a piece on it. The Japanese lover in *Hiroshima Mon Amour* has learnt French to read about the French Revolution.

79 See Greenaway's gloss on the murderer fleeing right to left, the 'sinister' direction, in Prud'hon's *Divine Justice Pursuing Crime: Flying Out of This World*, p 176. The scene, in fact, is complicated in this respect by the camera turning, as Miranda reaches it, and following her as she moves from the right to the left of the screen. It is clear that such movements are carefully considered by Greenaway; Milo enters first from right to left and this direction is linked to her character throughout *A Zed and Two Noughts*. Spica, as aggressor - attacking Patricia, harassing Michael, hectoring Richard, torturing Pup - is often on the right of the screen, facing left. The warp and weft of the choreography of *The Cook*, of processions and recessions, is not simplistic but it is simplified by the set: the characters move from right to left for sex (Michael and Georgina; Fitch and Patricia) and violence and vengeance (Spica, on several occasions). The bad news of Pup is brought to the lovers by Richard from right to left, and this is followed by Georgina's visit to his hospital, where she enters from left to right, a ministering angel. Left to right is how we read in the West, and Hockney has suggested this is what we project onto paintings. I tried reading the compositions of contemporary Japanese photographs in a recent exhibition against this habit, and my readings were transformed.

80 p 45.

81 And another image which could have had a section to itself - pages, or feathers, or confetti, or money, falling through the air. It is first found in the text of *A Walk Through H*: 'Tulse Luper on the evening of my last illness waded through that worthless ephemera with a frown, tossing the papers into the air like confetti.'

82 The bathroom is not only the location of Georgina's first encounters with Michael; it is also the location for Albert's infantile sexual demands. We learn this from Georgina's monologue, but it comes as no surprise after Spica's obsessive linking in his conversation of sexuality and toilets. This - if this is not too realist, too 'psychological' a reading - might also explain why he is so blind to the affair; his thinking about what Georgina might be doing in the toilet is dominated by their own sex life.

83 See *Fear of Drowning*, p 57.

84 *The Origin of Species*, chapter 2.

85 *Rosa*, p 117.

86 *A Zed and Two Noughts* (London 1986), pp 13-14.

87 Like Milo in *A Zed and Two Noughts*. Van Meegeren, the surgeon, is also described as a stitcher.

88 Greenaway nods in this passage, giving the quote to Maupassant. It is reworked, with the same slip of the pen, in *The Stairs Munich*, p 27. The Phillips text reads: 'Everything in the world exists to end up as a postcard (Mallarmé adapted).' (*Works and Texts*, p 77.)

89 pp 74-91.

90 p 125.

91 Caux et al., pp 81-2. (On the same video as *M is for Man, Music, and Mozart*, Nyman appears in *Letters, Riddles and Writs*, a tricksy but unimaginative programme - talking busts of Beethoven and Haydn, dream and trial sequences - and suggests how one composer can use another.)

92 *Flying Out of This World*, p 84.

93 p 85.

Art Caught in the Act

1 'A Stipulation of Terms from Maternal Hopi', *Circles of Confusion*, p 176.

2 *Watching Water*, section 12.

3 'How I Became a Film Director', *Notes of a Film Director*, p 13.

4 Cited in Christopher Williams, ed., *Realism and the Cinema* (London 1980), p 42. Vision itself here seems to be defined as uncomfortably close to a cinematic editing process. Bazin's offering of deep focus (specifically, William Wyler's) as in some way restoring this freedom is bathetic, but it is interesting that other techniques which he claims for realism - long shots and long takes - are also used by Greenaway to allow the audience something of the freedom of the viewer of a painting.

5 Hollis Frampton, 'The Whithering Away of the State of the Art', *Circles of Confusion*, p 164.

6 'Grids', *The Originality of the Avant Garde and Other Modernist Myths*, New York 1985. Krauss is here referring to the modernist grid, which she carefully distinguishes from the perspective grid; but her phrase is equally true of the perspective grid.

7 'Montage in 1938', *Notes of a Film Director*, p 69.

8 p 46.

9   It is not suggested that the killer has consciously edited it in advance of this, his first view of his first killing. Similarly, there is a discrepancy between the view of the camera held at chest level and the following point of view shots, which are taken from eye level.

10 (California 1993).

11 *Transcript*, I.2 (1995), p 56.

12 Sotheby's.

13 *The Stairs Geneva*, p 84.

14 *The Stairs Geneva*, p 80.

15 *The Stairs Geneva*, p 12.

16 *The Origin of Species*, chapter 3.

17 Bertolt Brecht, *The Messingkauf Dialogues*, (trans. John Willet, *Dialogue aus dem Messingkauf*, Frankfurt Suhrkamp Verlag, 1963), p 12.

18 p 12.

19 'Fourth Appendix to the Messingkauf Theory', *Messingkauf Dialogues*, p 105.

20 There is a similar image in Eisenstein's *October*.

21 *Messingkauf Dialogues*, p 104.

22 Script (Paris 1994), p 34.

23 pp 92-3.

24 *Rosa*, p 66.

25 Robert Graves, 'Minos and His Brothers', *The Greek Myths*, first published 1955.

26 p 87.

27 p 42.

Irony and Tragedy (Six Necessary Elements)

1   p 15.

2   From a proposal dated May 1994.

3   See Walter Kaufmann, *Tragedy and Philosophy* (New York 1968), section 9.

4   pp 46-7.

5   pp 35-7.

6   *Rosa*, p 93.

7   Volume XIX, chapter 20.

8 *Freud and Man's Soul* (Harmondsworth 1991), pp 90-1.

9 p 134. (On Primaticcio's drawing for a ceiling painting, *The Chariot of Apollo*.)

10 *The Stairs Geneva*, p 4.

11 p 131.

12 *The Stairs Geneva*, p 37-9.

13 A word without a penumbra of association, quite apart from its innate strangeness. Around *Schaulust* are: *Schau*: view; inspection; show; exhibition; spectacle; *Schaubild*: chart; graph; diagram; curve; *Schaubühne*: stage; *Schaulock*: peephole - all from the *Langenscheidt Concise Dictionary*, which defines *Schaulust* itself as curiosity, and *Schaulustige(r)* as onlooker, curious bystander; sightseer.

14 Gambon, incidentally, is forced into a Last Supper: he drinks (white) wine instead of blood, but then he eats flesh instead of bread. Cannibalism is the central, participatory, ritual and myth of Christianity.

15 Caux et al., p 114.

16 (London 1995), p 114.

17 p 68.

18 *Rosa*, pp 97-8.

Filmography etc.

<table>
<tr><td colspan="2">FILMS</td></tr>
<tr><td>1966</td><td>TRAIN</td></tr>
<tr><td>1966</td><td>TREE</td></tr>
<tr><td>1967</td><td>REVOLUTION</td></tr>
<tr><td>1967</td><td>5 POSTCARDS FROM CAPITAL CITIES</td></tr>
<tr><td>1969</td><td>INTERVALS</td></tr>
<tr><td>1971</td><td>EROSION</td></tr>
<tr><td>1973</td><td>H IS FOR HOUSE (re-edited 1978)</td></tr>
<tr><td>1975</td><td>WINDOWS</td></tr>
<tr><td>1975</td><td>WATER</td></tr>
<tr><td>1975</td><td>WATER WRACKETS</td></tr>
<tr><td>1976</td><td>GOOLE BY NUMBERS</td></tr>
<tr><td>1977</td><td>DEAR PHONE</td></tr>
<tr><td>1978</td><td>1-100</td></tr>
<tr><td>1978</td><td>A WALK THROUGH H</td></tr>
<tr><td>1978</td><td>VERTICAL FEATURES REMAKE</td></tr>
<tr><td>1979</td><td>ZANDRA RHODES</td></tr>
<tr><td>1980</td><td>THE FALLS</td></tr>
<tr><td>1981</td><td>ACT OF GOD</td></tr>
<tr><td>1982</td><td>THE DRAUGHTSMAN'S CONTRACT</td></tr>
<tr><td>1983</td><td>FOUR AMERICAN COMPOSERS</td></tr>
<tr><td>1984</td><td>MAKING A SPLASH</td></tr>
<tr><td>1985</td><td>INSIDE ROOMS - 26 BATHROOMS</td></tr>
<tr><td>1986</td><td>A ZED AND TWO NOUGHTS</td></tr>
<tr><td>1987</td><td>THE BELLY OF AN ARCHITECT</td></tr>
<tr><td>1988</td><td>DROWNING BY NUMBERS</td></tr>
<tr><td>1988</td><td>FEAR OF DROWNING</td></tr>
<tr><td>1988</td><td>DEATH IN THE SEINE</td></tr>
<tr><td>1989</td><td>A TV DANTE, CANTOS 1-8</td></tr>
<tr><td>1989</td><td>HUBERT BALS HANDSHAKE</td></tr>
<tr><td>1989</td><td>THE COOK, THE THIEF, HIS WIFE AND HER LOVER</td></tr>
<tr><td>1991</td><td>PROSPERO'S BOOKS</td></tr>
</table>

1991	M IS FOR MAN, MUSIC AND MOZART
1992	ROSA
1992	DARWIN
1993	THE BABY OF MÂCON
1994	THE STAIRS GENEVA
1996	THE PILLOW BOOK

OPERA

1994	ROSA, A HORSE DRAMA (Music by Louis Andriessen)

CURATORIAL EXHIBITIONS

1991	THE PHYSICAL SELF
	Boymans van Beuningen, Rotterdam, November
1992	100 Objects to Represent the World
	Academy of Fine Arts,
	Hofburg Palace and Semper Depot, Vienna, October
1992	LES BRUITS DES NUAGES (FLYING OUT OF THIS WORLD)
	Louvre, Paris, November
1993	WATCHING WATER
	Palazzo Fortuni, Venice, June
1993	SOME ORGANISING PRINCIPLES
	Glynn Vivian Art Gallery, Swansea, October
1993	THE AUDIENCE OF MÂCON
	Ffoto Gallery, Cardiff, October
1994	THE STAIRS GENEVA
	Geneva, April
1995	THE STAIRS MUNICH
	Munich, October
1996	SPELLBOUND (IN THE DARK)
	Hayward Gallery, February

ONE-MAN SHOWS

1988	Broad Street Gallery, Canterbury
1989	Arcade, Carcassonne
1989	Palais de Tokyo, Paris

1990	Nicole Klagsbrun Gallery, New York
1990	Australia Center of Contemporary Art, Melbourne
1990	Ivan Dougherty Gallery, College of Fine Arts,
	The University of New South Wales, Paddington
1990	Cirque Divers, Liège
1990	Shingawa Space T33, Tokyo
1990	Altium, Fukoa
1990	Dany Keller Galerie, Munich
1990	Video Galleriet, Copenhagen
1990	Kunsthallen Brandts Klaedefabrick, Odense
1990	Galerie Xavier Hufkens, Brussels
1991	Watermans Gallery, Brentford
1991	City Art Centre, Dublin (If Only Film Could Do The Same)
1992	Gesellschaft für Aktuelle Kunst, Bremen
1992	Nicole Klagsbrun Gallery, New York
1994	Arizona State University Art Museum, Tempe, Arizona
1994	Gesellschaft für Max Reinhardt-Forschung, Salzburg

BOOKS

1984	THE DRAUGHTSMAN'S CONTRACT
	(L'Avant Scène, Paris; English and French)
1986	A ZED AND TWO NOUGHTS
	(Faber and Faber, London; English and Finnish)
1987	THE BELLY OF AN ARCHITECT
	(Faber & Faber, London; English; Haffmans Verlag, Zurich; German)
1988	DROWNING BY NUMBERS
	(Faber and Faber, London; English)
1988	FEAR OF DROWNING
	(Disvoir, Paris; English and French)
1989	THE COOK, THE THIEF, HIS WIFE AND HER LOVER
	(Disvoir, Paris; English and French; Haffmans Verlag, Zurich; German)
1990	PAPERS
	(Disvoir, Paris; English and French)

1991	PROSPERO'S BOOKS
	(Chatto and Windus, London; English; Haffmans Verlag, Zurich; German)
1992	PROSPERO'S SUBJECTS
	(Yobisha and Co., Japan)
1992	PETER GREENAWAY
	(Filmstellen, VSETH/VSU, Zurich; German)
1992	PETER GREENAWAY Fête et Défaite du Corps
	Agnès Berthin-Scaillet (L'Avant-Scène, Paris)
1993	WATCHING WATER
	(Electa, Milan; English and Italian)
1993	ROSA
	(Disvoir, Paris; English and French)
1993	THE BABY OF MÂCON
	(Rogner and Bernhard, Hamburg; German)
1993	THE FALLS
	(Disvoir, Paris; English and French)
1994	THE BABY OF MÂCON
	(Disvoir, Paris; English and French)
1995	THE WORLD OF PETER GREENAWAY
	Leon Steimetz (Journey Editions, Boston)

CATALOGUES

1991	THE PHYSICAL SELF
	(Boymans van Beuningen, Rotterdam; English and Dutch)
1992	100 OBJECTS TO REPRESENT THE WORLD
	(Academy of Fine Arts, Vienna; English and German)
1992	LES BRUITS DES NUAGES (FLYING OUT OF THIS WORLD)
	(Louvre, Paris; English and French)
1993	WATCHING WATER
	(Electa, Milan; English and Italian)
1993	SOME ORGANISING PRINCIPLES
	(Glynn Vivian Art Gallery, Swansea; English and Welsh)

1993	THE AUDIENCE OF MÂCON
	(Ffoto Gallery, Cardiff; English and Welsh)
1994	THE STAIRS GENEVA
	(Merrell Holberton, London; English and French)
1995	THE STAIRS MUNICH
	(Merrell Holberton, London; English and German)

Index

Illustrations

The Blinding Beam

OF THE PROJECTOR IS SWITCHED OFF

EISENSTEIN P-R-K-F-V